AF477792

Conceptions of God, Freedom, and Ethics in African American and Jewish Theology

Black Religion/Womanist Thought/Social Justice

Series Editors: Dwight N. Hopkins and Linda E. Thomas
Published by Palgrave Macmillan

"How Long this Road": Race, Religion, and the Legacy of C. Eric Lincoln
Edited by Alton B. Pollard, III and Love Henry Whelchel, Jr.

*African American Humanist Principles: Living and Thinking Like the
Children of Nimrod*
By Anthony B. Pinn

White Theology: Outing Supremacy in Modernity
By James W. Perkinson

*The Myth of Ham in Nineteenth-Century American Christianity: Race, Heathens, and
the People of God*
By Sylvester Johnson

Loving the Body: Black Religious Studies and the Erotic
Edited by Anthony B. Pinn and Dwight N. Hopkins

Transformative Pastoral Leadership in the Black Church
By Jeffery L. Tribble, Sr.

*Shamanism, Racism, and Hip Hop Culture: Essays on White Supremacy and
Black Subversion*
By James W. Perkinson

Women, Ethics, and Inequality in U.S. Healthcare: "To Count Among the Living"
By Aana Marie Vigen

Black Theology in Transatlantic Dialogue: Inside Looking Out, Outside Looking In
By Anthony G. Reddie

Womanist Ethics and the Cultural Production of Evil
By Emilie M. Townes

Whiteness and Morality: Pursuing Racial Justice through Reparations and Sovereignty
By Jennifer Harvey

The Theology of Martin Luther King, Jr. and Desmond Mpilo Tutu
By Johnny B. Hill

Conceptions of God, Freedom, and Ethics in African American and Jewish Theology
By Kurt Buhring

Black Theology and Pedagogy
By Noel Leo Erskine
(forthcoming)

Conceptions of God, Freedom, and Ethics in African American and Jewish Theology

Kurt Buhring

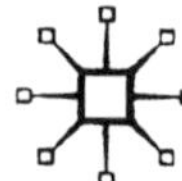

CONCEPTIONS OF GOD, FREEDOM, AND ETHICS IN AFRICAN AMERICAN AND JEWISH THEOLOGY
Copyright © Kurt Buhring, 2008.

First published in 2008 by
PALGRAVE MACMILLAN™
175 Fifth Avenue, New York, N.Y. 10010 and
Houndmills, Basingstoke, Hampshire, England RG21 6XS
Companies and representatives throughout the world.

PALGRAVE MACMILLAN is the global academic imprint of the Palgrave Macmillan division of St. Martin's Press, LLC and of Palgrave Macmillan Ltd. Macmillan® is a registered trademark in the United States, United Kingdom and other countries. Palgrave is a registered trademark in the European Union and other countries.

ISBN-13: 978–1–4039–8479–1
ISBN-10: 1–4039–8479–4

Library of Congress Cataloging-in-Publication Data

Buhring, Kurt.
    Conceptions of God, freedom, and ethics in African American and Jewish theology / by Kurt Buhring.
        p. cm.—(Black religion/womanist thought/social justice)
    ISBN 1–4039–8479–4
    1. Black theology. 2. Suffering—Religious aspects—Christianity. 3. African Americans—Religion. 4. Black power. 5. Cone, James H. 6. God (Judaism) 7. Suffering—Religious aspects—Judaism. 8. Holocaust (Jewish theology) 9. Fackenheim, Emil L. I. Title.

BT82.7.B84 2008
231—dc22   2007041189

A catalogue record for this book is available from the British Library.

Design by Newgen Imaging Systems (P) Ltd., Chennai, India.

First edition: June 2008

10 9 8 7 6 5 4 3 2 1

Printed in the United States of America.

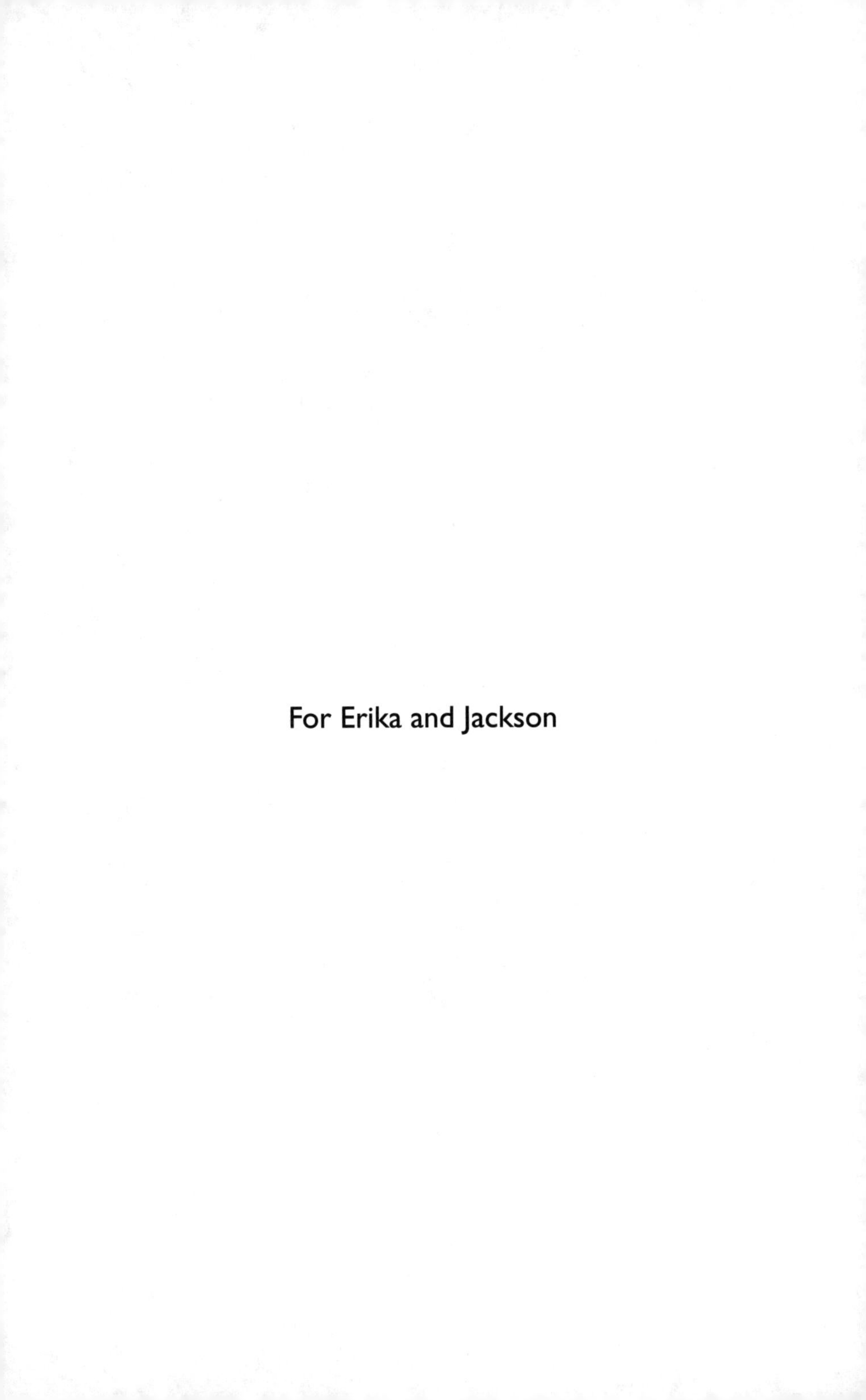

For Erika and Jackson

Contents

Acknowledgments   ix

1. Introducing Black and Jewish Responses to Experiences
    of Moral Evil and Suffering   1

2. What Does the Christian Gospel Have to Do with the
    Black Power Movement?: James Cone's God
    of the Oppressed   15

3. Why Divine Goodness or Power? Why God? Why
    Liberation?: Critiques and Affirmations of James Cone   61

4. A New Sinai? A New Exodus? Divine Presence
    During and After the Holocaust in the Theology
    of Emil Fackenheim   85

5. After the Holocaust: The Destruction of the God
    of History, of Chosenness, and of Patriarchy; Critiques
    and Affirmations of Emil Fackenheim   131

6. A Consideration of Humanocentric Theism, Resistance,
    and Redemption   159

Notes   197

Bibliography   233

Index   255

Acknowledgments

As is always the case, this work would not have been possible without the support, encouragement, and guidance of many individuals. The present book is a revised version of my doctoral dissertation at the University of Chicago Divinity School. I appreciate the helpful suggestions of my committee readers, David Tracy and Paul Mendes-Flohr. Earlier versions of portions of the book have been presented at conferences and I am particularly grateful to Gary Dorrien and Anthony Pinn for their feedback and salient critiques. I am thankful to my students at Saint Mary's College in Notre Dame, Indiana, who so often provided me a fresh perspective of material related to this book's content. In addition, I would like to thank my colleagues at Saint Mary's, especially in the Religious Studies Department. They have been both patient and enormously supportive of my work. I thank my editors and the staff at Palgrave Macmillan for their enthusiasm and trust in accepting my manuscript proposal and for their professionalism in helping throughout the book's production. I would also like to acknowledge Linda Thomas and Dwight Hopkins, editors of Black Religion/Womanist Thought/Social Justice series, with which I am honored to be associated. Further, Dwight Hopkins has had a unique and enormous role in the process of bringing this book to fruition. He has been my teacher in several classes, my doctoral dissertation advisor, my advocate and promoter with publishers, and my mentor and friend. This book would not have been possible without his passion and expertise. Finally, I would like to thank deeply my friends and family, especially my parents, Ed and Pat Buhring, my sisters Laura and Debra, and my mother-in-law, Marty Schuh. They have always been incredibly understanding and supportive throughout this process. My greatest appreciation goes to my son, Jackson, and my wife, Erika. Jackson has been extremely good-natured in understanding why I was not always able to play Star Wars with him as I was working on my "God book." Because he is a creative and imaginative five-year old, his incredibly insightful and thought-provoking questions often prompted me to rethink and clarify my beliefs and my writing. There is no possible way of adequately expressing here my thanks to Erika. She has inspired and supported all my work and served as patient, enthusiastic, and brilliant interlocutor for me. I am unspeakably grateful for her humor, support, respect, and love. She is my best friend and greatest love.

1

Introducing Black and Jewish Responses to Experiences of Moral Evil and Suffering

This introductory chapter seeks to draw the reader into the perennial philosophical and theological issue of theodicy through the lens of black experiences of American slavery and racism on the one hand and Jewish experiences of the Holocaust on the other. It is asserted that these historical realities demand a serious consideration and reformulation of traditional understandings of God, including divine goodness, power, and presence, and of humanity. The chapter explains the roles of the various interlocutors in the subsequent chapters and begins to point toward the final constructive perspective of humanocentric theism and the ethical category of resistance. I believe these concepts of God and humanity are relevant to anyone interested in theology and theological anthropology in an encounter with suffering and evil, whether black, Jewish, or other.

Problem

The senseless murder of an innocent child. The random nature of terminal illness. The prosperity of the wicked and the suffering of the good. We are confronted daily with such examples of life's realities. How do we explain these instances? Is it possible to rationalize them? More importantly than how we rationalize them, how do we deal with them on a practical level? Most of the time we maintain that suffering and injustice are simply the way of life. Whether we like it or not, life certainly is not always fair. Indeed it often is not.

Seeing the suffering and deaths of people half way around the world on television, sadly enough, often does not elicit much more than a temporary feeling of sympathy and a more lasting feeling of relief that we ourselves are not involved. Complicating our apathetic attitude toward life's problems is the sense that, even if we did care enough, even if we devoted all our efforts, money, and time to solving all the world's problems, or even one in particular, it still would not make any difference.

For most of us, it takes a direct, personal encounter with suffering or injustice for us to deal with it in more than a superficial way. It is only when *I* get fired from my job, only when *I* am injured, only when *my* loved one is diagnosed with cancer, only when *my* country is at war, that I will think about or deal with these issues. Whether we are more compassionate toward the sufferings and injustices of others immediately, or toward our own sufferings and injustices, we quickly turn to the perennial philosophical and theological question of "Why?" When one is forced to consider life's meaning head-on, one's thoughts often turn to God.

Now the previous questions are reformulated, this time with God in the equation. The issue is no longer so much why this happened as why God let this happen. If God is all-good (omnibenevolent) and all-powerful (omnipotent), how could this not have been prevented? What possible reason could God have for allowing this to happen? Ultimately, why did God choose me to experience this?

In classical philosophy and theology this is the problem of theodicy. How are we to justify God's goodness and God's power in the face of suffering and evil? The two primary problems I struggle with in this work are, given the reality of suffering, evil, and injustice in the world, first, "How we are to understand God?" and second, "How are we to understand ourselves?"

The fact that so many people can affirm faith in an all-good, all-powerful God despite the reality of suffering and evil in the world is fascinating to me. For *anyone* to believe in God a leap of faith is needed, which may not be based on a rational analysis of this problem.[1] But what can be said about a person who has suffered through life, and has been confronted with the evils of the world directly? How is faith maintained in this instance? How does this person understand God? What does her theology look like?

I am often asked to explain my interest in these issues of evil and suffering, given my social location as a white, heterosexual, middle-class,

American male. Though I myself have thus far led a life relatively free of personal, direct experiences of radical moral evils or even any serious and significant suffering, I still feel empathy for and have solidarity with people who suffer from injustices. Though honestly I cannot really point to reasons for my concerns that would be obvious and clear to many beside myself, I believe there have been two primary spheres of influence that have brought me to this topic, my parents and my academic experiences.

First, my parents instilled in me a sense of justice, compassion, and concern for those who are less fortunate. Though I never remember lacking for any necessary material possessions as a child, I would label my family's socioeconomic class as lower-middle class. My father worked a variety of jobs, including as a construction worker, bartender, and draftsman. My mother has worked as an office manager and bookkeeper at a variety of small companies. They have lived through several economically difficult periods of job loss and layoffs, pay cuts, medical illnesses, and bankruptcies. I experienced moderate poverty and knew of families that were not as comfortable as we were; my best friend throughout my childhood seldom had a winter coat to shelter him from the midwestern winters. Whether as a result of these experiences, fairly typical ones for working-class families, or otherwise, I find that I side with poor and working-class people in economic, social, and political issues. Furthermore, the nebulous and persistent problem of poverty is unarguably and *intimately* related to other social evils such as sexism and racism. In the end, I have gained a conviction from my parents that all people should be respected and cared for, particularly *people who have the least in society.*

In addition to the influence of my parents, my undergraduate and graduate work was the second force luring me into the present topic of evil and suffering. I was baptized and confirmed in the Lutheran Church-Missouri Synod. As a teenager, I considered myself a good Christian, or at least I tried to be one. At that stage in my life, being a good Christian to me meant having faith in God and in the divine love incarnate in Jesus Christ. Though never expressly discouraged from asking questions, it was implicit to me that true faith left little room for doubts or for critical inquiry into religious matters. Once at college and away from home, my religious faith and ideals were challenged and enriched by my academic experiences, most significantly in courses with Howard Burkle and Harold Kasimow at Grinnell College in Iowa.

In my classes with Howard Burkle, "Major Western Religions" and "Existentialism," I encountered a mentor who taught me how to critically read and analyze religious and philosophical perspectives that shook the foundations of my intellectual and personal worlds. Though never explicitly stating his own views in class, Burkle implicitly indicated his beliefs by interacting with the selected texts first as a proponent of each particular thinker and later, after allowing student criticism, offering incisive and profound opinions of the viewpoint of the text. In this way, I found myself first wholly swayed and challenged by the reading, my Christian faith nearly destroyed by Jewish and Muslim beliefs and atheistic and nihilistic claims, only later to be renewed and enriched by Burkle's method of integrating such challenges while still maintaining an unexpressed Christian faith. I learned that an unexamined faith is not worth having.

In addition to Burkle, Harold Kasimow guided my introduction to various world religions, especially Judaism, Islam, and Hinduism. Kasimow is a practicing Jew who draws from Zen Buddhism and is a staunch advocate of interreligious dialogue. I remember being initially confused about his religious identity when I learned he was Jewish but practiced Buddhist meditation. How was this possible? In contrast with Burkle's performance of detached objectivity, with a clearly strong subjectivity beneath the façade, Kasimow's religious beliefs were worn on his sleeve. From him I learned that one's religious faith is deeply enriched through encounters with other, previously foreign or strange, beliefs. Following his own mentor, Abraham Joshua Heschel, and thinkers such as Wilfred Cantwell Smith and Hans Kung, Kasimow argued that a diversity of religions was the will of God and that there could be no peace in the world unless there were peace among religions. From Burkle and Kasimow then I learned that religious faith is important and that such a faith is often most strongly enriched and deepened through serious and critical inquiry and through an encounter with beliefs and ideas that seem, and many times are, most at odds with one's own.

Upon returning home on breaks from school, I would often find it difficult to sit through a church service without constantly asking critical questions. I came to see much of what was represented in church as anti-intellectual, anti-Semitic, patriarchal, and racist. I also came to think of my former religious views as trite and naïve. This was particularly so when it came to traditional responses to the issues of suffering and moral evil. I was disturbed and unsatisfied with claims that human suffering is always the result of deserved punishment, or that it will be outweighed by heavenly reward, among other traditional formulations of theodicy. I refused to understand my father's heart disease or my mother's employment difficulties in these ways. I began searching for more coherent and satisfying ways of understanding suffering and evil.

At this point in my life I am not actively participating in any organized religion and I am largely critical of many aspects of traditional Christianity that many Christians would believe to be valid for, and perhaps necessary to, Christian identity. Despite this, however, I still label myself as a Christian. I regard the life and teachings of Jesus of Nazareth as revealing profoundly divine goodness, love, and presence and as providing an ethic of love and justice, particularly about care for the least of society. While I connect this aspect of my religious life with values initially instilled by my parents, my reflective, critical, and pluralistic concept of Christianity is impacted by my academic experiences. From this perspective then developed my interest in and passion for innovative and creative theological responses to suffering and moral evil that are rationally compelling, existentially satisfying, and ethically responsible and inspiring. The theologies of James Cone and Emil Fackenheim meet and exceed these criteria.

The present work attempts to compare and draw from two primary thinkers, James Cone and Emil Fackenheim, who address racism and the Holocaust respectively. Perhaps a more direct comparison could be made between treatments of slavery and the Holocaust, as historical events, or between racism and anti-Semitism as social phenomena, which to be sure are historically situated. My emphasis on racism on the one hand and the Holocaust on the other follows from the concerns and focus of Cone and Fackenheim. For Cone, slavery is a part of the larger evil of racism; the end of slavery did not bring with it an end to the existential, social, economic, and political oppression of African Americans. The problem of anti-Semitism, though setting an important context for the Holocaust, does not explain the Holocaust, according to Fackenheim. It is the event of the Holocaust that so profoundly ruptures our conceptions of God, humanity, covenant, and redemption, not the more general, but still very serious issue of anti-Semitism. The present work is therefore concerned primarily with theological statements made in *the light of racism and the Holocaust*.[2]

The issue of faith in God despite suffering and evil is raised to an even higher degree when the suffering and evil confronted are of a collective, social, enduring, and not at all random nature. It is one thing to ask why God allowed a loved one to die; it is entirely another to ask why God allowed six million Jews to die during the Holocaust, or countless millions of Africans to die during the European slave trade. The sufferings and deaths of African Americans and Jews demand an answer from God. Four hundred years of slavery and racism, thousands of years of anti-Semitism and the Holocaust should force anyone, the theologian in particular, to wrestle with God until some understanding is reached.

As a white Christian academic, my consideration and analysis of black and Jewish theology are self-consciously undertaken as an outsider, with all the accompanying reservations and limitations this entails. However, this position also allows me to consider ideas and claims to which I would not have access if I had explored only white and Christian theologies. In other words, as a white Christian, my examination of Cone's thought enriches my faith in ways not possible if my focus were exclusively or primarily on white thinkers; likewise, exploring Fackenheim allows for greater and more diverse possibilities than if I had restricted myself to Christian responses to suffering and moral evil. Their work demands that I look at both whiteness and Christianity in new and critical ways. I believe this point is especially relevant when it comes to my white Christian consideration of an issue with which I have little or no personal experience, that is, radical suffering and moral evil.

Furthermore, my selection of African American and Jewish suffering in confronting the nature of faith and the question of theodicy is by no means intended to mitigate the evils perpetrated on other communities. The responses of black and Jewish thinkers, specifically Cone and Fackenheim, to the questions posed by suffering and evil are some of the most profound and relevant I have encountered. By an exploration of the particularities of the histories of these two groups, I hope to be able to provide a basis from which to address the sufferings and evils that individuals and groups face.

Thesis

Humanocentric theism is the theological perspective that is explored and articulated in this work. This perspective develops out of a conversation with various thinkers, especially James Cone, Emil Fackenheim, William R. Jones, Dwight Hopkins, and Melissa Raphael. The thesis of this book is that humanocentric theism is an intellectually coherent and existentially satisfying theological position to deal with suffering, evil, and injustice; the ethical corollary to my notion of humanocentric theism is that it is through human freedom, grounded in divine gift, that suffering and evil are to be resisted. Though this stance does not "solve" the philosophical question of evil, I hope it can provide a meaningful way of understanding suffering and moral evil, and also a firm foundation from which to respond to suffering and moral evil through resistance.

According to this position of humanocentric theism, divine power is essentially limited to allow for human freedom. Being created in the image of God means being created as free, moral agents. We have the potential for both radical good and radical evil. If God were to step into human history each time one of us was about to commit an evil act, we would not truly be free. The cost of this freedom is the possibility that we may carry out evil deeds and that we are responsible for these actions.

In other words, in terms of the theodicy question,[3] I affirm the reality of evil, the goodness of God, and reinterpret the nature of God's power. By necessity, true human freedom means that God's freedom must be limited. This does not mean that God is not active in history, but simply that God is active in a manner that differs from our common notions of the nature of a divine agent. God is still powerful, but the notion of power is understood differently.

According to this understanding, which shares much with process theologies,[4] we are to understand perfect power as a force that creates us as free, moral agents, and provides enough space for us to fully develop *our* freedom and power. True power and true love allow for both a distance and the potential for mistakes. God is not truly powerful or loving unless we are powerful and loving. This understanding of God rejects a patriarchal, dominating, and authoritarian understanding of God's perfection in its notion of divine perfection as loving, giving, and creative.

My assertion is that this God is neither weak, nor lacking in power. Power should be understood as the ability to bring about certain ends. God is still able to bring about certain ends, even if not meeting our expectations of what those ends should be or how they should be brought about. According to such an understanding, God is active in human history through persuasion, not coercion. God persuades us to act toward liberation and redemption. By reconceiving of human agency and freedom, and consequently, of divine activity and presence, it is apparent that the responsibility to resist evil and suffering lies with *both* God *and* humanity. It is only through resistance to oppression and despair that humanity may find hope and redemption.

Method

The theological position proposed takes black and Jewish suffering as its starting point. I employ the black and Jewish religious conceptions of the ideal of social justice and the necessity and possibility for human contribution toward redemption. Specifically, I explore the theologies of James Cone, a black theologian of liberation, and Emil Fackenheim, a post-Holocaust Jewish theologian. Each thinker and his tradition are addressed in regard to (1) how God acts in the world; (2) the concepts of human freedom, responsibility, and resistance; (3) what the role of suffering does play and should play in black theology and Jewish theology; and (4) the potential tension between the understanding of God's active and historical taking of sides with particular communities, or chosenness, and the reality of continued structural and personal oppression and suffering in those communities.

I take human freedom and agency to be my theological norm. This norm is distinct from theologies that consider themselves to be dealing with theodicy in general, which assumes God's goodness or power as norm and proceeds to formulate a notion of humanity. By using human freedom as the norm of theology, I do not assume God's omnipotence. Starting from suffering and using the ultimacy of human freedom, as grounded in our creation in divine freedom, I endeavor to make a statement about how humanity deals with suffering and oppression. Admittedly, a central aspect of my methodology is the assertion that human freedom is ultimate because it is founded upon divine activity and will. Nevertheless, the seemingly subtle distinction in norms manifests itself in my conclusions.

The interpretation of humanocentric theism presented here, though not advocated by either Cone or Fackenheim, draws from each of these thinkers and emphasizes particular aspects that are present, though perhaps not stressed in their work. I present and analyze the thought of Cone and Fackenheim as a foundation for a constructive theology. I believe Fackenheim and Cone assert that human resistance is a theological response to oppression that is founded on God's will and command. Fackenheim says that God's Commanding Voice was heard even at Auschwitz. We are commanded to resist terror and despair. Cone says God works for the liberation of the oppressed and that, to be truly free, we too must struggle for the least of society. Both Fackenheim and Cone respond to their existential reality of suffering, oppression, and death through resistance. Both interpret this resistance as a theological category, as commanded of us by God. It is only through resistance, they insist, that liberation, redemption, and hope are possible. Cone and Fackenheim are explored independently of one another initially and brought into conversation in the final analysis.

Chapters 2 and 4 focus on the thought of James Cone and Emil Fackenheim because I am interested and challenged by their writings and excited by the potential for dialogue between the writings of these two thinkers. I believe that these two figures, perhaps more than any other theologians within their traditions, deal most honestly, fruitfully, and creatively with the issues of theodicy, agency, and chosenness. Each of the two chapters examines their understandings of God, the divine-human relationship, human freedom and agency, the idea of resistance, and suffering and chosenness.

It is important to point out that while Cone and Fackenheim are utilized here as foundational for a constructive theology, voices of dissent and critique in response to these writers are vital to my own enterprise. In addition to the many works of each of these authors, I also draw materials from other Black, Womanist, and Jewish theologians in my study. This approach is useful because it places each of these thinkers within the context of his tradition, shedding light on both representative and unique aspects of their thought.

Thus, in chapter 3, I place four thinkers in conversation with Cone. First, I discuss William R. Jones' critique of Cone's methodological and theological assumptions. Jones, one of the earliest critics of Cone, argued that he had no grounds for claiming that God is a benevolent and liberating force in the lives of African Americans. Jones challenged Cone's belief that African American liberation in history was inevitable. As an alternative to Cone's traditional theism, according to which God is all-good and all-powerful, Jones proposed humanocentric theism. According to this stance, which I too advocate with some additions, God's goodness and power are not assumed.[5] Rather, a robust notion of human freedom, based on divine gift, is the basis for the potential of liberation in history.

Next, Anthony Pinn, who also challenges Cone's methodological assumptions, is examined. Continuing Jones' work, Pinn moves even further away from theism, advocating a black humanism. Pinn's writings show that humanism has been and is now a viable black religious response to suffering and evil.

Then, I look at Delores Williams, who asserts on the basis of the Bible and the history of African Americans that, it is survival, not liberation, which is the proper motif of black theology. Along the lines of Jones' critique, Williams argues that there has been no definitive divine act of liberation on behalf of African Americans. Using the story of Hagar and Sarah, along with the historical experiences of African American women, Williams asserts that black theology must be a theology of survival. In addition, Williams also strongly maintains that the suffering of Jesus, and that of African Americans in general, is not to be embraced as redemptive. As she provocatively states, there is nothing redemptive about the bloody death of Jesus. Williams looks to the loving ministry of Jesus to the poor and outcast during his life as the fundamental revelatory significance of Jesus.

Finally, I examine the work of Dwight Hopkins, who more than any other second-generation black theologian takes up Cone's legacy and refines it. Hopkins' work develops the notion of the everyday social and cultural phenomenon of African American experience as a source for constructive theology. Looking at African American folk culture, humor, music, and literature, as well as religion during slavery, Hopkins shows how black people have resisted oppressive white culture and maintained a liberating alternative worldview and way of life. Though not explicitly a critic of Cone's, Hopkins does stress the idea of divine-human partnership in striving toward liberation more than the notion of God being the primary actor in this pursuit as Cone does.

In chapter 5 I treat Fackenheim's interlocutors in a parallel fashion. First, I examine the Holocaust theologian, Richard L. Rubenstein, who argues that Auschwitz destroys any faith in a good and active God of history. Rubenstein claims that we must turn to a God of nature or God as Holy Nothingness, and stresses the sociological and psychological role of religion in his advocacy of the primacy of ritual. Further, Rubenstein takes issue with Fackenheim's 614th commandment because it deems as sinful the understandable and valid stance of the Jew who, after Auschwitz, believes neither in God nor in remaining a Jew.

Next, I look at the controversial and provocative Marc Ellis, who takes Jewish theology to task on the notion of Jewish chosenness and on the theological importance of Israel. Ellis challenges Fackenheim's support of the state of Israel as a fundamental aspect of Jewish identity and faith. Ellis also provides a fertile basis for comparison between black theology of liberation and Jewish theology of liberation.

Following Ellis is an examination of Melissa Raphael, who develops a feminist Jewish post-Holocaust theology. Raphael argues that male post-Holocaust theologians, including Fackenheim, attempted to confront the event of the Holocaust with traditional models of God as patriarchal and dominating in mind. If divine power and presence are reinterpreted along feminist lines, the Holocaust remains an event of horrific stature, yet many of the theodicy problems are rephrased.

Finally, paralleling Hopkins' relation to Cone, Michael L. Morgan is studied as a contemporary theologian who further develops Fackenheim's thought. Morgan's work is used to illuminate Fackenheim's ideas of revelation, history, and redemption for the twenty-first century.

Chapter 6 is the constructive portion of the book in which I explore and develop the theological stance of humanocentric theism and the ethical response of resistance. This contribution to the conversation draws from Cone and Fackenheim, as well as Jones, Hopkins, and Raphael. Cone and Fackenheim demand that relevant theology must address racial and ethnic oppression and suffering. Cone argues that liberation is the key to understanding God's relationship to humanity, oppressed humanity in particular. I claim that God acts with humanity, persuading us to resist oppression and struggle for the liberation of the least of society. God wills freedom, liberation, and hope, but these goals are not inevitably reached, as Jones wrote.

Fackenheim cites the Voice of Auschwitz as commanding that Jews resist slaughter and despair. I assert that it is through resistance to suffering and despair that we become fully human and that God's will is enacted in history. In other words, it is only through resistance that *tikkun olam*, or a mending of the world, is possible. I clarify how I understand resistance as an ethical and ontological category.

The category of humanocentric theism is taken from Jones, though I differ from his formulation in that I do maintain divine goodness and use this as a basis on which to attempt to flesh out exactly what it is that God persuades us to do. Through persuasion, God guides us toward freedom and liberation, love and justice, and hope and redemption. In other words, God does have a goal in mind for us, but it is up to humanity to accept it and work toward it, or to reject it and continue the cycle of oppression and evil.

Though drawing from Cone and Fackenheim, I modify or challenge aspects of their work. My understanding of God is humanocentric theism. I believe that God creates humans with the purpose of becoming free and independent creatures, living in loving and just community with one another. Being created in God's image means being free to create our own characters and communities. I reject Cone and Fackenheim's traditional theistic concept that God is involved in human affairs in a direct and coercive manner. Instead, the concept of divine presence and activity developed here owes much to Melissa Raphael's understanding of *Shekhinah* (the female aspect of divine presence). God's involvement is in creating us as free beings, and persuading us to use our freedom toward good and just ends. God is active in the world by acting with and through human freedom and the natural processes of the world. Finally, though my ethical category of resistance is possible from a humanistic philosophy, I maintain belief in God as the ground of human existence, freedom, and resistance.

Resistance is both a way of being and a way of doing. Resistance must be understood as resistance against existential despair and against social, cultural, and historical forces of dehumanization. It is any stance taken against people, forces, or events that impede full and complete human fulfillment. Resistance should also be taken up for the least of society, the oppressed, the economic poor, the socially outcast, and those who lack power in its traditional forms. Resistance must also be a positive, constructive response to dehumanization. Resistance should ultimately envision and strive toward a loving, just, and peaceful society. This goal is not to be understood as inevitable, triumphalistic, or naïve. It may quite possibly remain an ideal rather than an actuality, but it must be a goal. Actions or beliefs of resistance need not necessarily be understood by an individual or a community who carries them out as being religious in character, but may be. For it is in human resistance to despair, oppression, and dehumanization that our full humanity and our link to God are manifested.

Resistance may be the seemingly simple act of Jewish prayer at Auschwitz or the religious meetings of enslaved blacks in woods. In some cases, existence itself may take on the character of resistance when existence becomes a crime or existential absurdity. Resistance is present in communal movements of social and political justice; importantly, it also is present in the everyday activities of people when they employ humor as a response to suffering, when they carry out small acts of kindness for another person, or when they survive another day.

This notion of resistance need not necessarily be understood as militaristic or violent. Ideally, resistance should be actively nonviolent.

However, if called for, resistance may take on violence as a method, but only as a last resort. In the end, it must be remembered that resistance is a human activity and, as does any human activity, holds the potential for both good and evil. I explore a few examples of resistance with the purpose of further clarifying it as a theological category.

Finally, the assertion that God persuades us toward liberation from oppression and toward redemption, as opposed to enacting these goals without us, has an important corollary. Suffering and evil are caused by human wrongdoing. Neither does God will suffering, nor is God able to end it unilaterally. Suffering, though potentially transformative, is to be resisted; suffering is not redemptive. On this point, my stance is closer to Fackenheim, who rejects the notion of Jews as martyrs during the Holocaust, than to Cone, who asserts that suffering may be redemptive, as it was in the case of Jesus. My understanding of resistance to suffering does not mean that one should avoid suffering because of apathy or fear. Instead, resistance means that one must struggle against suffering, not embrace it.

I feel that a final word concerning my project is necessary. As a white, non-Jewish male I am admittedly an outsider to both groups I examine in this book. Certainly, this means that my work has particular limitations and must be read as such. I do not wish to be presumptuous in my analysis of either black theology or Jewish theology. The analysis and ideas presented must be read as those of an outsider. In the end, readers of either community must judge for themselves how the position of an outsider is to be regarded in relation to these particular traditions.

Despite these possible dangers and limitations, I feel it necessary to delve into the work of Cone and Fackenheim because I believe their work must not be dismissed as relevant only to their particular communities. Their theologies demand and deserve greater attention from both whites and Christians. Cone and Fackenheim have exhibited sustained passion and brilliant creativity in their concern for human suffering, oppression, and despair. Without sacrificing intellectual integrity, they managed to remain faithful to both God and to the human condition.

Furthermore, I believe the theological traditions these two individuals represent have a relevance that transcends particularities. I am excited by the potential for theological exchange between two traditions that are not always viewed as sharing a common ground. The goal of such interfaith and intercultural dialogue is not to ignore genuine points of difference or conflict between various participants.

Rather, the aim is to explore questions of theology and ethics from multiple perspectives in the hope of coming to a richer, more complex understanding of ourselves as well as each other.

In this particular study, I recognize both the dangers and the potentials of utilizing a Christian theologian and a Jewish theologian for a constructive theology. The history of Christian-Jewish relations has led to much turmoil and destruction, to put it very mildly. Furthermore, the fact that I am comparing African American with Jewish thought involves additional complexities that are treated briefly in chapter 6. It is because of these tensions, not despite them, that I believe there is a potential for a fascinating and relevant theological development.

In this work I am concerned with formulating a theological attempt at dealing with moral evil and suffering broadly and with black and Jewish suffering in particular. This attempt is focused on the suffering of two particular communities of faith because general treatments of theodicy lack relevance when not applied to specific people, times, and places. I believe the theology developed, though in conversation with black theology of liberation and Jewish Holocaust theology, has relevance for any theological context that wishes to deal honestly and concretely with human suffering and redemption. In the end, the questions of how we conceive of God and how we understand our place in society and history must concern us all.

2

What Does the Christian Gospel Have to Do with the Black Power Movement?: James Cone's God of the Oppressed

> Blackness gave me new theological spectacles, which enabled me to move beyond the limits of white theology, and empowered my mind to think thoughts that were wild and heretical when evaluated by white academic values. Blackness opened my eyes to see African-American history and culture as one of the most insightful sources for knowing about God since the Bible was declared a canon. Blackness whetted my appetite for learning how to do theology with a black signature on it and thereby make it accountable to poor black people and not to the privileged white theological establishment. (James H. Cone, *Risks of Faith*, xxii)

In the above lines, James Cone reflects on his own early theological journey and emerging frustrations with and rage against the theological powers-that-be. With an explosive and creative merging of Martin Luther King, Jr. and Malcolm X in his body and soul, in the 1960s Cone denounced his doctoral advisor, and really by implication the entire white, Christian theological establishment, as racist. How could any Christian in America at this time keep silent in the face of enormous racial tensions and violence? he asked. Cone credits blackness as the key to unlocking the theological shackles that had been placed on him and as the existential source for a revolutionary way of doing theology, a new set of concerns, and a new primary audience. Cone's conversional "return to blackness" remains one of the most significant events in the history of Christian theology.

Before beginning a fuller discussion of Cone, which is the intent of this chapter, I feel it is necessary to briefly explain the connections I see between the concerns laid out in the previous introductory chapter and the exploration of the present one. In other words, why *am* I exploring African American theology, and Cone in particular, in an effort to address the more general issue of suffering and moral evil? How did I come to my encounter with the work of James Cone?

As I trace back to the roots of my awareness of Cone I find the improbable starting point of an undergraduate course, "Modern Hindu Thought." From a fascination with Gandhi and the idea of nonviolence, I made the short jump to Martin Luther King, Jr. I now sense that this is an interest and a connection that are probably fairly common among intellectually eager and idealistic undergraduates. After a discussion of thesis papers during a senior capstone seminar class, another student asked me if I had ever read Cone.[1] In researching King I had drawn from Cone's *Martin & Malcolm & America*, but I had not read Cone beyond this. It was in a graduate school class at the University of Chicago Divinity School on black theology with Dwight Hopkins that I began my own theological conversion to greater awareness of the blackness of which Cone and others wrote.

While my familiarity with King and Hopkins' class allowed me the opportunity to fully consider and evaluate Cone's theology, I believe the space in which I did most of my reading and the period of my nascent adult life that I was in also played a part in my encounter with Cone. I had just then moved to the Chicago area and was living in Aurora, Illinois. My wife worked as a residential counselor at a residential, public high school for gifted math and science students. As I came to learn, Aurora is about as far away from Chicago as one could be and still be taken remotely seriously when claiming to be from the "Chicago area." To get to the University of Chicago in Hyde Park, on the city's South Side, I took a commuter train into downtown Chicago, walked several blocks through downtown to another train station, and got on another commuter train to 59th Street. At the time I saw this daily trip, which could take up to three hours each way, as an inconvenience and nuisance. In retrospect, it allowed me plenty of time to do reading for my classes and, relevant to the present discussion, I now recognize that I was reading Cone and simultaneously getting a better sense of race relations and the intimately related issues of socioeconomic class. I was not entirely unaware of race and class in

America before this, but I was reading Cone while witnessing many other dynamics at the same time. The train from Aurora to Union Station was full of well-dressed, white, suburban business people, often obnoxiously on cell-phones. Moving through the incredible diversity of people and places in downtown Chicago, I saw working-class people, homeless individuals asking for food or money, Streetwise vendors, tourists, students, and business people. Once in the station waiting for the southbound train from downtown to Hyde Park, I saw business and working-class people, only this time they were predominantly black. Then, at the stop for the University, mostly white students got off. My understanding of Cone's work benefited greatly from my growing sense of de facto racial segregation, links between race and class, the invisibility of the poor, and the privileges of whiteness in the United States.

Quite regularly I was sitting in the downtown train station, reading Cone, and involuntarily nodding my head in agreement. I found his analysis of race in America and his correlation of the life of Jesus Christ with this contemporary context to be compelling and inspiring. Now, let me be careful and clear here. As a white person, I do not intend to claim any special access to "blackness." I can never place the theological spectacles that Cone describes in my field of vision. However, I do believe that, as a white theologian, I can and must take notice of what Cone and others can see through this lens of blackness. Through such a perspective I have come to regard "African-American history and culture as one of the most insightful sources for knowing about God." Furthermore, when considering and making theological claims, I absolutely feel compelled to hold myself accountable to "poor black people." Finally, I hope that I am at least beginning to recognize that my whiteness privileges my option to, in turn, stop and start seeing the world through the "blackness"-tinted spectacles of others with rather disturbing freedom. I began to wonder why my Divinity School was still not taking the issues of which Cone spoke very seriously. Why were there only one African American member of the faculty and only a handful of black students? Why were there only five of us in Dwight Hopkins' wonderfully amazing and eye-opening class on black theology? And, by following Cone's own intellectual development, I started to consider how these issues of race were linked to class and gender. While there were very few black students, there were certainly also very few poor students or women. Finally, there was little offered in the curriculum that I felt related directly to these contemporary issues.

So, in dealing with the topic of possible understandings of God and humanity in the face of suffering and moral evil, the appropriateness of using Cone seemed rather obvious to me. As Cone asserts, given the nature of the topic, it is crucial to approach the issue of suffering, evil, and theodicy from a very particular perspective to avoid falling into irrelevant abstraction. It is because of this very specific focus of Cone's theology that I believe Cone's analysis of the nature of suffering and evil and his theological and anthropological claims warrant much more serious and wider attention from non-African Americans than has been evident. Therefore, in my own constructive efforts at formulating a meaningful, relevant, and compelling theological position on suffering and moral evil, I feel that I cannot afford to ignore Cone, and his interlocutors, and that in fact I must place him very centrally.

In this chapter, after providing a brief biographical sketch of James Cone, I examine Cone's theological methodology. Cone's method places the black experience in dialectical relation to the Bible, and thus sets a framework for discussing the human-divine relationship in general. After outlining Cone's methodology, the major part of the chapter focuses on Cone's thoughts on God and humanity, and human resistance to oppression. In chapter 3, the critiques of William R. Jones, Anthony Pinn, Delores Williams, and Dwight Hopkins are brought into discussion with Cone. In chapter 6, Cone is placed in conversation with Emil Fackenheim and both are utilized as sources for a constructive theology. In particular, I hope to draw from Cone to assert that God does side with the oppressed in history and to make clear the imperative for humans to act as collaborators with God in resistance efforts taken for liberation and redemption.

Biographical Background

The method, content, and form of one's theology are fundamentally shaped by one's identity and by one's cultural and historical context, as in any discipline. Therefore, it is necessary and desirable that the context of a thinker be understood before her thought may be properly encountered. With this claim in mind, my analysis of James Cone's theology begins, as that of Emil Fackenheim's, with a look at their respective lives.[2]

Born on August 5, 1938, James Cone was raised in Bearden, Arkansas, a rural community of four hundred blacks and twice as many whites. Cone was greatly influenced by the black church experience at Macedonia African Methodist Episcopal Church (A.M.E.). There, he writes, "I encountered the presence of the divine Spirit, and my soul was moved and filled with an aspiration for freedom."[3] The God encountered at Macedonia was a God who loved black people and would one day relieve them of their earthly sufferings. Cone was further influenced by the theology and ethics of Martin Luther King, Jr. and the civil rights movement.

In addition to finding divine love in Bearden, Cone also found white hatred. Cone encountered white racism in its social, political, cultural, and theological forms. Segregation, Jim Crow laws, and disenfranchisement were combined with claims of black inferiority and a divinely sanctioned status quo. The contradiction between black religious understandings and racist social conditions influenced Cone's interest in religion and philosophy.

After earning an undergraduate degree from Philander Smith College in Little Rock, Arkansas, Cone studied at Garrett Biblical Institute in Evanston, Illinois, earning his doctorate in 1965. The journey north from Arkansas showed Cone that white racism was not unique to the rural South. For example, Cone recounts an episode when he was refused service in a white barbershop because he was black.[4] The racism encountered in the North illustrated just how deeply entrenched the phenomenon was.

Cone faced racism in both the community and in the seminary. On a personal level he describes the oppressive mentality of many of his professors and fellow students, citing instances when he was told he could not even qualify for the doctoral program at Garrett. On a more systematic level, Cone criticizes his program for not including even one book written by a black thinker. Already recognizing that theology must address contemporary social and political issues, Cone asks, "What could Karl Barth possibly mean for black students who had come from the cotton fields of Arkansas, Louisiana and Mississippi, seeking to change the structure of their lives in a society that had defined *black* as nonbeing?"[5] Though he himself wrote his dissertation on the anthropology of Karl Barth, it is clear that Cone understood the racist character of much of white Christian theology.

While teaching at Adrian College in Michigan in the late 1960s, Cone once again reflected on the relevance of the Christian gospel to the black experience in America, which at the time included Malcolm X and the Black Power Movement, King's assassination, and rebellion in Watts, Detroit, and Newark. Cone asked, "What has the biblical message to do with the black power revolution?"[6]

He addressed this issue in several articles, essays, and speeches, and especially in his first two books, *Black Theology and Black Power* (1969) and *A Black Theology of Liberation* (1970). In these early works, and throughout his career, Cone created and developed a black theology of liberation. Cone argues that Christianity is a religion of liberation. He correlates experience and theory, black experience and theology in particular. He finds a middle path, so to speak, between the nonviolent beloved community of Martin Luther King and the demand for justice "by any means necessary" philosophy of Malcolm X. Though consistent throughout his career in his assertion of God's liberating activity on the behalf of the oppressed, Cone's thought did not stagnate, but developed in significant ways since his early work.

In chapter 4 of his *For My People: Black Theology and the Black Church* (1984) and in the preface to the 1990 edition of *A Black Theology of Liberation*,[7] Cone cites particular areas that he had ignored or neglected in his initial work. First, his early work was marked by a sexist disregard for the experiences of black women. He explained that black male religious scholars and preachers failed to address the oppression of black women in society, and in the black church as well. In addition, black males did little to support the theological reflections of black women.[8]

Second, when working on his early publications, Cone was not aware of the links between oppression in America and oppression in the third world. Cone writes, "I am convinced that no one should claim to be doing Christian theology today without making the liberation of the Third World from the exploitation of the First World and the Second World a central aspect of its purpose."[9] Cone's involvement in the Ecumenical Association of Third World Theologians (EATWOT) indicates his matured appreciation and understanding of the connections and relationships between black oppression in the United States and oppression throughout the world.[10]

Cone points out that a third weakness in his early theology was a lack of the type of an economic class analysis that characterized Latin American liberation theology. He writes, "An exclusive focus on racial injustice without a comprehensive analysis of its links with corporate capitalism greatly distorts the multidimensional character of oppression and also camouflages the true nature of modern racism."[11] Like his recognition of sexism, Cone's acknowledgment of classism exhibits his belief in the interconnectedness of various forms of oppression.

Finally, a fourth mistake Cone admits is his "methodological dependence" on white theology and philosophy, in terms of both sources and method.[12] Though Cone used black experience and history as the primary sources for his theology, he also relied on many white thinkers in his analysis of black oppression and liberation.[13] He describes this as a "negative overreaction to white racism." For black theology to have continued relevance, a constructive methodology, independent of white racism and utilizing black and African thought, had to be developed.[14]

Methodologically, Cone explains that were he given the chance to rewrite his earlier work, he would not begin with an abstract notion of revelation and move on from there to explicate the traditional topics of Christian theology. Instead, he would make theology a second step to praxis on behalf of the oppressed, as Gustavo Gutierrez, a Latin American liberation theologian, had claimed was proper.[15] Cone's theological method is a good starting point for a discussion of his theological reflections.

Theological Method

To best understand the thought of James Cone, I believe one must begin with an examination of his methodology. In the late 1960s and early 1970s, James Cone formulated and crafted a theological framework and thus created a revolution. A core component of this revolution was his methodology. Cone's method started from the context of the oppressed of society, used this oppression coupled with the revelation of Jesus Christ as the norm, and maintained a dialectic of action and reflection.

After Cone's early writings, especially *Black Theology and Black Power* (1969), *A Black Theology of Liberation* (1970), *The Spirituals and the Blues* (1972), and *God of the Oppressed* (1975), the vocation of the theologian could no longer be limited to reflections made in an isolated study or university office. The influential Protestant theologian Karl Barth had said that a theologian must work with the Bible in one hand and a newspaper in the other. He meant that a theologian must reflect on both the message of the Bible and the current events of the day. Cone added that a theologian must work, not only with the Bible and a newspaper in hand, but also with the plow, hammer, and perhaps even the gun in hand, because these objects better reflected the lives of those for whom theologians should be writing and living.

Now the theologian has to be active with and among the people, particularly the oppressed members of society.[16] Certainly, the Bible must still be in the mind of the theologian, but now it is reflected upon only after the context for such reflection is established. Only after the action of existentially becoming one with the oppressed, after exposure to the experience of oppression, and after viewing the world through the eyes of oppression, can the theologian begin to reflect on these realities in the light of the Gospel. In other words, as Gustavo Gutierrez asserted, action must precede reflection. Cone argued that theology could not be an objective or disinterested discourse about God. It must be passionate and must respond to both God's revelation in Jesus Christ *and* the reality of suffering and oppression in the world.[17] I concur with this argument that for Christian theology to be true to the message of the Bible, the voices and experiences of the oppressed must be its starting point. Likewise, for Christian theology to be relevant to these very people, it must combine prophetic reflection with liberative action, as Jesus Christ did.

Cone maintained that since theology is a human word about God, one must consider the background and context of the theologian when examining his or her claims. The mistake of theology, white, European theology especially, was that it believed that objectivity was possible and that one's own life experiences could be separated from one's theology. For too long it had been the oppressive white, European male context that had shaped modern theological discourse. For example, when Paul Tillich referred to the existential questions of human existence,[18] he was essentially pointing to the existential questions of white, male, Western existence. As a result, the theology produced was manifested in the voices of this group and focused on its concerns and worldview.[19] Cone argued, first, that one must be conscious of one's context and audience and, second, that his own context and audience was the African American experience of the twentieth century. He asked, "[W]hat did Barth, Tillich, and Brunner have to do with young black girls and boys coming from the cotton fields of Arkansas, Tennessee, and Mississippi seeking to make a new future for themselves? This was *the* major question for me. And it was further intensified by the civil rights struggle. The contradiction between theology as a discipline and the struggle for black freedom in the streets was experienced at the deepest level of my being."[20] Cone reasoned his own theology must reflect this context if it were to be relevant to this audience.[21]

Furthermore, Cone agrees with the important and central role of Jesus Christ in Christian theology, but adds that it is Christ understood as liberator that is vital. The message of the Bible is that God sides with the oppressed and is active in history, working toward their liberation. Cone asserts that the vocation of the theologian must start and finish with a commitment to the oppressed and marginalized, just as God's does. This explains Cone's need for a new starting point and a new set of sources for doing theology.[22]

The starting point of Cone's black liberation theology is the dialectic of the Bible and the black experience. The core of his system is the assertion that Jesus Christ lived and lives even now for the liberation and freedom of the poor and marginalized, and for black poor and marginalized in particular.[23] Cone claims that the message that explodes from the Bible is that God sides with the oppressed of the land and works for them and with them to liberate them from oppressive and demonic structures. From the exodus of God's Chosen People, through the voices of the prophets, culminating in the life, death, and resurrection of Jesus Christ, the Bible displays God as liberator of the oppressed. Like the Bible, one can see God working in and through the lives and experiences of black folk. Through black resistance and survival, joy and tribulation, God lives among the oppressed, Cone asserts.

Cone's dialectical methodology, oscillating between the black experience and scripture, is evident in the fact that he begins both his *God of the Oppressed* and *My Soul Looks Back* by relating his experiences growing up in Bearden, Arkansas. In the preface to *God of the Oppressed*, Cone argues that he is black first and "every thing else after that." That is, he begins from his existential location as a black American male and *then* examines the claims of Christianity.[24] He writes, "We cannot be 'objective,' . . . Our theology must emerge consciously from an investigation of the socio-religious experience of black people, as that experience is reflected in *black* stories of God's dealings with black people in the struggle of freedom."[25] The question driving his theological life is—what does the Gospel of Jesus Christ have to do with the struggles of the oppressed for liberation? He claims the essence of both the black experience and the Bible is the message of Jesus and his liberation of the oppressed. After explaining what Cone means by black experience, history, and culture, I explore his interpretation of the Bible.

Cone asserts that the existential reality of being black in a white world is to live an absurd life. Cone describes this absurdity as the sense of "the absolute contradiction between *what is* and *what ought to be*."[26] He further explains, "Absurdity arises as the black man seeks to understand his place in the white world. The black man does not view himself as absurd; he views himself as human. But as he meets the white world and its values, he is confronted with an almighty No and is defined as a thing. This produces the absurdity."[27] Thus, absurdity is shaped by the confrontation between black identity and white racism.

There are both negative and positive consequences to this encounter. Cone explains that the black experience deconstructs the white, oppressive understanding of society, even as it constructs its own alternative view of the world. Here both a "No" to white racism and a "Yes" to Black Power are evident.

On the deconstructive side, black experience is shaped by white racism. Cone writes,

> The black person knows that a ghetto is the white way of saying that blacks are subhuman and fit only to live with rats. The black experience is police departments adding more recruits and buying more guns to provide "law and order," which means making a city safe for its white population. It is politicians telling blacks to cool it or *else*. It is George Wallace, Hubert Humphrey, and Richard Nixon running for president. The black experience is college administrators defining "quality" education in the light of white values. It is church bodies compromising on whether blacks are human.[28]

Though Cone's references speak of America in the 1960s and 1970s, his evocative description is still applicable today. It may take on new forms, but white racism has not been eradicated.

On the constructive, positive side, the black experience, according to Cone's account, includes a love and respect for one's black identity *because* one is black. Cone explains the power of the black experience:

> It is the sound of James Brown singing, "I'm Black and I'm Proud" and Aretha Franklin demanding "respect." The black experience is catching the spirit of blackness and loving it. It is hearing black preachers speak of God's love in spite of the filthy ghetto, and black congregations responding Amen, which means that they realize that ghetto existence is not the result of divine decree but of white inhumanity.[29]

Cone explains that the black experience includes the idea of "black soul," including joy and pain. It is manifest in the pride of a strong black man or woman being black, the joy of the sheer tenacity that forbids white oppression to impede one's happiness, and the absolute resolution to end this oppression today, not tomorrow. It also includes knowing for certain that the day of victory will surely arrive because you are on God's side. The tradition of survival and resistance, in addition to liberation, is also in evidence here.[30]

Alongside the black experience as a second source for Cone's theology is black history, which is the litany of black individuals and communities who have lived the absurd existence. Cone explains that black history "began when black mothers decided to kill their babies rather than have them grow up to be slaves. Black power is Nat Turner, Denmark Vesey, and Gabriel Prosser planning a slave revolt. It is slaves poisoning masters, and Frederick Douglass delivering an abolitionist address."[31] This record of the black experience includes the non-Christian black religious tradition, including African religions, Afro-Caribbean spiritual traditions, and the Nation of Islam, among others.[32]

A third source to which Cone points is black culture. Here he considers creative forms of expression such as music, art, and literature. This source includes black folktales, slave secular songs, the blues, and personal accounts, particularly in slave narratives and the writings of Harlem Renaissance and the 1960s and 1970s. One may include the influences and impact of African cultures as well.[33]

It is from the context of black experience, history, and culture that Cone comes to the Bible and the Christian tradition. Thus, an additional source alongside this context is an amalgamation of the traditional Christian theological sources of revelation and scripture. For Cone, revelation is witnessed to in the Bible, but is not limited to the biblical text. Cone explains that revelation is God's self-revelation of the liberative intent and power of the divine. This revelation is evident in the first three sources of black experience, history, and culture. It also is present in the historical events of the Bible such as the Exodus, Incarnation, and Resurrection. Given this understanding, Cone explains that revelation occurs wherever there is liberation or struggle for liberation.[34]

The major theological concern for James Cone is how to interpret the Bible so that it would address the needs of African Americans in the United States. Again the dilemma of how to be both black and Christian was at the forefront of Cone's consciousness. By doing a detailed analysis of Cone's biblical hermeneutics, the dialectical exchange between experience and text becomes evident.[35]

The Bible is integral to Cone's theology. In fact, he claims, "Black theology is biblical theology."[36] Cone believes that, though black experience should always serve to temper the authority of scripture,[37] the theological attempt at interpreting revelation through the lens of oppression was inherently a biblical approach to understanding God's Word.[38] Though not infallible, the Bible's role in Cone's system is "an indispensable witness to God's revelation" and "a guide for checking the contemporary interpretation of God's revelation."[39] The Bible is witness to the revelation of God working in history for human liberation.[40] For Cone, the biblical story shows that God was a liberating God throughout Israel's history and most profoundly in the Incarnation of Jesus.

Just as the exegetical method of reading the Bible through the eyes of the oppressed is an inherently biblical approach for Cone, the resulting message of liberation in black theology is inherently biblical.[41] Cone asserted that if one understood the Bible correctly, then the only notion one could come away with would be that God actively identified with the oppressed Jews and helped to liberate them.[42] In God's descent to the oppressed, God fully identifies with the oppressed, most fully in the form of Jesus Christ. This identification is so complete that it has a sociocultural meaning alongside the more abstract philosophical meaning. The incarnation is significant not only because it marks a miraculously new divine-human relation, but also because of who Jesus was and what he did in history. He was a Jew who lived and worked among the socially outcast and the least of society. Cone points to scripture as the witness to this theologically significant fact of Jesus' life.

One may understand Cone's use of the Bible by comparing his interpretation of scripture with the use to which Albert Cleage puts the same text in his *Black Messiah*, issued in 1968, the year before Cone's *Black Theology and Black Power*. Cleage and Cone were similar in their desire to apply their interpretation of Bible to the modern black community and to affirm the validity of the Christian religion for modern blacks. In fact, both men claimed that the Bible spoke specifically to the black community. However, they differed in their understandings of the central message of scripture and their resulting solutions for contemporary blacks. These differences are nuanced and slight on a certain level, but nevertheless shed light on their divergent views of the true meaning of the Bible and of their solutions for modern black oppression.

Cleage read the Bible as part of black history, while Cone reads it as part of God's history. Cleage believed that the Nation Israel was the root of the modern Black Nation and that Jesus was one of the Black Nation's greatest leaders. The lessons of the Old Testament are the lessons of the Black Nation.[43] Cone understands the Bible to be a witness to the liberating force of God in the lives of the oppressed. The Old Testament tells us that God takes sides with the oppressed and the New Testament is the story of God's most imminent identification within the oppressed. Cleage used the Bible as a kind of handbook for revolution, learning from past mistakes.[44] Cone uses it as proof that, because all humans are made in the image of God, and God is righteous and loving toward us, we too should rise up against oppression wherever we see it. In the end, Cone's unique understanding of the resurrection of Jesus means that God fights on the side of any group of oppressed peoples and so should we.

James Cone views the Old Testament as evidence that God takes sides with oppressed peoples and helps them to fight for liberation. He does not disagree with Cleage concerning the race of the biblical patriarchs, but he does not explicitly agree either. Cone emphasizes the fact that the ancient Jews, who may have been black, were oppressed, whatever their race may have been historically.

Just as Cleage had learned from the Ancient Jews that the oppressed must fight with God and not remain passive,[45] Cone understands that the election of Israel in the Old Testament was a "terrible responsibility,"[46] because "the covenant requires obedience to the will of Yahweh." That is, the Chosen People of God cannot simply relax and reap the benefits of God's favor. Rather, "to accept the covenant means that Israel must now live as Yahweh's liberated people, becoming the embodiment of freedom made possible through his freeing presence. The covenant not only places upon Israel the responsibility of accepting the absolute sovereignty of Yahweh as defined in the first commandment; it also requires Israel to treat the weak in her midst as Yahweh has treated her."[47] More than any other group of people, the Chosen of God must live up to this special designation by remaining faithful and righteous. In addition, just as Cleage had recognized that the loss of community had been Israel's downfall,[48] Cone defines sin as the denial of "the values that make the community what it is."[49]

Cone believes it was when Israel forgot its Exodus-Sinai tradition of social justice and moved into the period of the monarchy that the status of the oppressed in society was ignored. This failure prompted the rise of prophecy. Cone explains, "The prophets were almost unanimous in their contention that Israel disobeyed the first commandment. The people failed to recognize Yahweh's sovereignty in history, and thus began to trust their own power and the power of political alliances with other nations (Isa. 31:1). . . . The disobedience of the first commandment always has consequences in the social life of the community. Israel, therefore, began to oppress the weak and the poor in their own community."[50] This sin, then, is what led to the exile, according to Cone.

For Cone, the righteousness of a person depends on what role that individual plays in the liberation of oppressed peoples. The Bible exhorts us to "share in [God's] creative involvement in the world on behalf of men."[51] Cone understands the Bible, not as a singular revelation of God, but as a witness to one of many of God's liberating activities in the world. That is, just as God was immanent within the Jewish community in the Bible because they were the oppressed of their times, God is immanent in the modern black community because that is where there is oppression. For Cone, the Old Testament shows that God takes sides with the oppressed, then the Israelites, now blacks, and serves as a liberating force in the lives of these oppressed peoples.

Both Cleage and Cone continued their respective theologies by applying the same principles to the New Testament as they had used in reading the Old Testament. Cone asserts that "If Yahweh is to keep his promise to bring freedom, then the Old Testament cannot be the end of Yahweh's drama with Israel. The Old Testament pushes beyond itself to an expected future event which Christians say happened in Jesus Christ."[52] While Cleage saw in Jesus a political revolutionary,[53] Cone sees a liberator of the oppressed. As Cone emphasizes ancient Israel's oppression over their race, he refers to Jesus as not-white, but still also not *black* as Cleage did.[54] Cone writes:

> It seems to me that the *literal color* of Jesus is irrelevant, as are the different shades of blackness in America. . . . The importance of the concept of the black Christ is that it expresses the *concreteness* of Jesus' continued presence today. If we do not translate the first-century titles into symbols that are relevant today, . . . Jesus becomes merely a figure of past history.[55]

Cone explains that it is useful to envision the historical Jesus as black because that would make him more relevant to the modern situation. "The blackness of Christ clarifies the definition of him as the *Incarnate* One. In him God becomes oppressed humanity and thus reveals that the achievement of full humanity is consistent with divine being."[56] Cone calls God black, explaining "the blackness of God means that God has made the oppressed condition God's own condition. This is the essence of the biblical revelation."[57] Unlike those of Albert Cleage's, Cone's notions of race seem to imply a quality of character more than a quantity of skin pigment.

There is a tension in Cone's distinction between literal blackness and symbolic blackness. On the one hand, Cone argues for a literally black Christ and is interested in addressing his theology to the experiences and needs of African Americans. On the other hand, though, Cone seems to mitigate his stress on race by allowing that the category of blackness may be symbolic. Cone's category of symbolic blackness serves to allow nonblacks to identify with Christ and with Cone's theological goals. However, I believe the main reason Cone stops short of identifying Jesus as literally black is that such a move prevents African Americans from assuming a higher status in God's eyes only because of skin color. By identifying blackness as a quality of character, Cone does indeed open the door for some progressive whites who agree with Cone's goals and methods to play some part in the liberation of the oppressed. In addition, Cone's symbolic blackness is inclusive of non-black minorities who suffer oppression. Ultimately though, Cone makes this move because he does not want to claim that God identifies and sides with blacks because of a phenotypical characteristic. God identifies with blacks, not because they are black, but because they are oppressed. Since the oppressed now are black, Jesus is black.[58]

Like Cleage,[59] Cone also analyzes the white corruption of true Christianity.[60] He recognized that Christianity had been abused by whites to pacify blacks and "keep them in their place." Whites had used the Bible to justify slavery[61] and to encourage blacks to stop concerning themselves with the atrocities and sufferings of this life. Cone struggles with doubts about whether the Christian Scriptures could still speak to contemporary blacks despite these abuses.[62] In the end, Cone triumphantly and passionately concludes that "Christianity . . . is Black Power."[63]

Cone understands Jesus to be God's most complete and immanent identification with the oppressed of the earth. He cites Luke 4:18–19[64] as the pronouncement of God's liberating force in the person of Jesus: "The Spirit of the Lord is upon me, because he has anointed me to bring good news to the poor. He has sent me to proclaim release to the captives and recovery of sight to the blind, to let the oppressed go free, to proclaim the year of the Lord's favor." Just as God had taken sides in the Old Testament with the Israelites, Jesus continues to side with the oppressed in the New Testament. "In the New Testament, Jesus is not for *all*, but for the oppressed, the poor and unwanted of society, and against oppressors."[65] This liberation should not be misunderstood to mean only a paradisiacal afterlife, since Cone saw salvation as "release from slavery and admission to freedom . . ."[66]

The significance of God's Incarnation for Cone was that, from God's descent to earth, humans learn that God cares about their oppression on earth. God is not some abstract, transcendent, and thus for Cone, irrelevant force. "In Christ, God enters human affairs and takes sides with the oppressed. Their suffering becomes his: their despair, divine despair."[67] The life of Jesus is a testament to his identification with the oppressed and socially outcast. Jesus was born in the modern "equivalent of a beer case in a ghetto alley."[68] His baptism implied that Jesus was a sinner like us, while his ministry placed him squarely within the existence of oppressed outcasts.[69] The most significant fact about the Incarnation though is the death and resurrection of Jesus. In death, Jesus is evidence that God fully identifies with human suffering and existence, and in resurrection he is proof of God's awesome liberating power.[70] "[Jesus] is God himself coming into the very depths of human existence for the sole purpose of striking off the chains of slavery, thereby freeing man from ungodly principalities and powers that hinder his relationship with God."[71] Cone's concept of the importance of the death and resurrection of Jesus differs from Cleage's.

Cone's understanding of the Incarnation of God points to his understanding of revelation and biblical interpretation. For Cone, the Bible tells of some, not all, of God's actions through history. The relevance of the Bible for Cone is "its power to point beyond itself to the reality of God's revelation and in America, that means black liberation."[72] The Bible for Cone is not an account of the singular divine identification with the poor, rather it is proof that it happens all the time.[73] "If the gospel is a gospel of liberation for the oppressed, then Jesus is where the oppressed are and continues his work of liberation there."[74]

Because God is the God of history, Cone believes that if one can make the case for God acting a certain way in the past, then one can assume and claim that God acts in such a way now. "If the historical Jesus is any clue for an analysis of the contemporary Christ, then he must be where human beings are enslaved. To speak of him is to speak of the liberation of the oppressed."[75] Because Jesus sided with the oppressed of the first century, Jesus sides with the oppressed of the twentieth century, Cone concludes. In contemporary America, the African American community is where Cone finds the Incarnate Jesus. So, Cone asserts, one can speak of Jesus as the Black Christ.[76]

Cone believes that the significance of Jesus is found not simply in his life of service for and fellowship among the oppressed, though this is vital as well, but also in the cross and resurrection, which show the length to which God is willing to go to liberate and the power which God holds to liberate. Cone understands the resurrection to be the evidence that God is still fighting for the liberation of the oppressed. In the life of Jesus, God most certainly took sides, and through the resurrection God continues to side with the oppressed of the world. The resurrection made Jesus's life both universal and eternal.[77]

Obviously, Cone understands Jesus to be most strongly manifested in the modern age within the black community since that is where one finds the harshest oppression. Black Power, Cone proclaims, is "Christ's central message to twentieth-century America."[78] The force of Cone's biblical hermeneutic was that he applied it smoothly and consistently to contemporary America. Cone questions, "What does the Christian gospel have to say to powerless black men whose existence is threatened daily by the insidious tentacles of white power?"[79] His answer is that the Bible is inherently a liberating story of the God of Liberation. Therefore, black theology's "sole purpose is to apply the freeing power of the gospel to black people under white oppression."[80]

Cone uses a dialectical theological method that moves between the sources of black experience, history, and culture and the Bible and the Christian tradition because he believes that it is in this interchange that God is revealed to humanity. After an analysis of Cone's understanding of God, his consequent notions of humanity are explored.

James Cone on God

James Cone understands God as the liberator of the oppressed. This understanding is based on both the black experience and the Bible. More precisely, it is through the black experience that the Bible is read, and this reading in turn shapes the black experience.[81] At the core of this theology lies a belief in a God of both love and justice without which God is incomplete. Cone cites the Bible as the foundation of his assertion that God is liberator. It is in the Bible that one encounters a God who set Israel free from Egyptian bondage, sent prophets with messages of freedom, and ultimately became Incarnate in Jesus Christ, who lived among and ministered to the oppressed and outcast of society. For Cone, God is the God of the oppressed who liberates and whose love *is* justice. Because of the life, death, and resurrection of Jesus, Cone believes that humans must take up God's fight for freedom and struggle with the oppressed for liberation. He claims that the God of the white tradition and of white theology is not a deity who deserves worship. Cone outlines how and why the black God was encountered in the lives of black folks and manifested in the black experience.

Though Cone's original impetus for his work was the white racism evident throughout society and the academy, methodologically he started his naming of God with revelation, most importantly, the Bible. Cone understands revelation to mean divine self-disclosure. Though this self-disclosure took place in the Bible, it has also occurred throughout history. Cone believes that divine self-disclosure takes place in relation to human reception. He wrote: "Divine revelation is not the rational discovery of God's attributes, or the assent to infallible biblical propositions, or an aspect of human self-consciousness. Rather, revelation has to do with God as God is in personal relationship with humankind effecting the divine will in our history."[82] Cone reasoned that "[w]e can only know God in relation, not in essence."[83]

Though I agree with this claim, I believe that Cone, in his own theological assertion of God as liberator, does try to say something about God's essence. To argue that we know God only in relation is one thing, but to say that we should know God in relation as liberator of the oppressed is another, because it limits the content and nature of our relation to God. That is, if one claims that this is the only relation we can or should have with God, then one is making a statement about the God in essence, as well as about God in relation. That God acts as liberator of the oppressed defines God's essence in a particular way. Rather than saying we know God in relation, not in essence, Cone should more precisely say we know God's attributes, not essence. One of these attributes is how God relates to humanity.

For Cone, God's revelation takes place in the lives of humanity, particularly in the lives of oppressed humanity. Cone went as far as to claim that revelation is intended only for the oppressed and takes place only in the context of liberation history. He explained that "[r]evelation is God's self-disclosure to humankind *in the context of liberation.*"[84] Since revelation was for the oppressed and it occurred in the context of liberation, Cone could write: "In a word, God's revelation means liberation—nothing more, nothing less."[85]

I believe this view of revelation too narrowly defines God's relation to humanity. As with his above epistemological claim, Cone sacrifices clarity for rhetoric. If liberation refers only to the sociopolitical liberation of African Americans, one could argue for other forms of revelation, both throughout history and in the contemporary context. Because of his understanding of how God reveals Godself and the contemporary realities of American society, Cone argued in 1970 that "the black revolution in America is the revelation of God. Revelation means black power."[86] However, Cone's definition of liberation has become deeper and broader over time to include cultural and psychological liberation, while encompassing all oppressed peoples, not only African Americans.

Cone claims that he was not simply collapsing ideology into theology when he explained the nature of divine revelation in such a way.[87] Instead, he understands his work to be a description of how God really acts. "The identification of the story of liberation with God's story, which troubles my critics, is not derived from the human situation. Christian theology does not move from human needs to God, but from God's revelation to our needs."[88] This distinction is not as clear in Cone's theology as he claims. In his claim Cone seems to side with Karl Barth's understanding of revelation as a phenomenon that originates with God and is transmitted below to humanity. In making this move Cone denies Paul Tillich's method of correlation whereby God's revelation is partially in response to the human existential condition. However, in practice Cone uses Tillich's method more than Barth's. In using his theology to answer how it is possible to be both black and Christian, Cone correlates black existence with the Christian Bible as a first step. His ideology *does* influence his theology as much as any theologian's ideology does and should impact theological claims. The problem is not that one's context shapes one's understanding of the human condition and divine revelation. Rather, the problem is not consciously acknowledging this fact; there is no "pure" revelation unmediated by ideology, experience, or context. In practice Cone acknowledges this, but in theory he tries to distance himself from his white predecessors who claimed that God's revelation supported slavery, racism, or oppression. Revelation, for Cone, is not a set of abstract philosophical principles, nor a collection of rigid moral mandates. Rather, revelation is God acting for oppressed humanity. These actions, Cone believes, could only be manifested within human history. "In fact, there is no revelation of God without history. The two are inseparable."[89] The Bible was an example of the recorded revelation of God acting in history.

In the Bible, one encounters a God who is active in history. "Unlike the God of Greek philosophy who is removed from history, the God of the Bible is involved in history, and God's revelation is inseparable from the social and political affairs of Israel."[90] Cone's God is a historical, political deity who most certainly takes sides with the oppressed. He writes, "There is no knowledge of Yahweh except through his political activity on behalf of the weak and helpless of the land."[91] The entire biblical account, for Cone, is proof of God's actions in history for the oppressed.

Cone understands God as liberator to be rooted initially in the doctrine of creation. "God as creator means that humankind is a creature; the source of its meaning and purpose in the world is not found in oppressors but in God."[92] Human meaning and purpose find their source in the concept of the image of God. Cone understood being created in God's image as being created for freedom. Freedom is both our drive for our own liberation and our efforts at liberating others.[93] "To affirm that liberation is an expression of the image of God is to say not only who God is but also who I am and who my people are. Liberation is knowledge of self; it is a vocation to affirm who I am created to be."[94] Freedom, for Cone, is not the ability to do what one pleases, but rather, the freedom to do as God wills.[95] In other words, our freedom comes with responsibility. God wills that we act for the oppressed, alongside God.

The Bible, from the Old Testament through the New Testament shows how God acts as liberator, for Cone. "It is a fact in almost every scene of the Old Testament drama of salvation, the poor are defended against the rich, the weak against the strong. Yahweh is the God of the oppressed whose revelation is identical with their liberation from bondage."[96] Along with the time of the prophets, the Exodus narrative is a central account in the Old Testament for Cone. "In the Exodus event, God is revealed by means of acts on behalf of a weak and defenseless people. This is the God of power and strength, able to destroy the enslaving power of the mighty Pharaoh."[97] This powerful, liberating God acts in history, and, by doing so, establishes an expectation, or a covenant that freed humans will also act in history according to the will of God. "By delivering this people from Egyptian bondage and inaugurating the covenant on the basis of that historical event, God is revealed as the God of the oppressed, involved in their history, liberating them from human bondage."[98] The story of God liberating the oppressed on earth continues with the life of Jesus.

In response to the claim that liberation is a motif throughout the Bible, Delores Williams argues that if one reads the text through the eyes of non-Hebrews or non-Christians, the message of liberation is not very clear. Williams points to the story of Hagar to show that survival, not liberation, is God's way to deal with oppression. God gives the land of milk and honey to the Israelites and commands them to conquer the people already living there.[99] What does this say about God's relation to the native inhabitants of the land? ask Palestinian Christian and Native American liberation theologians.[100] Though it can be acknowledged that God does take sides and acts as liberator throughout portions of the Hebrew Bible and the Christian scriptures, these challenges must be considered by any theologian, such as Cone, who views the Bible as an unmitigated liberative message. These are important points to consider when we later examine Cone's understanding of God taking sides with the oppressed and acting in history for their liberation.

The message of liberation that Cone extracts from the Bible reaches its culmination in the incarnation of Jesus Christ. Cone claims "Christian theology begins and ends with Jesus Christ. He is the point of departure for everything to be said about God, humankind, and the world."[101] Cone also defined his theological norm as Jesus: *The norm of all God-talk which seeks to be black-talk is the manifestation of Jesus as the black Christ who provides the necessary soul for black liberation.*"[102] Cone speaks of Jesus as black because of his notion of incarnation and resurrection. The incarnation of Jesus means that God took on human form and did so in such a way that he undeniably identified with the oppressed. Throughout the existence of Christ on earth he lived an oppressed life, lived among the oppressed, and struggled to bring liberation to the economically poor and socially outcast.[103] This life spent among the poor, struggling for the dignity of the outcast takes on cosmic ramifications because of who Jesus is. Cone asserts:

Jesus was not simply a nice fellow who happened to like the poor. Rather his actions have their origin in God's eternal being. They represent a new vision of divine freedom, climaxed with the cross and the resurrection, wherein God breaks into history for the liberation of slaves from societal oppression. Jesus' actions represent God's will not to let his creation be destroyed by non-creative powers. The cross and the resurrection show that the freedom promised is now fully available in Jesus Christ. This is the essence of the New Testament story without which Christian theology is impossible.[104]

Cone understands the life of Christ to be a continuation of the Old Testament emphasis of God siding with the oppressed. It was through the death and resurrection of Jesus that such a divine preference became universal and eternal.

Cone explains the shift of the story from particular and historical to universal and eternal: "If the history of Israel and the New Testament description of the historical Jesus reveal that God is a God who is identified with Israel because it is an oppressed community, the resurrection of Jesus means that all oppressed peoples become his people."[105] The rebirth of Christ also means a rebirth of his way of life.

Cone views the cross and resurrection as two sides of the same coin that signified that God won our freedom from oppression and gave us the gift of fighting for that freedom as well.[106] "*The finality of Jesus lies in the totality of his existence in complete freedom as the Oppressed One who reveals through his death and resurrection that God is present in all dimensions of human liberation.* His death is the revelation of the freedom of God, . . . his resurrection is the disclosure that God is not defeated by oppression but transforms it into the possibility of freedom."[107] The phrase "the possibility of freedom" implies that work is left to be done for humanity. The work of Jesus Christ is a start, not yet complete. Our struggle for freedom returns the story to the particular and historical. For it is in history that individuals and communities struggle for the liberation of the oppressed on earth.

Cone locates this struggle in twentieth-century America in the African American community. He reasons that "[i]f the historical Jesus is any clue for an analysis of the contemporary Christ, then he must be where human beings are enslaved. To speak of him is to speak of the liberation of the oppressed."[108] In contemporary America, for Cone, the oppressed are African Americans. Cone argues that "Christ is black, therefore, not because of some cultural or psychological need of black people, but because and only because Christ *really* enters into our world where the poor, the despised, and the black are, disclosing that he is with them, enduring their humiliation and pain and transforming oppressed slaves into liberated servants."[109] For Cone, blackness is theologically identical to being oppressed. Again, as cited above, he writes, "The blackness of Christ clarifies the definition of him as the *Incarnate* One. In him God becomes oppressed humanity and thus reveals that the achievement of full humanity is consistent with divine being."[110] Cone's logic is that God was incarnate among the oppressed of the first century in Israel, and, because of the resurrection, God is Incarnate always, among the oppressed of all times. In twentieth-century America this means that Jesus is black.

Once one understands the nature of Jesus in the theology of James Cone, one may examine Cone's notion of God. For, as stated earlier, the concept of Jesus Christ in black theology radically impacts the resulting naming of God. "The Christian understanding of God arises from the biblical view of revelation, a revelation of God that takes place in the liberation of the oppressed Israel and is completed in the incarnation, in Jesus Christ."[111] For Cone, Jesus is the liberator and hence God is a liberating God. He wrote that "God is the political God, the Protector of the poor and the Establisher of the right for those who are oppressed. To know God is to experience the acts of God in the concrete affairs and relationships of people, liberating the weak and the helpless from pain and humiliation."[112] As liberator of the oppressed, God has certain powers.

But, given the reality of oppression, Cone does not understand these vast powers of God to encompass all imaginable feats. He explains, "Omnipotence does not refer to God's absolute power to accomplish what God wants."[113] Instead, Cone's God uses a power that affirms human worth and dignity, illuminating human freedom, particularly for the oppressed. In his words, "God's omnipotence is the power to let blacks stand out from whiteness and to be."[114] Oppression attempts to crush this human freedom and self-worth. In America, one form of oppression is slavery and racism.

In the midst of the American Dream a nightmare has existed. For about 250 years, slavery was understood by black Americans as white hypocrisy, which would be punished by God. "The theological assumption of black slave religion as expressed in the spirituals was that *slavery contradicts God*, and *God will therefore liberate black people*."[115] For Cone, God does take sides, and in America that means God sides with African Americans against the white power structure and against white racism.

Cone asserts that his liberating God must be black. He explains that "the blackness of God is the key to our knowledge of God."[116] Blackness for Cone is not only skin pigmentation; it is an existential standpoint from which one resists oppression, thus transcending race. According to Cone, a person with black or white skin can be "black." Likewise, "though one's skin is black, the heart may be lily white."[117] To be black means that you resist social, political, cultural, and psychological oppression in whatever form you encounter it. In Cone's words, "Being black in America has very little to do with skin color. To be black means that your heart, your soul, your mind, and your body are where the dispossessed are."[118] It is because God sides with the oppressed, throughout the Bible and throughout history that God is black. "The blackness of God means that God has made the oppressed condition God's own condition. This is the essence of the biblical revelation."[119] Cone does not claim to describe a physical attribute of God, nor does he claim an inherent value in a particular human physical characteristic. Rather, he asserts that God is black and has chosen black people because God identifies with and sides with the oppressed, who happen to be black. Relating this understanding of blackness to the traditional concept of the Christian Trinity, Cone writes:

> The blackness of God means that the essence of the nature of God is to be found in the concept of liberation. Taking seriously the Trinitarian view of the Godhead, black theology says that as Creator, God identified with oppressed Israel, participating in the bringing into being of this people; as Redeemer, God became the Oppressed One in order that all may be free from oppression; as Holy Spirit, God continues the work of liberation. The Holy Spirit is the Spirit of the Creator and the Redeemer at work in the forces of human liberation in our society today.[120]

Cone challenges contemporary theologians to take his concept of blackness seriously: "My point is that God came, and continues to come, to those who are poor and helpless, for the purpose of setting them free. And since the people of color are his elected poor in America, any interpretation of God that ignores black oppression cannot be Christian theology."[121] Cone compellingly demands that once the Christian theologian acknowledges that Jesus was for the outcast and downtrodden, it is impossible not to make the jump to understanding that God is with black people. Given his understanding of incarnation, resurrection, and power, one can examine his notions of immanence and transcendence.

For Cone, God's immanence is identical to God's incarnation and resurrection. That is, immanence for Cone means that God is active in history, fighting for and among the oppressed, and that God does so for all time. "The immanence of God means that God always encounters us in a situation of historical liberation. . . . According to biblical religion, God is involved in the concrete affairs of human history, liberating the oppressed."[122] This historical, worldly force does not diminish the transcendence of God for Cone, though.

Cone maintains God's transcendence to emphasize that, ultimately, liberation is in God's hands. For Cone, the biblical account of God liberating the oppressed in history is coupled with a belief that God also transcends history and human understanding. On the one hand, Cone places his faith and hope in a God who is present to empower the oppressed. In this way, he puts the burden of liberation efforts on human shoulders. When speaking of the beliefs of enslaved blacks who carried out acts of resistance and insurrections, Cone writes, "The only hands God had were their hands and . . . without the hazards of escape or insurrection slavery would never end."[123] On the other hand, Cone is hesitant to simply equate human culture, ideology, or efforts with divine activity or will, because he saw such a move made and abused by white theologians. Thus, while he believes God is indeed active in history, liberating the oppressed, he explains, "God is always more than our experience of God."[124] This point is made clear in Cone's interpretation of the Exodus: "The biblical writer wishes to emphasize that Israel's liberation came not from her own strength but solely from the power of Yahweh, who completely controls history."[125] According to Cone's view, humans must fight against oppression, but he is confident that God will certainly be there if we fall short of the goal. "Ultimately (and this is what God's transcendence means) black humanity is not dependent on our power to win."[126] As we see in chapter 3, William R. Jones is critical of the possible tension between Cone's imperative for human liberative efforts and his confidence in God's goodness and power in this respect.

Simultaneous immanence and transcendence are not in contradiction with each other for Cone, nor are the simultaneous love and righteousness of God.[127] In Cone's naming of God, love is the most important divine attribute because all other qualities flow from love. "Black theology agrees that the idea of love is indispensable to the Christian view of God. The exodus, the call of Israel into being as the people of the covenant, the gift of the promised land, the rise of prophecy, the second exodus, and above all the incarnation reveal God's self-giving love to oppressed humanity."[128] Cone explains that the problem with overemphasizing love was that it made God weak and uninvolved in human existence, thus contradicting the biblical characterization of the divine-human relationship. He wrote of most theologies that "[t]he most common procedure is to emphasize God's love as the dominant motif of Christianity and then interpret God's righteousness in the light of it. But this approach fails to take seriously the concept of God's righteousness and tends to make God's love mere sentimentality."[129] A God whose love is mere sentimental affection and warm-heartedness is not a liberator God for Cone.

According to Cone, one should not separate love from justice, wrath, and righteousness. "It is important to note in this connection that the righteousness of God is not an abstract quality in the being of God, as with Greek philosophy. It is rather God's active involvement in history, making right what human beings have made wrong."[130] Without righteousness and God's active concern for earthly affairs, love would mean that God loves all humanity and all human enterprise, regardless of the character or actions of humanity. Love without righteousness would mean that the status quo is divinely willed.[131]

Given the fact that racism is part of the status quo, Cone argues God's love cannot stand apart from God's righteousness. As a result, divine love for the oppressed manifests itself in divine justice against the oppressor. "The wrath of God is the love of God in regard to the forces opposed to liberation of the oppressed."[132] For Cone, the oppressor/oppressed language took on concrete form in the arena of race relations and the Black Power movement of the late 1960s and early 1970s.

Cone believes that God fought on the side of African Americans out of love and against white Americans out of wrath. "Righteousness is that side of God's love which expresses itself through black liberation."[133] The two emotions cannot logically be separated. "Black theology cannot accept a view of God which does not represent God as being for oppressed blacks and thus against white oppressors."[134] The Black Power movement, for Cone, was an example of how humans took up the side of righteousness and fought alongside God for their freedom.[135] He summarizes that "[t]his means that in a racist society, we must insist that God's love and God's righteousness are two ways of talking about the same reality. Righteousness means that God is addressing the black condition; love means that God is doing so in the interests of both blacks and whites."[136] Through God's love for the oppressed, manifested in God's wrath against the oppressor, God is working to save both the oppressed and the oppressor from their conditions. Cone's linking of love and justice serves as a corrective to theologies that stress love at the expense of justice.

Oppression as a generic, abstract phenomenon is difficult to struggle against in the real world. Cone's insistence on particularization of oppression, putting a face to it, so to speak, is necessary. Perhaps Cone's particularization might best be accompanied by an admission that oppression is complex and that no individual or community is beyond oppressing fellow human beings. Such a move might still encourage people to resist oppression, but not to assume that they are blameless in all circumstances. One may be oppressed in one instance, yet be an oppressor in another. For example, is an African American male who is sexist or homophobic deserving of divine love as oppressed by white America despite his own oppression of women or homosexuals? Cone would be hard pressed to maintain unequivocally that God is "on his side." God's love and God's justice are inextricably linked in such a way as to prevent any self-righteousness on the part of humanity.

In regard to this issue, Reinhold Niebuhr made a helpful distinction between the equality of sin and the inequality of guilt. Niebuhr claimed that though we are each equally sinful in the eyes of God, some are more guilty than others. He understood guilt to be the "objective and historical consequences of sin" and asserted the "simple religious insight . . . that the men who are tempted by their eminence and by the possession of undue power become more guilty of pride and of injustice than those who lack power and position."[137] Niebuhr's point serves to nuance Cone's assertion while maintaining the force of its indictment of oppressors.

James Cone views God as liberator of the oppressed. This naming of God is profoundly shaped by Cone's reading of the Bible in the light of the black experience. He believes that from Creation, through the Exodus, through the time of the prophets, and ultimately in the life, death, and resurrection of Jesus, God is a liberating God. In the crucifixion and resurrection of Jesus, God set humanity free to labor for its own liberation in partnership with God. Because of the resurrection, Cone asserts that Jesus' fellowship among the oppressed of the first century and struggle for their human dignity and freedom could be understood to exist for the oppressed of all centuries. Given African American oppression, Cone reasons, Jesus must be among the black community of today. The presence of God within this oppressed community means that God is with the oppressed, God fights for the oppressed, and ultimately, God will liberate the oppressed. The role of humanity in this process must be further examined to better understand Cone's theological enterprise.

James Cone on Humanity

For Cone the notion that theology is the study of God leads him necessarily to the study of humanity. We cannot know God apart from

God's relationship to humanity. Cone explains the character of theology: "It is the *divine* involvement in historical events of liberation that makes theology God-centered; but because God participates in the historical liberation of humanity, we can speak of God only in relationship to human history. In this sense, theology is anthropology."[138] Theology itself is based on theological anthropology for Cone because God is involved in human affairs. We know who God is by what God does in human history. In turn we get a glimpse of who we are and what we may become by understanding who God is in relation to us.

Cone's theological anthropology is formed partly in response to the claims of earlier theologians. Cone indicts white Christian theologians as racists when they prefer to discuss theology as an abstract, philosophical issue—God in Godself—at the expense of dealing with theology as a practical, ethical discipline—God as active in human history. This failure leads to a lack of concern for those with whom God is concerned—the oppressed.[139] This mistake had been manifested, in different ways, in at least two theological schools of thought.

Cone is critical of neo-orthodoxy because it fails to relate claims about God to social justice. He asserts, "The Barthians have confused God-talk with white talk, and thus have failed to see that there is no real speech about God except in relationship to the liberation of the oppressed."[140] The neo-orthodox hesitancy to connect or equate the Word of God with any particular word of humanity led to the irrelevancy of theology to the conditions of the oppressed. In other words, God is too separated from humanity. For Cone, since God is concerned with the oppressed, any theology that fails to place a similar concern at its core simply serves to reinforce the oppressive status quo.

Liberal theologians are no safer from Cone's analysis than neo-orthodox ones. In distinction from neo-orthodoxy, liberalism makes the error of a facile identification of human ideals with divine ideals. Ignoring human evil and oppression, liberalism believed that humans are essentially good and are progressing toward perfection. Cone explains that such claims of human goodness are misguided at best and racist at worst. He writes, "Blacks know that a person can be lynched in other ways than by hanging from a tree. What about depriving blacks of their humanity by suggesting that white humanity is humanity as God intended it to be? What about the liberal emphasis on human goodness at the same time whites were doing everything they could to destroy blacks?"[141] Cone explains that it was irresponsible and hypocritical to discuss God's goodness and the ideal of love in the midst of black suffering and white oppression.[142]

Though Cone is critical of both neo-orthodoxy and liberalism, he also takes up themes from both schools of thought. Cone's theological anthropology shares with neo-orthodoxy its denial that human ideology be equated with the Word of God. In Cone's case though, it is white ideology in particular whose divinity is denied. White theology must not be the final word on God and humanity. Barth's "No!" to Nazi ideology and equation of the Third Reich's program with divine will is transformed by Cone into a "No!" to white racism and white claims that God is white and wills the theological and social success of white ideology.

As for his affinity with liberalism, Cone's theological anthropology is similar to liberal anthropology in its evaluation of history and culture, though for Cone it is black history and culture that provide a hint of God's nature, and thereby of human nature. Cone's pessimism concerning human nature is reserved largely for the white culture of racism. He is, however, optimistic concerning the ideals and possibilities of black culture because he believes it is within the lives and experiences of black people, the oppressed, where God is truly manifest.

With his denial of white racism and his affirmation of black culture, Cone simultaneously critiques and employs aspects of earlier theological methodologies. Once again, Cone's method shapes, and is shaped by, his commitment to the oppressed. It is this commitment that leads him to assert, "Because black theology begins with the black condition as the fundamental datum of human experience, we cannot gloss over the significance and the concreteness of human oppression in the world in which blacks are condemned to live."[143] Thus, humanity, black humanity in particular, stands at the very center of Cone's theology.

Cone describes the nature of black humanity, and importantly humanity in general, as being both sinful and endowed with freedom. For Cone, sin is more of an existential category that a moral one. Sin is defined as estrangement from the source of one's being; it is the denial or ignorance of one's true self. For whites, sin is pretending to play God in the realm of human affairs. For blacks, sin is the "desire to be white," meaning having the belief that blackness is wrong or lacking in some way. In each instance it is a misunderstanding of one's character and nature, and the consequent activity in the world of fulfilling the role of oppressor, for whites, and oppressed, for blacks.[144] Thus, for Cone, the biblical Fall may be interpreted as leading to sin[145] or to our rational limitations in knowing God; Cone avoids using the doctrine of original sin as an explanation for an inevitable moralistic failure of humanity. For Cone, sin at its root is the failure to recognize and strive for our own freedom and that of others, specifically the oppressed of society.[146] The notion that we need not be redeemed by God before we strive to attain the freedom for which we have all been created, is developed in the pages that follow.

For Cone, human freedom is based on divine freedom. Again, we can talk of God only by talking of the God-human relationship. He explains, "God's being as freedom not only affirms the divine will to *be* in the divine-self; it is also an affirmation of God's freedom to be *for us* in the social context of human existence."[147] Both divine and human freedoms are historical realities. Freedom must be manifested in history. Cone writes, "When freedom is separated from history, it is no longer authentic freedom. It is an opium, a sedative which makes people content with freedom's opposite, oppression."[148] Cone cites the presence and activity of God in the Exodus and the incarnation as evidence that God is for the oppressed in human history.

As divine freedom means God is for the oppressed in history, human freedom means that we in turn act for God. In relating human freedom to the theological concept of the *imago Dei* (the image of God), Cone argues that the image of God should not be characterized as rationality, but rather as freedom and as revolt against oppression in striving for that freedom. He asserts that being created in the image of God means being created for freedom. Cone writes:

> The image of God refers to the way in which God intends human beings to live in the world. The image of God is thus more than rationality, more than what so-called neo-orthodox theologians call divine-human encounter. In a world in which persons are oppressed, the image is human nature in rebellion against structures of oppression. It is humanity involved in the liberation struggle against the forces of inhumanity.[149]

It is when society tries to take away the freedom for which we are created and negate this divine gift that struggle must occur to regain this measure of freedom. "It is the biblical concept of the image of God that makes black rebellion in America human."[150] The liberation struggle takes place in history, not in theory, according to Cone.

Cone denies the value of theoretical debates on the nature of the image of God and on free will. He asserts, "Freedom, then, is not an abstract question. It deals with human existence in a world of societal enslavement. We cannot solve the question of freedom in a college classroom, theoretically debating the idea of 'freedom versus determinism.' Freedom is an existential reality. It is not a matter of rational thought but of human confrontation. It is not solved by academic discussion but by risky human encounter."[151] The idea that freedom involves struggle in history means that freedom is not an individual concept, but a social one.

For Cone freedom is not the freedom to do whatever we want to do, but rather the freedom to act toward the liberation of the oppressed. He explains, "Being human means being against evil by joining sides with those who are the victims of evil. Quite literally, it means becoming oppressed with the oppressed, making their cause one's one cause by involving oneself in the liberation struggle. *No one is free until all are free.*"[152] Thus freedom, rather than being an individualistic concept, is a social responsibility. Elsewhere Cone asserts, "Authentic freedom of self is achievable only in the context of an oppressed community struggling for liberation."[153] Cone understands God's liberating power toward the oppressed to mean a responsibility for humans to struggle for freedom. "In this sense, liberation is not a human possession but a divine gift of freedom to those who struggle in faith against violence and oppression. Liberation is not an object but the *project* of freedom wherein the oppressed realize that their fight for freedom is a divine right of creation."[154]

Only the oppressed, and those who resist oppression with them, are truly free because only they can overcome oppression by using their God-given freedom to do so.[155] Cone understands this to be the freedom of a Christian: "The free Christian man cannot be concerned about a reward in heaven. Rather, he is a man who, through the freedom granted in Christ, is ready to plunge himself into the evils of the world, revolting against all inhuman powers which enslave men."[156] Freedom comes through acting for liberation without the expectation of reward.

By viewing the image of God as the inherent desire and drive toward freedom, rather than as rationality, Cone allows humans a responsibility and a role in pursuing their own freedom with God. He asserts, "The image of God then is not merely a personal relationship with God, but is also that constitution of humanity which makes all people struggle against captivity. It is the ground of rebellion and revolution among the slaves."[157] Cone's interpretation of the image of God as freedom makes human social justice necessary for both oppressor and oppressed to be freed from the chains of sin and for complete human fulfillment.

In addition, the appeal to human freedom as a universal entitlement broadens Cone's notion of liberation to include oppressed peoples of all religious faiths, and even agnostics or atheists. In the traditional Christian scheme of sin and salvation, one could be saved only through Jesus Christ. In contradistinction, in Cone's system of oppression and liberation Jesus liberates, but is not the exclusive conduit of freedom. Though not explicitly stated, Cone seems to prioritize liberation through any path over exclusivistic claims of liberation through Christ alone.

Because God creates us to be free, sides with the oppressed in the Hebrew Bible, and becomes oppressed in Jesus Christ, when we struggle for liberation we struggle with God. For Cone, injustice is a denial of one's humanity, as well as an affront to the divine gift of freedom. Because we were created in the image of God we cannot and should not accept oppression or injustice anywhere.[158] To do the work of God is to fight against oppression, just as God has always done.

According to Cone, it is in the life of Jesus that God manifests the divine identification with the oppressed and in his resurrection that this identification is made eternal. In Jesus, God concretely identifies with the lives and concerns of the oppressed. Jesus serves two purposes, according to Cone. He both frees us to act for freedom, by his redeeming act, and he shows us how it is done, by his ministry to the oppressed, afflicted, and outcast. In Cone's words, "God in Jesus meets us in the situation of our oppressed condition and tells us not only who *God* is and what *God* is doing about our liberation, but also who *we* are and what *we* must do about white racism."[159] Jesus acts as a mediator between God and humanity. We are given hope and confidence by his divine nature, and the knowledge that God indeed fights for the oppressed; we are given responsibility in an initiative to take up this fight ourselves.

Ideally, then, the work of God is aided by the human struggle for liberation. Differing from Barth, who was interested in salvation history, in which humanity plays a passive role, Cone understands humanity as actively pursuing salvation, or liberation—Cone makes little distinction between the two concepts. In the fight for the liberation of the oppressed we earn our own liberation. Following the commandments is not enough to earn some heavenly reward, according to Cone. "To participate in God's salvation is to cooperate with the black Christ as he liberates his people from bondage. Salvation, then, primarily has to do with earthly reality and the injustice inflicted on those who are helpless and poor."[160] We should act as though this life, this world, were our only reality. Injustice here is worse than some imagined hell, for Cone. Cone believes that the proper human response to God's liberating will and power is to fight with God for the liberation of the oppressed. Cone understands salvation and liberation to be identical, both of them already but not fully achieved realities.[161] In other words, the actions of Jesus were complete, and yet, humans still must contribute to the process.

In the course of fighting against evil and striving toward freedom, one always faces opposition. Cone argues that "freedom is inevitably associated with suffering."[162] In the course of liberating activity, humans will inevitably encounter setbacks and suffering, claims Cone. To be sure, he is resistant to assigning any role to God in black suffering: "Despite the emphasis on future redemption in present suffering, black theology cannot accept any view of God that even *indirectly* places divine approval on human suffering."[163] That said, Cone understands a particular type of suffering to be redemptive, if it occurs in the context of the struggle for freedom, because *God* makes it so. "Israel's suffering is redemptive, because it is suffering with and for its Lord who is always identified with the little ones in agony. Therefore, it is God who makes human suffering redemptive!"[164] The freedom to fight for liberation would always be coupled with the pain of suffering, just as responsibility always follows freedom, according to Cone.

Suffering is part of divine election for those willing to fight for liberation, just as it had been for Israel. "There is no divine election without the call to suffer for justice."[165] In fact, it was the suffering of Jesus that freed us to perform the activity that would bring our suffering: "God in Christ became the Suffering Servant and thus took the humiliation and suffering of the oppressed into God's own history. This divine event that happened on the cross liberated the oppressed to fight against suffering while not being determined by it."[166] This type of positive suffering, positive because it effects change and takes place within a divine context, can even bring satisfaction and happiness to those who struggle with and for the oppressed.

The joy of which Cone speaks is a result of our partnership with God. "There is joy in our suffering insofar as we have to suffer for freedom. There is joy not only because we know that God has defeated evil but also because God is present with us in our fight against suffering and will come again fully to consummate the freedom already given in Jesus Christ."[167] James Cone understands suffering, at least suffering voluntarily undertaken in liberation efforts, to be the consequence of the struggle toward freedom. Suffering is an inevitable result in the struggle against evil and oppression, according to Cone. In this way, both God and humanity fight against oppression, and both suffer. Citing Martin Luther King, Cone explains: "King's suffering, and that of freedom fighters around the world is redemptive when, like Jesus' cross, it inspires us to resist evil, knowing that suffering is the consequence. To resist evil is to participate in God's redemption of the world."[168]

Even after considering the critiques of William R. Jones and Anthony Pinn, which are presented in chapter 3, Cone asserts that an understanding of some forms of suffering is redemptive because he believes it to have the potential to be liberating in the lives of Black people. He explains: "Listening to black Christians, I am not convinced that Jesus' cross and suffering are always negative for women and poor people, never empowering and liberating, and thus must be discarded. The evidence is ambiguous and complicated."[169] Cone acknowledges that evil and suffering pose a serious threat to faith. Specifically, black suffering presents a serious stumbling block to black faith. However, for Cone, the assertion that suffering destroys faith fails to take into consideration those who respond to suffering with faith.

According to Cone, though there may be no solution to the philosophical problem of suffering, one finds a hint in the response of black believers. He holds it is only from the stance of black faith that one can acknowledge the reality of black suffering and simultaneously maintain belief in God's goodness and efficacy to liberate the oppressed. From such a stance, divine goodness and power are most profoundly evident in the death and resurrection of Jesus. Cone asserts: "[Ordinary blacks] really believed that Jesus' death expressed God's solidarity with the little ones—making them human in every sense of the word. This faith not only gave blacks an identity that whites could not take away, it also empowered them to resist, with all the power they had."[170] Cone believes that suffering, encountered in the fight for freedom, could actually empower blacks to struggle for liberation and to resist the dehumanizing force of white racism.[171]

James Cone on Resistance

Now that Cone's theological method and understanding of God and humanity have been examined, I provide a more detailed discussion of what Cone identifies as positive, human acts of liberation in the hope of further clarifying the nature of Cone's view of resistance and liberation. Cone's notion of resistance is based on the Bible and includes the ideals of justice and hope; it arises out of the particularity of black oppression in the United States, and thus depends on black history and culture for its form and content; it advocates self-defense in the face of dehumanization, but not necessarily violent means; and it is global in scope in its recognition that oppression is a worldwide reality.

Cone understands black resistance as a response to white oppression. It is the idea that one will no longer accept the absurdity of living in a white world subserviently, but will instead revolt against such a condition. It is a movement of emotion, intellect, body, and spirit against forces, structures, and individuals who maintain this absurd reality. Simultaneously, it is a realization that what the white world offers to the black experience is not all that life has to offer.[172] Therefore, resistance is a movement against the forces of oppression and also, importantly, a movement for liberation. Cone writes, "Black history is . . . the record of black people's resistance, an account of their perceptions of their existence in an oppressive society. What whites did to blacks is secondary. The primary reality is what blacks did to whites in order to delimit the white assault on their humanity."[173] Resistance may be defined, at least initially, by the entity against which it resists, but eventually it has the potential to become a constructive force, developing independently from the reality that made it necessary.

Resistance is an existential reaction to dehumanizing forces that may take on philosophical, theological, political, and cultural manifestations. Cone's black theology of liberation is an example of philosophical and theological resistance. Cone claims that the revolutionary intent of black theology is not based on ideology but on the Bible. He writes, "The Christian man is obligated by a freedom grounded in the Creator to break all laws which contradict human dignity. Through disobedience to the state, he affirms his allegiance to God as Creator and his willingness to behave as if he believes it. Civil disobedience is a duty in a racist society."[174] Elsewhere Cone explains it is only because God struggles for the oppressed that "we are granted the freedom to share in the divine movement of liberation."[175] In the Bible, both in the Hebrew Bible and in the New Testament, Cone finds the justification for resistance to injustice and oppression.[176]

In addition to the biblical call to set the captives free, Cone looks to black history and experience to define his notion of resistance. As is seen in Emil Fackenheim's understanding of resistance, for Cone black resistance is possible now because it was actual in the past. He looks to the insurrections of enslaved blacks, led by Gabriel Prosser, Denmark Vesey, and Nat Turner; progressive black religious leaders during the nineteenth century such as Richard Allen, Henry Highland Garnet, and Henry McNeal Turner;[177] black music, especially spirituals; and the lives of Malcolm X and Martin Luther King, Jr. as examples of black resistance.

Cone views these examples of black resistance as fundamentally religious in character, which, he believes, lends the ideal not only of justice, which is present in secular black resistance, but also of hope. Religious faith inspires acts of social justice and also supports these efforts if they fall short. Cone asserts the belief that God is on the side of black resistance against white oppression allows blacks to maintain hope against the odds and to continue to struggle despite real and apparent setbacks. In other words, religion-based acts of resistance include an aspect of hope against despair that is lacking in primarily secular acts of resistance, according to Cone.

The experience of hope is an important reason for Cone's rejection of black humanism, as characterized by thinkers such as William R. Jones and Anthony Pinn, as a viable option in the fight for social justice.[178] Humanism, including its assertion that humanity must fight for justice without appeal to God, is bound to fail, Cone asserts. He maintains that both God and humanity must strive toward liberation, and that God will step in to inspire, support, and complete human efforts. Ethically, Cone's black theology of liberation is similar to Jones' humanism. Theologically and philosophically, however, they differ regarding the rationale behind and the potential for human efforts of social justice.[179] The point relevant for our present purpose is that Cone believes religious faith, usually a specific form of Christianity, to be exact,[180] is a central aspect of resistance. For faith in God, according to Cone, is the impetus for resistance as well as the assurance of its success, because it encourages both justice and hope. Now that Cone's conception of resistance has been described in general terms, it will be helpful to explore a few specific examples of black resistance. These examples are the spirituals and the work of both Malcolm X and Martin Luther King, Jr.

In response to black critics who claimed that Cone's early theology relied too heavily on white sources and methodology, Cone began to search black history and culture more thoroughly for potential sources for constructive theology. The result was his 1972 work,

The Spirituals and the Blues. In this book, Cone illustrates the presence of the theme of liberation in the early expressions of African American suffering and hope. Cone responded to critics, both white and black, who claimed that the spirituals and black religiosity in general, promoted an otherworldliness and a lack of concern with justice in earthly history. Cone's analysis shows that black spirituals represented both a form of resistance against white understandings and teachings of Christianity and a fervent faith in a God who would liberate the oppressed and call the oppressors to account, both in this world and in the world to come.

Cone explains that the spirituals present an alternative to white oppression and white corruption of the liberating Christian message of the Bible. He writes:

> The basic idea of the spirituals is that slavery contradicts God; it is a denial of God's will. To be enslaved is to be declared *nobody*, and that form of existence contradicts God's creation of people to be God's children. Because black people believed that they were God's children, they affirmed their *somebodiness*, refusing to reconcile their servitude with divine revelation. They rejected white distortions of the gospel, which emphasized the obedience of slaves to their masters. They contended that God willed their freedom and not their slavery.[181]

The belief that God willed their freedom encouraged them to demand that enslaved blacks resist white forces that stand in their way.

In reply to Karl Marx's indictment of religion as the "opium of the people"[182] and to non-Christian, militant black supporters of black power, Cone asserts that the spiritual was a form of resistance in itself and in that it inspired more active forms of resistance.

> When it is considered that Nat Turner, Denmark Vesey, and Harriet Tubman may have been creators of some of the spirituals; that "Sinner, please don't let this harvest pass" probably referred to a slave resistance meeting; that after 1831 over 2000 slaves escaped yearly; and that black churches interpreted civil disobedience as consistent with religion; then it is clear that many slaves recognized the need for their own participation in God's liberation. Indeed many believed that the only hands God had were their hands and that without the hazards of escape or insurrection slavery would never end.[183]

In other words, Cone would agree with the critique of the spiritual, and of Christianity in general, by Marx and black power advocates, if it induced passivity. A central tenet of Cone's theology, then, is that true Christianity, including his interpretation of the spiritual, is revolutionary and liberating. In addition to leading to these active forms of resistance, the spirituals also indicate a complex eschatological notion of hope, according to Cone.

Cone denies that spirituals were not concerned with earthly oppression. Citing historian Miles Fisher, as well as the testimony of Frederick Douglas and Harriet Tubman, Cone explains that "heaven for early black slaves referred not only to a transcendent reality beyond time and space; it designated the earthly places that blacks regarded as lands of freedom. Heaven referred to Africa, Canada, and the northern United States."[184] Thus heaven could be code or metaphor for earthly liberation from slavery, suffering, and oppression.

Simultaneous with these worldly meanings of hope were the transcendent, future, otherworldly assurances that the justice of God would eventually prevail over white oppression. Cone describes that "the concept of heaven was not exhausted by historical reality or present existence. It expressed something besides the capacity of black people to be human in the midst of suffering and despair. In the spirituals, heaven was also hope in the future of God, an expectation that the contradictions of slavery were not ultimate. They believed that life did not end with death and that somewhere in the 'bosom of God's eternity,' God would rectify the wrongs against black people."[185] Though resistance should ideally take on a more active, this-worldly emphasis, resistance must also be understood as resistance against despair and resignation. That the spiritual could simultaneously instill the imperative for revolt, escape, and various forms of active resistance, along with the faith and hope that God would "make a way out of no way" indicates the profundity and complexity of this form of expression. In chapter 3, we see that, like the black spirituals, Jewish *midrash* (narratives that further explore and develop biblical pericopes and themes) may be a creative expression of life lived in absurdity and contradiction and yet one in which resistance is an imperative and hope survives.

While spirituals could be understood as artistic forms of resistance, the life and work of Malcolm X and Martin Luther King, Jr. may be understood as political and cultural forms of resistance. Cone declares, "Martin and Malcolm symbolize the two great resistance traditions in black history—integrationism and black nationalism."[186] Throughout his treatment of Malcolm X and King, Cone insists that these two leaders must be understood in dialectical relation to one another to fully appreciate the nuances and complexities of each. Furthermore, though real differences existed between Malcolm X and Martin Luther King, Jr., Cone contends that the trajectories of their philosophies were growing toward one another at the end of their lives. Cone explains, Malcolm X and King "struggled against the same evil—racism—and for the same goal—freedom for African-Americans."[187] Also, Cone makes clear that the social analyses of both Malcolm X and King were based largely on their religious beliefs, Malcolm's understanding of Islam and King's of Christianity. Finally, though largely differing in their assessments of the most effective means of resistance against injustice, in terms of robust self-defense versus nonviolent resistance, both Malcolm X and King came to understand their resistance struggles as global in scope and importance, and as including economic as well as racial and cultural dynamics. These traits that are characteristic of Malcolm X's and King's resistance against oppression are also true of Cone's theology and ethics of resistance.

In the Nation of Islam, Malcolm X found the self-esteem, self-respect, and appreciation of his identity that had previously been absent in his life. Cone points out that the Nation was attractive to Malcolm not only because of its stress on blackness over and against whiteness, but also because, "it was a religion specifically directed to the 'Negro in the mud'—dope addicts and pushers, pimps and prostitutes, prisoners—all of those blacks who saw no way out of the hell of their daily lives."[188] In the Nation, Malcolm discovered both his self-worth as a black man and a philosophy that explained the evil nature of whites.

According to Malcolm X, the white man did not simply have a history of evil or evil tendencies, but was actually satanic. How else can one explain the huge gap in the distribution of wealth, the overwhelming majority of prisoners being black, and the permanent underclass status of African Americans in this country and globally, Malcolm asked. In a 1963 speech delivered in Harlem, Malcolm explained:

Unemployment and poverty have forced many of our people into this life of crime; but . . . the real criminal is in City Hall downtown. The real criminal is in the State House in Albany. The real criminal is in the White House in Washington, D.C. The real criminal is the white man who poses as a liberal—the political hypocrite. And it is these legal crooks, passing as our friends, [who are] forcing us into a life of crime and then using us to spread the white man's evil vices among our own people. Our people are scientifically maneuvered by the white man into a life of poverty. You are not poor accidentally. He maneuvers you into poverty. You are not a drug addict accidentally. Why, the white man maneuvers you into drug addiction. You are not a prostitute accidentally. You have been maneuvered into prostitution by the American white man. There is nothing about your condition here in America that is an accident.[189]

Because white people were satanic, only God could conquer them. Malcolm believed that White America's Day of Judgment would arrive imminently, and that Allah Himself would carry out this justice.[190]At this stage of his life Malcolm believed there would be no human-divine partnership that would vanquish evil.

While awaiting Allah's imminent Judgment, Malcolm believed that separation was the only human answer to the problem of evil. Integration was not only impossible, but also "a sign of self-hatred."[191] Malcolm advocated separation not only because of his hatred of the oppressor, but also because of his love for the oppressed. He believed that black culture, black pride, and black unity could thrive in an all-black environment. Malcolm explained that black nationalism meant that blacks should control their own economy, their own politics, and their own communities.[192]

Furthermore, blacks had at least as much right to defend themselves as whites. Cone argues that Malcolm X did not advocate violence, but rather self-defense. He rejected King's nonviolence as "a ridiculous philosophy, one that whites would never embrace as their own." It is ironic that Malcolm's belief in self-defense and famous "by any means necessary" stance, which many whites called dangerous, reactionary, or racist, were in fact taken from white behavior throughout American history. Cone explains, "Malcolm could hardly contain his rage as he pointed out the contradictions between what whites advised blacks to do to get their freedom and what they did to attain their own. Patrick Henry did not practice the virtues of nonviolence. George Washington was no pacifist." Malcolm X's technique of self-defense differed from King's nonviolence because their goals differed. Whereas King envisioned a multiracial, unified beloved community, Malcolm advocated a black society in which black pride, culture, and development were held in esteem.[193]

Toward the end of his life, Malcolm X began to understand the larger reality of global oppression. He saw the connections between black struggles in the United States and black struggles in Africa and

Asia. Never relinquishing the centrality of the race critique to his philosophy, Malcolm added an economic analysis that actually served to deepen and nuance his understanding of racism. After his *hajj* (pilgrimage) to Mecca, Malcolm came to reinterpret whiteness as attitude and action rather than skin color. He saw that in the Islam of the East, racial identity was not important and that Elijah Muhammad had been wrong when he had told Malcolm that all Muslims were black. On his trip Malcolm witnessed whites, blacks, and all races coexisting harmoniously in a Muslim unity.[194]

If white devils, who could be conquered only by Allah, were not the source of evil, then perhaps human resistance to oppression and injustice could be effective. After his split with the Nation, Malcolm no longer advocated a separate nation for blacks, but instead believed that blacks should fight for their human rights within the United States.[195] Malcolm conceded that "the white man is *not* inherently evil, but America's racist society influences him to act evilly. The society has produced and nourishes a psychology which brings out the lowest, most base part of human beings."[196] After his break with the Nation, Malcolm no longer claimed that evil was whiteness, but he maintained that whiteness, understood as oppression and injustice, was evil. Though early in his public life Malcolm believed that the evils of white would be overcome only through the judgment of Allah, he later came to believe that humans could play a role, a fundamental one, in bringing about justice through resistance efforts.

James Cone's conception of resistance to black oppression is heavily influenced by the philosophy of Malcolm X. As for King, for Malcolm also resistance is religion-based, the religion in this case being Islam. For it is in Islam that Malcolm discovers human self-worth grounded in the gift of Allah, the idea of self-defense, and a respect for social justice. Malcolm's resistance is based on racial, economic, and cultural critiques of society, as is Cone's. Finally, just as Malcolm tied the welfare of black Americans to freedom struggles throughout the third world, Cone's initial concentration on racism in America broadens into a concern with the status of oppressed peoples worldwide. In the end, Malcolm X advocated resistance against racism and oppression and for black pride, welfare, culture, and freedom.

Just as Malcolm X's Muslim faith instilled a passion for social justice, Martin Luther King, Jr.'s Christian identity inspired his life's work for peace and justice. Profoundly shaped by his experiences in the black church tradition, Martin Luther King's presupposition of the inherent worth of humanity led him to reject segregation and racism. He argued that segregation denied both the presence of the *imago dei* (image of God) set forth in the Hebrew Bible and the new reconciled relationship that Christians have with God in Jesus Christ. King condemned segregation as an evil, not only culturally, but also theologically. The black church provided King with the knowledge that segregation was evil and also the tools to resist this evil through social protest. The boycotts and marches that King led were inspired by the church and were common techniques of black religious leaders such as A. Philip Randolph. King famously made this protest tradition his own when he fervently insisted that it be nonviolent.

Unlike Malcolm X, who advocated "any means necessary" to end racism and segregation, King believed in *agape* (unconditional love) manifested in nonviolent action because his goal was reconciliation between the races in America.[197] Peaceful ends may only be brought about by peaceful means.[198] Through nonviolent action, one does not try to conquer one's opponent, but rather one tries to transform the opponent.[199] King liked to point out that an "eye for an eye" strategy leaves everyone blind. He objected to violence in the civil rights struggle not only morally and theologically, but also practically. "How could a 10 percent Negro minority with no access to the weapons of warfare ever expect to wage a successful violent revolution against a white majority with the military technology of the United States?"[200]

King maintained that Malcolm X, the Black Power movement, white clergy, and white liberals all misunderstood his conception of love.[201] King's love, biblically grounded, was concerned with justice and reconciliation simultaneously; to ignore either aspect was to misunderstand the power of *agape*. Unlike the white clergy, King believed in civil disobedience: "One has a moral responsibility to disobey unjust laws";[202] unlike white liberals, King placed vital importance on his demands for justice in this life: "God has commanded us to be concerned about the slums down here, and his children who can't eat three square meals a day";[203] unlike Malcolm X and the Black Power movement, King fought for justice while maintaining his struggle for reconciliation and his love for all humanity.

According to Cone, just as Malcolm came to a fuller and deeper understanding of the global nature of oppression, King began to develop an economic critique of oppression later in his life and to link the resistance efforts of African Americans to the struggles of the oppressed throughout the world. After 1965, Martin Luther King began to examine the role of distribution of wealth in the lives of African Americans. King began to understand that, as Malcolm X had argued, integration would do more damage than good unless something was done about economic inequality. Just after the Watts rebellion in 1965, King lamented, "I worked to get these people the right to eat hamburgers, and now I've got to do something . . . to help them to get the money to buy [them]."[204] King chastised white America for its greed and apathy. He was indignant over the fact that there were still 40 to 50 million poor people in the richest nation on earth[205] and reminded whites, especially liberals, that "the daily life of the Negro is still lived in the basement of the Great Society."[206] Though he never believed in Communism, finding its materialism contradictory to Christianity,[207] after 1965 he nevertheless began to seriously consider the merits of an American form of socialism.[208]

In addition to the economic structure of the United States, King began to question the political conduct of America, particularly in Vietnam. In fact, James Cone argues that it was when he turned to domestic economic injustice and inequality that King began to place his struggle in the wider global context of the peoples of Africa, Asia, and Latin America.[209] He condemned "a rich and powerful nation that was blind to injustice at home and indifferent to world peace."[210] King protested against American priorities when the government would pour 35 billion dollars a year into the Vietnam War and deny funds to the slums of the United States.[211] King's response was not one of isolationism, but rather an attack on American hypocrisy. Not only was the war in Vietnam an oppressive and unjust effort, but it was also a slap in the face of economically and racially oppressed people worldwide. It was the hypocritical straw that broke the camel's back of King's faith in the ability of humans to defeat the forces of evil. Though King never entirely gave up on whites or humans in general, his last years were dominated by an unshakable faith in the power of *God* to set things right[212] despite *human* failings, and an interest in the value of black culture.

Thus, though King claimed that God needs humanity to conquer evil, he believed more importantly that humans need God and he redefined the power of this God: "If through sheer omnipotence God were to defeat his purpose [of granting human free will], he would express weakness rather than power. Power is the ability to fulfill purpose; action which defeats purpose is weakness."[213] According to King, humans are free instruments of God. God and humanity struggle *together* against evil; both are necessary partners in the struggle. Giving God too much credit leads to social apathy and complacency; giving humanity too much credit leads to blind arrogance and ignorance.[214]

King moved from an optimism concerning the potential for human resistance against injustice to a faith in the necessity for divine intervention. Forms of resistance such as protests, marches, and boycotts had improved the status of blacks within a racist American society, though they still left that society in place. In other words, human resistance, unaided by God, could only go so far. As Malcolm X came to believe that human resistance could improve the welfare of African Americans, and that humanity could act before Allah's judgment, King became more pessimistic about the possibilities of true social change brought about solely by human effort. In the end both men maintained it would be only through divine-human partnership that progress could be made.

King's resistance struggles religiously drew from the black church tradition and were founded on nonviolence. King also nuanced and deepened his initial race critique into an economic and global issue of oppression and inequality. He resisted the evils of segregation and racism and fought for social justice, unity, and his beloved community.

In James Cone's theology, and especially in his conception of resistance, one can see the profound dialectical influence of both Malcolm and Martin. Cone argues that resistance against oppression must be religiously based if one is to avoid despair. In the method of resistance, Cone stands closer to Malcolm's self-defense position but is always careful to point out he is not explicitly advocating violence.[215] Just as Malcolm X and King came to understand the economic connections with racism and the global reality of oppression, Cone broadened his initial theological concern with race into resistance against all forms of oppression. In fact, Cone's understanding of racism becomes fuller and more profound as he investigates other forms of oppression, such as sexism and classism. His work with EATWOT and his dialogues with other minorities within the United States point to Cone's understanding of the global nature of oppression and the scope on which resistance efforts must be mounted. Finally, like Malcolm and Martin, Cone believes resistance against oppression and despair must be a matter of divine-human effort. As liberator of the oppressed, God needs humanity to carry out resistance against oppression in the world; as fallen and finite human beings, we need to resist despair and maintain hope that God will "make a way out of no way," according to Cone.

Conclusion

James Cone's theology may be understood as a response to the problem of suffering and moral evil more than as a solution. In fact, I know of no theology that "solves" the problem of evil. Anyone who claims to do so has not understood the problem properly, in my view. That said, Cone does offer a profound, realistic, and hopeful response to the suffering of the oppressed and marginalized. He asserts that God is the liberator of the oppressed; divine goodness is made manifest in the fact that God sides with the oppressed, while divine power is evident in God's acts of liberation. This goodness is most readily evident in the divine incarnation of Jesus Christ, in his life and his work among the poor and marginalized, to the point even of death. Likewise, divine power is expressed in the resurrection of Jesus, wherein sin and oppression are conquered and the oppressed are given the freedom to work with God toward full liberation and redemption. Following the classical tradition of Christian theology, Cone views the event of Jesus Christ as already and not yet complete. According to Cone, humans must struggle for liberation along with God in the realm of human history, politics, and culture. In this fight suffering will be encountered. For Cone, however, suffering that is experienced in liberation efforts may be redemptive.

In my opinion, one of Cone's greatest contributions to Christian theology is his assertion that God takes sides with the oppressed and acts as liberator in human history. He reminds contemporary audiences that this claim is nothing new and it is in fact the dominant message of the Christian Gospel. Consequently, all thoughtful and sensitive Christians should recognize the validity of Cone's rationale in applying this claim to the modern context, so that one should also affirm divine solidarity with the poor, oppressed, and marginalized of our world today, including African Americans. In theological terms, I believe Cone's claim of divine benevolence manifested through such a preferential option for the poor is both challenging and compelling.

I also believe Cone's theology and theological anthropology serve as a foundation for human acts of resistance against oppression and despair. One cannot come away from a reading of Cone with the impression that he is satisfied with human apathy in the face of racism and oppression. His theology is at odds with any claim that God alone will "set things right." For Cone, divine power and transcendence provide the foundation for human hope and the imperative for human action. My disagreement with him on this point is in his particular understanding of divine power. As is discussed more fully in chapter 6, I find his concept of divine power too dominating and patriarchal. On a balance between divine power and human power, I think he still tips the scales a bit too far toward God, thus undermining for some people the very imperative he intends to convey. That is, the issue for me becomes whether an alternative understanding of divine power might still provide the foundation for human hope and an even greater imperative for human action. Along with other points of consideration, affirmation, and critique, chapters 3 and 6 return to this issue.

3

Why Divine Goodness or Power? Why God? Why Liberation?: Critiques and Affirmations of James Cone

The passionate and compelling theology of James Cone drew both intense support and strong criticism almost immediately after it was in presented in his initial publication. Now, as then, the same people often voice these two responses. Each of the four thinkers examined here, William R. Jones, Anthony B. Pinn, Delores S. Williams, and Dwight N. Hopkins critique at least some aspect of Cone's thought. Jones asserts theodicy must be the central category for black theology and argues that humanocentric theism or religious humanism could be the best way to encourage black resistance against suffering and oppression. Pinn believes the very category of theodicy begs the question of God's goodness and power. In distinction from Cone and Jones, Pinn argues for humanism, in which humanity is both functionally and ontologically ultimate. Both Pinn and Williams show the dangers of redemptive suffering theodicy and maintain that suffering has no redemptive qualities. As a womanist theologian, Williams represents here arguably the most significant critique of Cone's early work. Though able to see the disease of racism inherent in society and theology, Cone was blind to the sexism within his own theology. Along with his exposure to Latin American liberation theology's class critique, Cone's encounter with womanist thought forced him to see the interrelated quality of all forms of oppression. Hopkins is an important theological figure because, more than the other three scholars here, he most closely follows Cone's system while simultaneously incorporating into his work many of the earlier critiques of Cone's theology and carrying out his own interests in black folklore, literature, and political economy. Though each of these four figures is discussed separately, there are overlaps in their concerns, critiques, and proposals.

William R. Jones: Humanocentric Theism

Like Cone, William R. Jones asserts black liberation from economic, social, and political oppression to be the motivation for his work. What fundamentally differentiates Jones from Cone is the proposed theological foundation by which liberation may be brought about. The two differ in their conceptions of God, of the God-human relationship, and of ethnic suffering and oppression. Cone maintains that God is good and powerful, the liberator of the oppressed. Utilizing their free will, the oppressed will inevitably endure suffering along the road to liberation. Finally, though the oppressed must struggle for freedom, God's transcendence is the basis for these struggles and it provides hope for liberation. Jones, on the contrary, argues that the prolonged and intense suffering of African Americans brings into question the goodness and the potency of God. Developing a position of humanocentric theism in his early work, Jones asserts that humanity is functionally ultimate in the liberation struggle and that God does not take sides with the oppressed, or with any group for that matter. In his later writings, Jones' position of religious humanism extends his earlier claims to the argument that humanity is also ontologically ultimate and human freedom is no longer grounded in divine gift. Though Jones discusses suffering, claiming that it must be interpreted as a negative force for motivating humanity to fight for liberation, the brunt of his critique of Cone falls on traditional theism, and therefore it is the focus here.

In response to the nascent black theological project, represented by thinkers such as James Cone, Albert Cleage, and J. Deotis Roberts, William R. Jones challenged the very foundations of the movement with the article, "Theodicy and Methodology in Black Theology," which appeared in the *Harvard Theological Review* in 1971. In this precursor to his 1973 book, *Is God a White Racist?*, Jones took black theologians to task for assuming divine omnibenevolence and omnipotence despite what he saw as evidence to the contrary, that is, black suffering and oppression. He wrote, "We contend that the peculiar nature of black suffering raises the *question* of divine racism; we do not conclude that it *answers* the question. We do insist that black theology, precisely because of the fact of black suffering, cannot proceed as if the goodness of God for *all* mankind were a theological axiom."[1] Jones asserted that Cone and others could not logically claim that God is the liberator of blacks unless they could point to a specific divine act of liberation for African Americans. Jones asked, "In the absence of the liberation event *for blacks*, is it possible to speak of the liberation of blacks as implicit in God's innermost nature?"[2] Denying Cone's appeal to the Exodus or Christ's Resurrection as this liberative act, Jones stated that "the exodus may refute the accusation of anti-Semitism but not racism,"[3] since he saw no connection between the ancient Israelites and contemporary blacks in the United States.

Jones claims that God must be identified with the sum of his acts. That is, if we want to know the nature of God, we have no grounds to presuppose any character traits independent of God's activity in human history. Additionally, no appeal to a heavenly reward as compensation for earthly suffering would adequately address the charge of divine racism. In both the claim to know God from God's activity and in the denial of an exclusively eschatological liberation,[4] Jones actually follows Cone's own standards. Cone states, "If God is not for us, if God is not against white racists, then God is a murderer, and we had better kill God."[5] Elsewhere, Cone claims black liberation to be an already, but not fully, achieved reality through the death and resurrection of Jesus. Thus, Cone's own theology demands evidence that God is actually for black liberation. Without such evidence, Jones explains, either God is omnipotent but racist, that is, God could do something about racism but chooses not to, or else God's power must be reinterpreted in such a way that divine benevolence may still be defended.

At the end of *Is God a White Racist?* Jones begins his constructive task of putting forth forms of religion that, he believes, place theodicy at the center of black theology and that avoid the pitfalls of his predecessors that he had challenged. Jones argues that there are only two possible models for black theology that could adequately inspire blacks to fight against oppression:[6] humanocentric theism and what, at the time, Jones called secular humanism. He explains that, though he himself advocates humanism, he believes secular humanism would be rejected because he thinks that the correct system must be theistic to best respond to the reality of black religiosity;[7] that is, Jones feels that any theological or philosophical system that would meet the needs and desires of most African Americans must include faith in

God. Thus, in *Is God a White Racist?* Jones develops the category of humanocentric theism.

According to Jones, humanocentric theism's "special merits are its capacity to eliminate the charge of divine racism and its unambiguous impulse against quietism."[8] He explains further that "the distinctive feature of humanocentric theism is the exalted status it assigns to man and his activity."[9] From this perspective, humanity is functionally, though not ontologically, ultimate. If liberation is to come about, it will be through human efforts.

At this point it may be asked, what role God plays in such an understanding? Jones explains, humanocentric theism "assign[s] an exalted status to man, particularly to human freedom, but this status—and here we come to its theistic ground—is the consequence of God's will, and it conforms to [God's] ultimate purpose and plan for mankind."[10] Though he admits that there is not much difference practically between humanocentric theism and humanism, or even atheism,[11] Jones *does* maintain a distinction. Human freedom exists only because of the divine freedom that has willed it. From this perspective of humanocentric theism, divine sovereignty over human history is self-limited. Jones says, "It is the consequence of God's decision and will to respect the freedom He gave to man. This means that He relates Himself to man in terms of persuasion and not coercion."[12] Jones cites theologian Howard Burkle as a primary example of a humanocentric theist. Burkle writes, "Persuasion seems a kind of impotence. This objection is based on a misconception of power . . . . Among persons, persuasion and not compulsion is the highest form of power. Compulsion is a last resort . . . . Persuasion—the act of influencing another toward the better without deceit, threat or bribery—is power indeed."[13] In addition to this reconception of divine power, the certainty of human destiny must also be understood differently.

Since Jones maintains that humans are responsible for their own redemption, there is no guarantee of liberation. Humans, after all, are not perfect. "Talk about the inevitable liberation of blacks must also be muted. The actual character of human history is the product of human choices and actions. Human progress or moral improvement is not assured, particularly where black prospects are at stake."[14] The claim that liberation is not inevitable may be understood as destroying any ground for faith in God or hope for liberation. However, the claim that liberation is not guaranteed is the very impetus for human efforts, guided and inspired by God, for social justice and liberation.

Jones also asserts that God does not take sides with any group of people, including the oppressed, as Cone argues. God must be understood to be neutral in terms of events in human history, unless a particular event may be pointed to as an unequivocal liberative act of God, according to Jones. From Jones' perspective, there has been no such liberation event for African Americans. Without evidence for this liberation event, divine goodness cannot be assumed, at least in regard to divine goodness directed toward blacks, Jones claims. As is explored further in chapter 6 of this work, an alternative to Jones' line of thinking would be the reinterpretation of traditional notions of divine power as dominating, coercive, and overwhelming. In other words, Jones challenges traditional understandings of divine goodness, but does not really fully develop the concept of divine power as persuasive, which would mitigate his demand for an obvious "event" of black liberation.

Though Jones originally called his position secular humanism, he later clarifies that it should really be called black religious humanism. As we will also see Anthony Pinn do, Jones argues humanism is a valid option along the spectrum of religious perspectives. Both Jones and Pinn take issue with religion, especially black religion, being equated with theism, and specifically Protestant Christianity. They argue that such a narrow understanding of religiosity preemptively restricts potentially meaningful and useful perspectives that may be characterized by more adequate proposals for ending or alleviating black suffering.[15] In Jones' words, "because of the failure of white Christianity and because of the checkered success of black Christianity, it seems only reasonable to consider as candidate models for black-liberation theology other forms of theism or nontheism, if only to supplement black Christianity."[16]

A second and related point Jones and Pinn each make is that, not only is humanism a *religious* option, but it is also a genuine black option. Both thinkers explain that the tradition of black humanism is difficult to trace because of its lack of institutional structure and because of the theistic bias of most historians of African Americans. Nevertheless, in slave testimonies, slave seculars, the blues, literature, and rap of today, a voice critical of black theism may be heard.[17] Jones writes, "Whether we encounter black humanism during the slave period or more recent eras of oppression, it appears as a critic of black Christian theism, questioning the latter's capacity to make sense of the history of black oppression and to accommodate the prerequisites of a viable theology of liberation."[18] The presence of humanistic tendencies throughout black history is important not just to show that humanism is "black enough," but more importantly to show that as it had been a viable option in the past that served as a genuine and fulfilling response to black suffering, it could still serve today as an alternative to black theism.

As Jones himself admits, and as Pinn will later critique him on, it is difficult to distinguish between the humanocentric theism he outlined in *Is God a White Racist?* and the humanism that becomes the focus of his later apologetic work. Like humanocentric theism, Jones' humanism centers on the notion of the functional ultimacy of humanity in the struggle for liberation from economic, social, and political oppression of African Americans. It also meets his self-imposed standards of resisting quietism, in that liberation demands human action, and of denying the charge of divine racism, since earthly oppression is the result of human evil, in this case white racism. An obvious difference is that God seems to play less of a role in his humanism than in his humanocentric theism, but not substantially so. In other words, the functional ultimacy of humanity is not grounded on God within the humanist framework.[19] Perhaps Jones' humanism better meets his standards of denying both divine racism and quietism. In humanocentric theism, God is still at least partially responsible for moral evil and suffering because divine power has been self-limited to allow for the human freedom that results in moral evil and suffering. Also, in Jones' notion of humanocentric theism, theoretically God could be persuading humanity toward evil, as divine goodness is not assumed. In contrast, in humanism the blame for moral evil and the responsibility to overcome it is laid entirely at the feet of humanity.

James Cone ultimately rejects Jones' humanocentric theism, and any form of humanism, because of the potential he sees for the despair that may result in placing human liberation fundamentally in human hands.[20] He is sensitive to the theodicy challenges that Jones poses and, though finding them compelling, holds steadfastly to a faith in an active, good God. Cone admits in *God of the Oppressed* that faith in God is paradoxical, given the suffering history of blacks in the United States.[21] A radical difference between Cone and Jones is the fact that Jones does not utilize the Bible as a primary theological source. Cone looks to the Bible for the clue to the nature and character of his God. In it, time and again Cone discovers a benevolent God who sided with the oppressed and against oppression. From the Exodus, through the prophets, and through the life of Christ, God is portrayed as actively fighting against the powers of evil and oppression. In response to Jones, Cone does not claim a liberation event in history specifically for blacks. However, he responds to Jones' critique by deeming the cross-resurrection as the liberation event for which Jones searched as a sign of God's goodness and power. Because of the resurrection, Cone argues, the Christian may assume that God will eternally and universally continue his actions and intent evident in the Bible.[22] That is, because of the resurrection, Cone believes that Jesus will always heal the sick and maintain fellowship with the poor and outcasts. God will always take sides and will always fight against oppression. Cone sees the resurrection as both the defeat of evil and the bestowal of the power to fight against evil.

Again, a large part of what is at stake in the disagreement between Cone and Jones is which religious perspective best encourages black hope and black resistance against suffering and oppression. Cone's appeal to the life and resurrection of Jesus as a sign of hope and an inspiration for struggle is based on what he sees as the dominant view within black Christian faith itself. That is, he bases his claims on the faith content of nonacademics and nonprofessional theologians. As always, it is important to not simply remember for whom one does theology, but also to ground one's assertions, norms, and sources in the faith of this particular community. There is no doubt Cone does this. That said, Jones' work also articulates a vital expression of black religious experience that challenges the dominant view. Though addressed by Cone, Jones' challenge is still pertinent.[23] In raising the important question of divine goodness, Jones also opens the door for a creative interpretation of divine power that is explored in chapter 6.

Anthony Pinn: Atheistic Humanism

William R. Jones disagrees with both Cone's theocentric theistic stance and his redemptive suffering theodicy. While his criticism of Cone's theism has been explored, the subject of Cone's redemptive suffering theodicy has been left until now. This discussion of suffering lies at the heart of the critiques of both Anthony Pinn and Delores Williams. Here, Pinn's response is examined. Later, Williams is brought into dialogue with Cone and Pinn.

Though Jones' critique is compelling and challenges the very foundations of black theology, Anthony Pinn does not feel that Jones went far enough. He believes that Jones' humanocentric theism and demand that black theology be based on theodicy do not adequately address the depths of black suffering or the charge of divine racism. In moving from Jones' language to Pinn's here, it is helpful to distinguish among three types of humanism: theistic humanism, agnostic humanism, and atheistic humanism. Under this designation, Jones' humanocentric theism is an example of theistic humanism since, as we have seen above, Jones believes in God and argues that humans are functionally, but not ontologically, ultimate. In contrast, Pinn calls for atheistic humanism, or what he refers to as strong humanism, as the answer to black suffering. For Pinn, humans are both functionally and ontologically ultimate. Furthermore, Pinn rejects the category of theodicy altogether, since "[t]heodicy requires a compromise with suffering because it assumes the goodness of God and requires the finding of something useful in human suffering."[24]

Pinn argues that, although claiming to not presuppose the goodness of God, Jones' development of humanocentric theism posits a God whose power is reinterpreted as persuasive, but whose goodness implicitly remains. Pinn does not believe that Jones' humanocentric theism is adequate in philosophically renouncing a racist God. "In a word, the reduction of God's authority and the bolstering of human responsibility do not sufficiently alter the possibility of an evil (though limited) god or a God who persuades others to perform evil acts. If the latter is taken seriously, there is also the possibility of divinely approved and redemptive suffering."[25] In fact, Jones clearly argues that such a God may in fact persuade us toward evil. In other words, he never does explicitly presuppose God's goodness. He would concur with Pinn when he suggests, "Perhaps God's self-limitation is the ultimate slight [*sic*] of hand, the supreme alibi—with human abusers of freedom as the fall guys. Perhaps evil is not the result of human misdeeds against divine persuasion. Rather, it is possible that God is persuading white Americans to act in oppressive ways."[26] This is a valid point that must be addressed if humanocentric theism is to be a valid alternative to black liberation theology.

While Pinn claims that Jones misses the mark by focusing on theodicy, he criticizes James Cone primarily for offering a positive notion of some types of suffering that blacks can endure and that then turn into redemptive sources. He claims that, according to Cone, "[i]n short, out of suffering (properly addressed) comes a closeness to God and liberative consequences."[27] He continues, "Cone attempts, unsuccessfully, to draw a distinction between suffering *with* God (positive suffering) and suffering *because of* God (redemptive suffering).

However, positive suffering maintains the possibility of divinely sanctioned oppression." Pinn concludes, "In short, movement toward liberation should involve a desire for change brought about by a proper understanding of suffering as unquestionably and unredeemably evil."[28]

Pinn proposes the option of atheistic humanism as a position that denies both the theodicy issue and an understanding of suffering as redemptive. In contrast with "weak humanism," the label he gives to both Cone's and Jones' positions, Pinn's category of atheistic humanism, which he calls strong humanism, maintains that "moral evil in the world is easily understood as the result of misguided 'will to power' and nothing more. As a result, strong humanism also denies the existence of an evil God who is responsible for human suffering. Hence, strong humanism seeks to combat oppression through radical human commitment to life and corresponding activity."[29] Pinn believes that the understanding that evil must be fought by humans, with no hope of aid from God, is the most effective impetus in the struggle for freedom.[30]

Taking into consideration slave seculars, the blues, rap, and the literature of the Harlem Renaissance, James Weldon Johnson, James Baldwin, and Alice Walker,[31] Pinn defines African American humanism by the following five characteristics:

(1) understanding of humanity as fully (and solely) accountable and responsible for the human condition and the correction of its plight; (2) suspicion toward or rejection of supernatural explanation and claims, combined with an understanding of humanity as an evolving part of the natural environment as opposed to its having been created; (3) tied to this is an appreciation for African American cultural production and a perception of traditional forms of Black religiosity as having cultural importance as opposed to any type of "cosmic" authority; (4) a commitment to individual and societal transformation; and (5) a controlled optimism that recognizes both human potential and human destructive activities.[32]

Thus, as in Jones' humanocentric theism, in Pinn's atheistic humanism also liberation is not guaranteed. However, in Pinn's words, "What becomes important is not the 'end' of struggle—guaranteed outcomes—but that success is located in positive action itself."[33] Though suffering is inevitable in this Sisyphusian struggle, it must not be interpreted as redemptive in any way, Pinn asserts.

Pinn contends that "this form of humanism understands suffering as wrong and sees it as being solely a result of human misconduct.

Suffering is evil and it must end; contact with it and endurance of it do not promote anything beneficial. To think otherwise is to deny the value of human life by embracing a demonic force that effectively mutates and destroys the quality of life. *Suffering Has No Redemptive Qualities.*"[34] By redemption here, I take Pinn's provocative assertion to mean that there is no divine sanctioning nor divine co-suffering in human suffering, nor is there divine aid in its alleviation or termination. Suffering does and will occur, but this suffering does not aid the process of liberation in any way. Humanity is left with the terrifying and exhilarating challenge of liberation from oppression. Pinn concludes his *Why Lord?* by saying,

> [S]trong humanism does not guarantee an end to oppression. Human effort without superhuman assistance does not allow for such claims. However, sustained struggle takes place and is shaped by the possibility of change. And victories are not won because of or through suffering, but in spite of suffering. Possibility is enough. For what are the true possibilities for transformation when God's intervention is not apparent, but is desperately appealed to? How strongly does one fight for change while seeking signs of God's presence? Humanity is far better off fighting with the tools it has—a desire for transformation, human creativity, physical strength, and untapped collective potential.[35]

In response to Pinn, former Cone student and current black liberation theologian, Dwight Hopkins asserts, "Many black Christians believe in redemptive suffering because life has shown them that their black race would have undergone possible genocide without such an understanding of evil . . . . If belief in fruitful suffering motivates people of theistic faith to fight for a better earthly social reconfiguration, then redemptive suffering is beneficial." One of the issues at hand is—which philosophical or religious position best encourages human social action. Hopkins points out that "using [Pinn's] own criterion of 'experience' rather than doctrinal and theological obligations, one could strongly argue that experience has shown the most progressive social change organizations and movements in African-American history to have come out of black theistic religious influences, whereas the experience of non-theistic spirituals, rap music, folk tales, and black literature so far have not created sustained organizations for fundamental social change."[36] Hopkins' challenge of the social justice cash value of atheistic humanism is compelling, but not entirely fair. As indicated earlier, the fact that the manifestations and values of alternatives to black theism lack institutional structure does not mean they have been absent or ineffective. Hopkins' comment could just as easily point to the fact that these alternative frameworks have not been given full opportunity to transform society as that they have been unsuccessful.

I find Pinn's argument most important in the consideration of instances where human suffering is the result of humans oppressing humans. If one is to fight against oppression, some suffering is certainly inevitable, as Cone maintains. Further, suffering absolutely may build character and thus produce some positive results. However, to view the reality of suffering as identical to the efficacy of suffering is a dangerous theological move. Cone's understanding of suffering still leaves too much space for any "positive" suffering, as Pinn argues, and leaves in doubt the goodness of God, which both Pinn and Jones point out. As Jones explains, "To assign a positive quality to suffering, . . . dictates that we endure or embrace it; to define it as negative motivates us to crush it."[37] Though differing in important ways, both Pinn and Delores Williams center their criticism on Cone's notion of suffering—Pinn does so philosophically, while Williams does so existentially and historically.

Delores Williams: Suffering and Survival

Delores S. Williams' critique of James Cone's theology grows out of a womanist standpoint. Womanism, a theological and ethical school of thought of many black female clergy and religious scholars, had its formal beginnings in the late 1970s and early 1980s. Taking their starting point from Alice Walker's definition of womanist,[38] womanists critiqued both the racism of white feminist thought[39] and the sexism of black liberation theology.[40] Thinkers such as Jacquelyn Grant, Katie G. Cannon, and Delores S. Williams[41] argued that the particularity of black women's experience must be respected and understood as a central unique theological source.[42] Womanism has been characterized by its consistently holistic treatment of the interrelationship of various forms of oppression, such as racism, sexism, classism, and in some cases, homophobia and environmental degradation.[43]

In her profoundly challenging book *Sisters in the Wilderness*, Delores Williams critiques black liberation theology for positing the unambiguous character of the Bible as a liberating text, for advocating the doctrine of redemptive suffering, and for interpreting the death of

Jesus Christ according to traditional atonement theory. The critiques that Williams articulates in this text are not simply negative statements attacking the black theological enterprise in general, or James Cone in particular. With her critique as the base, Williams builds a constructive theological response to these challenges. This response includes an understanding of God as sustaining force in the survival of black women, a stress on the ministerial vision of Jesus Christ, and an interpretation of the resistance strategies of black women as religiously grounded.

Differing from Cone, Williams asserts that the Bible could not be understood as a wholly liberative text. Central to her treatment was the biblical pericope of Hagar and Sarah. Inspired by similarities between the figure of Hagar and the black American woman's experience, Williams challenges black theology's unquestioning acceptance of the Exodus story and the chosen nature of the ancient Israelites as the central message of the Hebrew Bible. She wants to know what God's special relationship with Abraham, Sarah, and Moses said about God's relationship to Hagar and the Canaanites, who the Israelites were divinely ordered to drive out of Palestine.[44] She discovers what she terms a "non-liberative thread" running through the Bible.[45] Williams states: "The fact remains: slavery in the Bible is a natural and unprotested institution in the social and economic life of ancient society—except on occasion when the Jews are themselves enslaved. One wonders how biblically derived messages of liberation can be taken seriously by today's masses of poor, homeless African Americans, female and male, who consider themselves to be experiencing a form of slavery—economic enslavement by the capitalistic American economy."[46] Williams concludes that the Bible must be viewed with a hermeneutic of suspicion and that black and womanist theologians in particular must begin to read the stories of the Bible from different points of view. She challenges the triumphalistic and liberative readings of the Bible that had characterized Cone's theology.

Just as she looks at the experiences of black women in history and in literature as sources for womanist theology, Williams looks at the biblical figure of Hagar as exemplar of black women's experience in the Bible. She describes Hagar's encounter with God, like that of many African American women, as a wilderness experience. "For many black Christian women today, 'wilderness' or 'wilderness experience' is a symbolic term used to represent a near destruction situation in which God gives personal direction to the believer and thereby helps her make a way out of what she thought was no way."[47] The story of

Hagar shows the reader a God who cares about the oppressed and serves to provide ways for the outcast to survive. God does not liberate Hagar from her bondage to Sarah and Abraham. God also does not encourage Hagar to leave her situation. Rather what one discovers is a God who sustains and empowers individuals to survive life's circumstances and hardships.

What does such a story say about how God acts in the world? What does Hagar's encounter with God teach us about human agency? It would certainly seem that we cannot take away the idea that God always acts in our lives in an intrusive and dominating manner, as many earlier Christian theologians have argued. Instead, we can claim that God is a caring God who respects human free will and agency, and who acts for the benefit of the oppressed in, sometimes, unexpected ways. The fact that the Bible may be, and has been, used in a variety of ways and used to support a variety of positions, serves to strengthen Williams' critique of black theologians' use of the Bible.

For Williams, the Bible is a collection of stories about survival, not liberation. The interpretation that the Bible is the story of God's liberating activity is true only from the perspective of those chosen by God to be God's people, the Israelites. In seeing the Bible as providing a message of liberation, James Cone and other liberation theologians have failed to realize that there are other oppressed people encountered in the Bible with whom God does not side. Williams, following the scholarship of Elsa Tamez, argues that one cannot read the story of Hagar and claim that God always sides with the oppressed. One cannot think of the Canaanites in the Promised Land who God commands the Israelites to conquer without wondering what such a command says about the status of the conquered in God's eyes. She does not deny that God does liberate in the Bible. She does claim, however, that, given the *complete* Biblical narrative, the Bible must be read with a hermeneutic of suspicion.[48]

In addition to her critique of the liberative interpretation of the Bible and use of Hagar as exemplary biblical figure, Williams also examines and challenges the historical roles into which black women have been categorized. She characterizes these as roles of surrogacy. Before the Civil War, when slavery existed, black women's experience could be described as one of coerced surrogacy. Black women took the places of white women in nurturing roles, white and black men in laboring roles, and white women again in sexual roles. In the postbellum period, this surrogacy continued, according to Williams, but this time as voluntary, though pressured, surrogacy. During this period, black women fulfilled nurturing tasks, worked as domestics, took on the role of head of household from many black men, and continued in their childbearing role for both the black and white communities.[49]

Williams traces the legacy of these roles over time. First, she argues the mammy figure resulted in the contemporary negative images of viewing black women as religious, fat, asexual, and self-sacrificing. Next, the worker role has resulted in a concept of the masculinized woman. Finally, the stereotype of black women as loose, oversexed, and amoral could be traced to the surrogacy role of concubine.[50] Williams concludes: "Surrogacy has been a negative force in African-American women's lives. It has been used by both men and women of the ruling class, as well as by some black men, to keep black women in the service of other people's needs and goals."[51]

In her treatment of the surrogacy roles played by black women, Williams does not simply maintain that surrogacy roles must come to an end, that God does not validate such roles, or that nothing can be learned theologically from such realities. Instead, she argues that black women should draw from the knowledge that Hagar was forced to play such a surrogacy role in her relationship with Sarah and Abraham. As Williams claims, the figure of Hagar has long been regarded as embodying black women's realities.

In addition to the story of Hagar as a source for womanist theology, Williams develops the literature of black women as a fount of theological ideas. Williams finds a "doctrine of resistance" based on black women's "resistance rituals" in the work of writers such as Zora Neale Hurston, Margaret Walker, and Alice Walker. This doctrine articulates God's sustaining force in the survival, resistance, and joy of black women. Williams points to at least four types of political strategies employed by black female characters against oppression. These strategies of resistance may be characterized as developing power, forging relationships, distancing themselves from oppression, and raising consciousness. First, developing power might mean either "assum[ing] defiant attitudes" or using physical strength. A defiant attitude may be the only resistance strategy available when physically overmatched; physical strength may mean working hard for oneself and one's loved ones or literally fighting back against those who terrorize or oppress, meeting "force with force." Second, forging relationships means that "women form strong bonds with other women and with men to increase self-esteem and to develop new possibilities for mutual relationships." Third, distancing oneself may mean either psychologically or physically removing oneself from the situation of oppression.

Finally, consciousness-raising "involves examining and changing [one's] consciousness about the meaning of values that have been fundamental to black women's early conditioning and to the ethical, moral, and religious foundations of the Afro-American community."

Importantly, these strategies of resistance are religion-based according to Williams. These strategies of "lifeline politics are informed by women's experience of transcendence, of faith, of ritual, and of God." She explains, "Lifeline politics are, then, religious in nature. The political strategies used by female characters in these novels are supported by women's religious practices. And, as Zora Neale Hurston's and Alice Walker's works reveal, these religious expressions are not all Christian. Yet they all sustain black women's efforts to oppose the many facets of oppression."[52] Thus Williams creatively and compellingly argues that womanist theology must be based on the experiences of black women as evidenced in both the Bible and in literature. In these sources one encounters a God who sustains, but does not liberate, and who empowers black women to resist oppression psychologically, intellectually, emotionally, and physically. Williams demands that the Christian tradition be viewed through the lens of these experiences and, if necessary, reinterpreted as a result of these experiences.

One particular doctrine that Williams asserts must be interpreted in the light of the experiences of black women in the Bible, in history, and in literature is the classic doctrine of atonement, which she believed had been assumed by mainstream black theology.[53] Williams sees Jesus portrayed by classic theology as the ultimate surrogate figure, who sacrificed his life so that humanity may be freed of sin and evil. She asserts, "Surrogacy, attached to this divine personage, thus takes on an aura of the sacred. It is therefore fitting and proper for black women to ask whether the image of a surrogate-God has salvific power for black women or whether this image supports and reinforces the exploitation that has accompanied their experience with surrogacy. If black women accept this idea of redemption, can they not also passively accept the exploitation that surrogacy brings?"[54]

Williams sums up her critique of the claim that Jesus's suffering was redemptive: "Humankind is, then, redeemed through Jesus' *ministerial* vision of life and not through his death. There is nothing divine in the blood of the cross."[55] She does not deny that the cross had meaning, but she simply rather wants to reinterpret that meaning in the light of the experiences of black women. "I am not suggesting that we forget the cross and Jesus' crucifixion. I am suggesting that we see them for what they are: symbols of violence and innocent suffering.

Neither violence nor suffering is good, nor should we attach positive value to them."[56]

Just as she does not entirely reject the use of the Bible in her challenge to its interpretation, Williams is also not willing to give up the value of the life and resurrection of Jesus in the New Testament. Her claim that there is nothing sacred in the blood of the cross shifts the focus on Jesus from his death to his life. In contrast with this potentially dangerous notion of salvation and redemption, Williams develops a doctrine of redemption based on the *life* of Jesus. Williams argues that the salvation of black women "is assured by Jesus' life of resistance and by the survival strategies he used to help people survive the death of identity caused by their exchange of inherited cultural meanings for a new identity shaped by the gospel ethics and world view."[57] The idea that Jesus shows us how to resist oppression in this life is drawn from the temptation accounts. Jesus resists death and the temptations of material wealth and of worldly monopolistic political power.

Williams goes on to claim that this understanding of redemption is also more scripturally sound. In the Gospels, the reader encounters a Jesus who "came to show humans *life*—to show redemption through a perfect *ministerial* vision of righting relations between body (individual and community), mind (of humans and of tradition) and spirit." This was the true gift of God; not some morbid human sacrifice of God's child, but rather, an exemplar of correct living and an invitation to participate in God's work toward redemption.[58]

In the end, Williams' theology results in a greater emphasis placed on the role of the human in the process of redemption and salvation than is evident in black theologians, such as Cone. She writes: "I believe the hope oppressed black women get from the Hagar-Sarah texts has more to do with survival and less to do with liberation . . . Human initiative "sparks" liberation—not divine initiative. In Genesis 16, Hagar liberates herself; she is a run-away slave. In Genesis 21, Sarah, her oppressor initiates Hagar's liberation. God merely agrees with Sarah."[59] In other words, God sustains humans, but humans must initiate their own liberation.

Delores Williams challenges the idea that God is always a liberating force in the lives of the oppressed. Often one discovers that faith in God may be maintained by understanding God's presence as aiding in survival. Such a shift from God as liberator to God as sustainer speaks volumes about human agency. According to Williams' shift, humans are forced into a greater role in their survival and liberation. The story of Hagar teaches us that God exists, God is caring, and that God will provide, but it also shows that we as humans must use our divine gift of free agency to sustain ourselves and to struggle toward our own liberation and the material and spiritual liberation of humanity. Williams admits that suffering may be a part of the journey through life but claims that our suffering, just like that of Jesus, should not be viewed as redemptive.

Anticipating the challenge of theodicy, it is interesting to me that Williams completely denies God any part in the crucifixion of Christ. If she is able to see the presence and the ambiguity of God in the story of Hagar, why is she reluctant to question the presence and the ambiguity of God in the story of Jesus? That is, in Hagar's story Williams claims that God sustained Hagar and aided in her survival. Even though God does not liberate her, God creates a space for her self-liberation and sustains her throughout her story. On the contrary, in Jesus's story, God does not liberate nor sustain, according to Williams. This story is simply a matter of human evil in which God plays no part. To deem the crucifixion of Jesus an act of murder, carried out by humans, does not explain the presence or absence of God in this murder. This characterization of God is not consistent with the portrait Williams claims to be evident in the Genesis pericope. Furthermore, beyond being inconsistent, the fact that Williams fails to consider God's part in Christ's death bars her from claiming a divine activity in the life and resurrection of Jesus. If God is present in sustaining Hagar and in the ministerial life of Jesus, then why cannot we consider God's presence in the death of Christ? Whether divine activity is providential, ambiguous, or punishing, it must be considered as playing a part in the crucifixion.

This issue aside, Williams' womanist critique of Cone's theology asserts that the experiences of African American women, the oppressed of the oppressed, must be employed as a central source for black theology. The experiences of black women in the Bible, especially Hagar, in history, particularly surrogacy roles, and in literature serve to deconstruct Cone's notions of liberation, servanthood, redemption, and human agency. Williams' theology constructively makes the case for God as sustaining force in the lives of black women such as Hagar and those found in the literature of writers such as Zora Neale Hurston, Margaret Walker, and Alice Walker. Williams argues that redemption is available, not through the death of Jesus, but through his life of ministry to the poor and outcast of society. It is this ministerial vision of righting relations that must inspire the resistance strategies and hope that are necessary to build a just society.

Dwight Hopkins: God as Spirit of Total Liberation in Us

In addition to the Bible, Cone uses the African American experience as a sign of God's taking sides with the oppressed and fighting for freedom. He groups Pinn's critique with that of Jones and believes that Pinn's strong humanism would not be adequate or honest enough to the black religious experience of faith in God.[60] Cone takes the reality of black existence as the center of his theology, even at the expense of God. He writes: "If God has made the world in which black people *must* suffer, and if he is a God who rules, guides, and sanctifies the world, then he is a murderer. To be the God of black people, he must be against the oppression of black people."[61] Cone also asserts, "Black Theology must take seriously the reality of black people—their life of suffering and humiliation. This must be the point of departure of all God-talk which seeks to be black-talk."[62] An illuminating and creative illustration of developing a theology from the reality and experiences of the black community is found in the work of Cone's former student, Dwight N. Hopkins.

In particular, Hopkins' *Shoes That Fit Our Feet, Down, Up, and Over*, and *Being Human* use the black experience as a source for theology.[63] In each of these books, Hopkins describes the faith and lives of black folk during and after slavery existed. In particular Hopkins' work provides both a theology and a theological anthropology developed from the black experience of slavery. After an examination of Hopkins' understanding of God, this section concludes with a look at his development of the category of resistance. Significantly, Hopkins' idea of God as the Spirit of Total Liberation in Us links these two spheres of theological concepts and anthropological claims. This naming of God is developed largely from the foundation built by Cone; it incorporates some of the critiques of the previous three thinkers, and expresses an imperative for a robust notion of human agency in the face of oppression.

Hopkins agrees with and builds upon Cone's assertion that God sides with blacks, with the oppressed.[64] Like Cone, Hopkins maintains that the Bible tells the story of a God, the Way Maker, who liberates the least of society. Hopkins' God is a God of justice, liberation, creativity, and humor. The aspect of Hopkins' thought upon which I wish to draw is his mitigation of Cone's emphasis on the role of God in actually carrying out liberation. Here Hopkins differs in degree from Cone rather than in kind. While Cone absolutely expresses the ethical conviction that humans, both oppressed and oppressor, must play a central role in the liberation process, Hopkins articulates a theology that asserts a form of divine presence as human agency, the Spirit of Total Liberation in Us. Thus, Hopkins emphasizes human responsibility and potential for liberation more than Cone does. Hopkins explicitly states that humanity must work with God as co-laborers to bring about liberation and implicitly shows how this is carried out in his use of sources.[65]

Though Hopkins clearly understands the Bible to be revelatory, he seems much more interested in how God is revealed in the lives of everyday black people and how these people understand the Bible.[66] In focusing on the black experience as a source for his theology, Hopkins shows how God acts in the world—not through overtly stepping into human history to alter its course, but rather through encouraging black resistance, hope, and joy.

Like Cone, Hopkins bases his theological method on the sources of the Bible and the black experience, among others. In practice Hopkins deals much more thoroughly with the black experience than with the Bible. When he touches on the Bible explicitly, it is through black experience. Hopkins asserts that enslaved blacks believed in a powerful and just God; he refers to this person of the Trinity as the Spirit of Total Liberation for Us. He writes: "The ultimate power in African American folk culture is the Way Maker, a being so infinite in abilities that anything is possible."[67] Indeed, Hopkins points out the belief in the Union victory in the Civil War and the Emancipation of the slaves as divine intervention and efficacy.[68] Hopkins outlines the various characteristics of the Way Maker in his discussion. He discusses the Creator Way Maker, a Co-laboring Way Maker, and a Stormy but Tender Way Maker.[69] It is in his exploration of the Co-laboring Way Maker that Hopkins extends and deepens Cone's trajectory of thought.

In distinction from Cone, Hopkins describes God's reality in the Exodus paradigm as an empowering force. For Hopkins, God does not simply defeat the Egyptians. Instead, God provides a space for the oppressed Israelites to act out their full humanity, meaning to develop and flourish as free and liberated beings. Hopkins writes, "Divine activity is revealed in the voice of the marginalized fighting to make a way out of no way. There is the action of Yahweh."[70] He argues that such a concept is found not only in the Bible but also in the black experience.

Hopkins understands that God fights with humanity: "The Way Maker plays the role of co-laborer in divine existence. God does not wish to go forth and work alone without other living realities aiding in the acts of creation, survival, and liberation."[71] Hopkins' theology certainly is not humanistic in the sense that Jones' and Pinn's are, but in a manner not so radically different from these two, he understands human agency as one way in which God's presence and activity is made manifest. It is not simply through any act of humanity that God is present, but especially in acts performed to coconstitute the New Self and the New Common Wealth. "In a word, God works with us through the act of freedom as we constitute ourselves from oppression to a full reality of the highest potential of a liberated humanity. God liberates us totally and holistically."[72] Again, though these sentences express the same convictions as Cone had before, the larger context of Hopkins' theology points to a greater role for humanity, because it is in humanity that one form of divine presence may be found. Ultimately God's presence for the oppressed is simultaneously God's activity in history and in the granting of human free agency. Both these divine forces work toward coconstituting the New Self and the New Common Wealth in an empowering covenantal relationship.

Significantly, one of the first characteristics that Hopkins examines is God as dynamic process. Here he points to the biblical self-naming of God, "I am who I am" (Exod. 3:14). Hopkins understands this dynamic process of God's ontology not as instability or unpredictability, but rather as fluidity and holistic presence for humanity and creation. In a sense God is unchanging in God's constant dynamism.[73]

One way in which this dynamic, all-powerful, and empowering God is present is in the life of Jesus Christ, the Spirit of Total Liberation with Us. Hopkins uses the story of Jesus to show that another component of the covenant with God is our caring for and liberating of others who are oppressed. He explains that "the co-laboring dynamic of Jesus Emmanuel with oppressed humanity entails defining our humanity based on the full attainment of others' humanity."[74] For Hopkins, it is the reality of Jesus that makes possible such a conversion from concern solely with the self to concern for the least of society. Insightfully, Hopkins claims, "conversion originates with the least in society undergoing a terrifying encounter with fear. Fear stands at the root of the oppressed person's entrapment to macropolitical structures of discrimination and microspiritual demons of self-imposed restraints."[75] Conversion toward the struggle to develop and attain the New Self and the New Common Wealth involves a journey into the depths of fear, with the knowledge that God is with us in Jesus Christ. It is with Jesus that we can attain our full humanity and struggle for the full humanity of all people, according to Hopkins.

In addition to God being with the oppressed in Jesus, based on the Gospel message of Christ, belief in Jesus also entails a hope in his return. "It is this hope that there is something different and better than this world of pain, oppression, and mere survival that engenders a profound faith and expectation among the economically poor, those heavy laden with worry and pain, poor and working people seeking better lives for their children and their children's children, and victims of all types of cruel and domineering structures."[76] For the oppressed then, there is hope that all will attain full humanity because God is for us and God is with us, not only in the Incarnation thousands of years ago, but also because of the resurrection, even now. In addition, postresurrection God is present as the Spirit of Total Liberation in Us.

Hopkins discusses the presence of the Spirit of Total Liberation in Us as freedom. In God's gift of life, we receive the breath of life, the Spirit of Freedom. "As an act of grace, God creates through divine freedom women and men by giving them the freedom and liberation inherent in God's own self."[77] The breath of God and the fact that we are created in God's image points to the divine gift of our inherent freedom. Hopkins envisions this freedom as holistic. It includes material and spiritual fulfillment. It should be evident both in this life and in the next to come.

Hopkins understands freedom primarily as a gift of God's gracious activity. However, humans often impede the freedom of other humans. When this occurs, as it did during the period when slavery existed, the oppressed have "a divine right to resist." He explains the resistance of enslaved African Americans was a theological reality:

> To claim control over and freedom for the black body (either individual or collective) was to assert that one's humanity reflected sacred creation—an attempt to position an ebony body for self-determination of space (that is, a political dimension) and for self-identity (that is, a cultural dimension). Both revolutionary aspects in the context of the slavery system removed one literally from the domain of the evil ones and their structures to sacred ground—a place where one sought a new life, "born again" in the hoped-for reality of new macro (political economic), micro (the everyday ordinary), linguistic, and cultural identity dimensions of what it meant to be a child of God struggling for full humanity.[78]

Thus, God creates us for freedom, not oppression. The attainment of our full human freedom is both divine gift and human project. At times, the human struggle for freedom must take the form of resistance. According to Hopkins, when humans resist oppression and seek liberation, God as the Spirit of Total Liberation in Us is revealed. To illustrate, Hopkins discusses several examples of resistance including Harriet Tubman's Underground Railroad, the slave rebellions led by Gabriel Prosser, Denmark Vesey, and Nat Turner, maroon communities, black folktales, and social, political, and cultural critics such as W. E. B. DuBois, Martin Luther King, Jr., and Malcolm X, and novelists such as Toni Morrison.[79] One of the often-ignored forms of resistance Hopkins explores is humor.[80]

Focusing especially on the antebellum period, Hopkins explains that enslaved African Americans employed humor and laughter both as a survival coping mechanism and also as a way to encourage more overt acts of resistance; often these effects overlapped. As a survival strategy, humor allowed the enslaved person to cope with and mock the sheer absurdity of living as a slave. Making fun of the system of slavery and/or the slave master could also be a way to undermine the oppressive system that valued some humans more than some others. As a form of resistance, humor is characterized by its psychological, communal, and religious aspects.

Psychologically, humor may be employed to feel better about one's self and one's identity. Humor may make one feel more human, more intelligent, and more valuable. Hopkins explains that "joking fosters a leveling of the apparent omnipotence of the monopolizers of divine creation. When the exploiter is laughed at, he or she can be better seen as just another human being and not some type of demi-god to be feared sheepishly and automatically by the least of society . . . . Thus one continues down the path of co-constituting the new self influenced by the Spirit."[81] Humor may psychologically make one feel better about oneself, despite what society dictates, as well as inspire one to act out on this new way of understanding one's identity and worth.

Next, Hopkins asserts that humor is a communal form of resistance. He explains, "[laughing] gains a great deal of its power of survival and resistance and draws on the liberating Spirit from within when it grows among family, friends, and allies . . . . [T]he notion of being fully human via laughter can only attain its fullness by interacting with community . . . . The humorous 'I' exists because of its impact on the 'we' and the 'we' receives nourishment from the 'I.' "[82] Again, this aspect of humor may be characterized as a survival mechanism, as a way of bonding with others over one's situation, but it also may be a practical method for undermining authority and encouraging outright rebellion.

Finally, Hopkins convincingly argues that humor as a form of resistance is consistent with and may be based on a particular interpretation of the Gospel. He writes, "Freedom pushes further toward actualization when a liberating laughter becomes a material force and a real truth for the least in society. Both by its role, its effect, and its definition, humor is the gospel of liberation."[83] In this way, humor allows the oppressed to become fully conscious of the image of God in which they were created and encourages freedom and attainment of full humanity despite oppressive social, political, or cultural structures.

In the end, Hopkins' theology covers much of the same ground as Cone's had before and there is much agreement between the two. In terms of methodology, both use many of the same sources. In my view, Hopkins develops these sources in much greater depth than Cone had before. In terms of theology, Hopkins' concepts of God as the Spirit of Total Liberation for Us and the Spirit of Total Liberation with Us (Jesus) are essentially identical to Cone's God of the Oppressed. What Hopkins expressly adds to this naming of God is the idea of God as the Spirit of Total Liberation in Us. This third characteristic of God, which in some ways combines traditional language of the Holy Spirit with a strong assertion of human agency provides a vital and significant component to a fuller development of the concept of resistance as a theological category.

As this chapter and the previous one explored Cone's theology and his critics and interlocutors with the intention of better understanding Cone's theology, the next two chapters (chapters 4 and 5) examine the work of Emil Fackenheim and four scholars who critically analyze his theology. It will be evident that, though Cone and Fackenheim started from different historical realities of oppression and different conceptions of God, they come to similar understandings of what the proper human response to suffering and evil should be—resistance against oppression and despair, grounded in a realistic and critical faith in both God and humanity.

4

A New Sinai? A New Exodus? Divine Presence During and After the Holocaust in the Theology of Emil Fackenheim

Only in this midnight of dark despair does post-Holocaust thought come upon a shining light. The Nazi logic of destruction was irresistible: it was, nevertheless, being resisted. This logic is a novum in human history, the source of an unprecedented, abiding horror: but resistance to it on the part of the most radically exposed, too, is a novum in history, and it is the source of an unprecedented, abiding wonder. To hear and obey the commanding Voice of Auschwitz is an "ontological" possibility, here and now, because the hearing and obeying was already an "ontic" reality, then and there. (Emil Fackenheim, *To Mend the World*, 25)

I began chapter 2 with an explanation of how I came to the work of James Cone and, more importantly, why I believe he provides a vital contribution to any contemporary discussion of suffering and moral evil, as well as of God and human freedom and ethics. So, the question here is, why put any Jewish theologian into an encounter with Cone, and why Emil Fackenheim in particular?

My personal journey toward Fackenheim began when I was an undergraduate. As mentioned in chapter 1, I had a Jewish professor and mentor, Harold Kasimow, who emphasized the importance and possibilities of interreligious dialogue. I was won over by Kasimow's erudite and compelling perspective that one's view of religion, really one's own religiosity, is deeply enriched by putting differing religious traditions into conversation with one another. So, the notion of drawing from a Christian and a Jew as the primary figures in this study has always seemed natural and necessary for me. Further, in my junior year I spent a semester abroad at Tel Aviv University. With European and other North American students, I took classes dealing with Judaism, Jewish Philosophy, and Politics of the Middle East. More than the classes though, my broader experience in Israel gave me a better sense of a Jewish culture and worldview. By this I mean that I began to see the great diversity among Israelis and among Jews, but I also got a sense of commonalities evident among many Jews in Israel. In the shadow of the Holocaust, there was the over-whelming assertion that such an atrocity must never happen again. I witnessed great pride in the existence and vitality of the Jewish nation-state, as both a homeland serving to prevent a second Holocaust, and also as a community of artists, athletes, and political and religious figures who make vital contributions to our world today. Manifesting key aspects of the Jewish tradition, many Israelis bore witness to the imperative for human activities of building equitable and compassionate communities, social justice, and con-cern for the least of society. I was intrigued by my encounter with the paradoxical theological concept of doubting and questioning God while simultaneously remaining faithful to God.

Between my time in Israel and my years in graduate school, I began reading Elie Wiesel, the modern-day Job. In his works I found a beautiful and haunting expression of the aspects of Jewish life after the Holocaust. Wiesel's writings bear powerful witness to the demand that the Holocaust never happen again and, given the ambiguity of divine power, goodness, and presence during such an event assert the necessity however impossible it may seem that we as humans must be the ones who prevent it. Wiesel captures and poetically articulates the theological tension that one encounters when one faces the perennial dilemma of why bad things happen to good people. He asserts that we must face moral evil directly and yet he still allows for the impos-sible possibility of fervent, stubborn faith in both God and humanity. Nevertheless, I decided not to put Wiesel into encounter with Cone primarily because he makes no claims to being a theologian and is not a systematic thinker or writer.

However, it was through my awareness of Wiesel that I came to Emil Fackenheim. In Fackenheim I found a more systematic theolo-gian and philosopher who dealt with the very themes raised by Wiesel. Though his earlier writings were less focused on the Holocaust per se, Fackenheim's works from around 1967 to 1982 represent a sustained and developing confrontation of the Holocaust and raise the question of the possibility of thought or action after this event. Fackenheim asserted that the Holocaust was a unique event in world history and ruptured all theology. I believe this claim of uniqueness and particularity is profound and important. I find Fackenheim's refusal to simply dismiss the Holocaust as another example of moral evil in a list of atrocities throughout history very appealing. From a Christian perspective I do not feel that sufficient number of Christians or Jews really took this claim seriously enough. As mentioned in chapter 1, I had personally encountered too many Christians who facilely and callously pushed away claims of radical evil that tests, if not destroys, one's faith. Wiesel and Fackenheim maintained that, after the Holocaust, if God is still to be found, it must be through a direct and honest engagement with these horrible realities, not in ignoring them.

It is in the midst of the horrors of the Holocaust that Fackenheim discovered the basis for maintaining faith in God and humanity. In several varied survivors' accounts Fackenheim found a tenacious and seemingly impossible will to endure and to survive. Many of these victims and survivors also attributed this will to something outside themselves. Fackenheim called this force or presence the Commanding Voice of Auschwitz. I quote Fackenheim's entire description here and again later in the chapter because of the centrality of this concept in his theology:

> What does the Voice of Auschwitz command? Jews are forbidden to hand Hitler posthumous victories. They are commanded to survive as Jews, lest the Jewish people perish. They are commanded to remember the victims of Auschwitz lest their memory perish. They are forbidden to despair of man and his world, and to escape into either cynicism or otherworldliness, lest they cooperate in delivering the world over to the forces of Auschwitz. Finally, they are forbidden to despair of the God of Israel, lest Judaism perish. A secularist cannot make himself believe by a mere act of will, nor can he be commanded to do so . . . . And a religious Jew who has stayed with God may be forced into new, possibly revolutionary relationships with Him. One possibility, however, is unthinkable. A Jew may not respond to Hitler's attempt to destroy Judaism by himself cooperating in its destruction. In ancient times, the unthinkable Jewish sin was idolatry. Today, it is to respond to Hitler by doing his work.[1]

Thus in his early writings Fackenheim asserted that God is evident during the Holocaust as a commanding presence, but not as a saving presence.

It is in Fackenheim's later work *To Mend the World* (1982) that he began to allow for the possibility of divine saving presence, at least in a fragmentary way. This divine saving presence may possibly be evident in *human* acts of resistance against oppression and despair. Specifically, as is discussed below, Fackenheim believed that human efforts to prevent a second Holocaust and to mend the world nearly destroyed as a result of the Holocaust might be redemptive. Further, as indicated by the quotation at the opening of this chapter, human acts of redemptive resistance are possible now only because they were actual during the Holocaust itself. These human activities might be signs that God is in fact still present, active, and, in a sense, saving.

Like Cone then, Fackenheim demanded that theologians honestly and directly face experiences of suffering and moral evil. They both argue that such considerations must take the particularity and uniqueness of such experiences seriously. Through their existential and philosophical experiences of suffering and moral evil, both thinkers assert the possibility of belief in God and in humanity, though for Fackenheim this possibility is more tenuous and fragmentary. As a result of their encounters with racism and the Holocaust, each of them develops creative and original concepts of God and expresses the imperative for human acts of resistance against oppression and despair.

As I did in my treatment of Cone, I begin with a brief biographical sketch of Fackenheim and move on from there to a discussion of his method. As Cone moves between the Bible and the black experience to develop his theology, Fackenheim remained loyal to both scriptural revelation and the Jewish experience, particularly the event of the Holocaust. Next, I provide an analysis of Fackenheim's notions of God and humanity, looking specifically at divine presence, human freedom, and resistance. In chapter 5, I use the work of Richard L. Rubenstein, Marc H. Ellis, Melissa Raphael, and Michael L. Morgan in conversation with Fackenheim to further explore his thought. Finally, in chapter 6 I use both Fackenheim and Cone to move toward developing my own constructive theology.

Biographical Background

As was mentioned before my sketching Cone's life in the second chapter, I believe that knowledge of a thinker's life is necessary if one hopes to fully understand that thinker's work. A theologian's method, concerns, and ideas are shaped by his or her personal background, as well as his or her cultural and historical context, even if this context is rejected. Fackenheim maintained that one's thought, to be authentic, must be involved in and influenced by one's historical circumstances and context.[2] Therefore, a brief examination of Fackenheim's biography is warranted, as this, I hope, will shed light on the content and form of his theology. It is with this assertion in mind that I provide the following brief account of Fackenheim's life.[3]

Emil Fackenheim was born in Halle, Germany in 1917. Though anti-Semitism had characterized much of Europe at the time, the ethos attained prominence under Hitler's Third Reich in 1933. It was in this environment of anti-Jewish hatred and persecution that Fackenheim began study in 1935 at Berlin's Hochschule fur die Wissenschaft des Judentums (Higher Institute for Jewish Studies). There he was ordained as a Reform rabbi.

In 1937 he returned to his hometown to study philosophy and theology at the University of Halle. Fackenheim explained that his thought at this point, as well as later in his life, was influenced most by Martin Buber, Franz Rosenzweig, Leo Strauss, and Soren Kierkegaard. Their neo-orthodox suspicion of the claims of the modern "enlightened" world as well as their emphasis on the importance of divine revelation as encounter with the radical Other had great impact on his thinking.

One aspect of Hitler's terror regime was the demand that universities, including Halle, conform to Nazi policies and philosophies. Fackenheim related that two of his professors, Paul Menzer and Otto Eisfeldt, courageously resisted the Nazi regime in the classroom, the one appealing to the ideal of morality in Kantian ethics, the other to the call for social justice of the Old Testament prophets. Fackenheim also said that he was later told that he was the last Jewish student at the University before his detainment in the Sachsenhausen concentration camp in 1938–1939.[4]

While at Sachsenhausen, Fackenheim was forced to participate in long, ordered marches from his living quarters to the factory in which he was made to work. He later explained that he immediately came to understand the reason for these marches, in which one was punished for going too slowly or falling out of line. He wrote, "I am certain that as early as 1938 the concentration camp had *one* purpose, i.e., slave labor, but also a *higher* purpose superseding slave labor and its benefits to the Nazi system, i.e., to rob its victims of their humanity if not yet their lives."[5] This hatred, denigration, and destruction of Jewish humanity, integrity, and dignity would characterize the Holocaust universe.

After his release from the camp in 1939, Fackenheim left Germany and went on to earn his doctorate from the University of Toronto in 1945, writing his dissertation in medieval Muslim thought. Fackenheim served as a rabbi in Hamilton, Ontario and was professor of Philosophy at the University of Toronto for several decades.

Fackenheim's early work focused on modern philosophy, specifically Hegel, Spinoza, Kant, and Rosenzweig.[6] For Fackenheim, the question driving the work of this period was "not whether this or that 'system' is true but whether there is 'the' Truth in philosophy at all, or whether indeed all such truth is somehow bound up with history."[7] Since he concluded that the truth is indeed "bound up with history," it becomes necessary to examine one's particular historical context. For Fackenheim, this meant an encounter with the Holocaust.

Like most other Jewish philosophers and theologians, Fackenheim did not directly address the Holocaust in writing until the 1960s. For many, the absurdity or profundity of the event shattered all attempts at analysis or reflection. Only after the release of a few autobiographical works of the Holocaust, including Primo Levi's *Survival in Auschwitz* (1958) and Elie Wiesel's *Night* (1960), did Jewish theologians begin to confront the Holocaust in print.

My focus here is Fackenheim's thought after 1967. For it is after, and in many ways prompted by, Israel's Six Day War of 1967 that Fackenheim offered in his work a full treatment of the Holocaust and the possibility of Jewish faith and response. For Fackenheim, the Six Day War raised the possibility of a second Holocaust so quickly after the first. A strong Jewish response to these events was demanded and this notion of response characterizes Fackenheim's thought. In 1987 he wrote:

> As I reflect at age seventy on the development of my thought, I can easily identify its dominating theme. In 1933 I was sixteen years old, being at the time a German still, as well as a Jew. Soon it became evident that Nazism was not a passing episode but rather a catastrophe for Jews, for Germany, for Christianity, for the whole modern world. With this, however, there came for me the growing conviction that Judaism had the resources to respond, and I set out to find what I could. By the time I became a rabbinical student in 1935 my goal was clear, and while later complexities came about that at the time I was too naïve and ignorant to suspect (as well as numerous excursions elsewhere), the goal itself has not really changed.[8]

Thus the challenge of Fackenheim's work, explicit since 1967, was to examine and articulate whether Jewish response to the Holocaust was possible and, if so, what the nature of such a response has been and should be.

Fackenheim's first two books on the Holocaust were *Quest for Past and Future* (1968), a collection of previous essays, and *God's Presence in History* (1970). In these works, Fackenheim examined whether faith in God or humanity is possible or even desirable after the Holocaust. It is in *God's Presence in History* that he asserted the centrality of the Holocaust for any future theology and began to develop his notion of the Commanding Voice of Auschwitz, evident in the 614th commandment, and the theological response to the event. In the 1982 *To Mend the World*, which Fackenheim called his "most important book,"[9] he presented his most complete theological treatment of the Holocaust, incorporating into this work his early philosophical analysis, his more developed theological reflections on the Holocaust, his notion of resistance as a Jewish response to the event, and his conception of the centrality of the state of Israel.

In 1983 Fackenheim immigrated to Israel and began teaching at the Hebrew University of Jerusalem. Particularly after that time, Fackenheim's support of the state of Israel may be understood as a theological response to forces that attempt to dehumanize and destroy Jewish identity and existence. Throughout his work, Fackenheim managed to maintain faith in the Jewish God of history and covenant, while always remaining true to the event of the Holocaust. This philosophically adept dialectic of faith in God and commitment to humanity even after the Holocaust characterize both the content of his theology and the form of his theology, that is, his method; the former of these is examined in the pages to follow.

Theological Method

James Cone's method moves dialectically between the Christian scriptures and tradition on the one hand and black experience, culture, and history on the other. Similar to Cone's, Fackenheim's theological method was developed by using the Torah and Jewish tradition along with Jewish experience, especially the Holocaust.[10] In Fackenheim's method, however, the Holocaust blocks access to the Jewish tradition and challenges all thought. Fackenheim's method involves an honest and intense encounter with the Holocaust, but never attempting to "explain" the event, as well as the effort to access the divine-human relationship of covenant that characterizes Jewish tradition. Thus, whereas for Cone the black experience serves as a theological source alongside the Christian tradition, for Fackenheim, the experience of the Holocaust serves negatively as a historical reality that brings the Jewish tradition into question, and that must be faced while attempting a return to the covenantal and biblical sources. The Holocaust also may be counted as a positive source for Fackenheim in that he claimed both God's presence and human response during and after the event.

After briefly relating Fackenheim's method to Paul Tillich's and showing how Fackenheim's thought developed over time, I show how Fackenheim understood the Jewish tradition, particularly what he termed "root experiences," and then move on to his discussion of the Holocaust, an example of an "epoch making event," and Israel. These two categories are central to Fackenheim's theological methodology. Fackenheim's theology involves the dialectical relationship of commitment to divine incursions into human history of a transcendent God into the particular history of the Jews and commitment to an encounter with contemporary historical events of Jewish history, namely the Holocaust and the emergence of the state of Israel. Fackenheim asked, given these enormous events, is it still possible for the Jew to connect with past incursions of the divine into history? Further, if such an experience is possible after the Holocaust and the reestablishment of the state of Israel, how is one's understanding of God and humanity altered? Finally, what is the character of such Jewish religious experience?

Like many aspects of Fackenheim's theology, his understanding of method developed and changed over time. In his earlier thought, he explained, he had agreed with Tillich's method of correlation, according to which, the role of theology is to mediate between the human, who formulates existential philosophical questions simply by existing, and the divine, which supplies the answers to these questions.[11]

Fackenheim rejected the methodology used by "classical theology,"[12] whereby the reality of revelation was assumed and theology "worked its way down." He explained that modern theology raised the question of the actuality of revelation. Modern theology, he believed, had to "work its way up." Theology now must begin with the human condition and illustrate the existential yearning for the divine to show the possibility of God.[13] In Fackenheim's words, *"the analysis of the human condition constitutes the necessary prolegomenon for all modern Jewish and, indeed all modern theology.* On the adequacy of this prolegomenon depends the foundation of its sequel, theology proper. For theology is the explication of the faith into which the leap has been made, and the analysis of the human condition alone can justify the leap into faith itself."[14] Thus, Fackenheim's early understanding of theological method was influenced by liberal theology's stress on the importance of the human condition, sometimes at the expense of the divine reality.

Later in his life, Fackenheim came to believe that his earlier use of a Tillichian method of correlation failed to affirm the true nature of God's revelation. Influenced by Buber, Rosenzweig, and perhaps Barth,[15] Fackenheim critiqued the method of correlation not only for creating false questions, but also, and more significantly, for not grasping the nature and scope of the divine answer, or "that 'incursion of a divine Other' (Rosenzweig) into the human world that modern criticism had disposed of all too lightly as a relic from the Middle Ages."[16] For that matter, the method falsely claimed that the divine answer responded directly to an already asked question.[17] On the answer side, it fails to take into account the incommensurability of the divine. In other words, the revelation at Sinai far exceeds any existential questioning or yearning for the divine. In the age of Auschwitz and the emergence of the state of Israel, Fackenheim reasoned, divine presence and revelation within human history are certainly not always what we expect.[18]

Fackenheim's new understanding of revelation as radical surprise meant that his definition of faith shifted as had his conception of method. In a 1951 essay, "Can There Be Judaism without Revelation?" Fackenheim stated, *"Faith may be defined as the sole positive answer to questions of ultimate importance, the asking of which is still reason's prerogative but which reason is no longer able to answer."*[19] However, in 1967, in the introductory chapter to the same volume of essays, Fackenheim said that his earlier definition of faith was not acceptable for him any longer.

In this later essay, "These Twenty Years: A Reappraisal," Fackenheim pointed out that an important fault in his earlier definition of faith was the "elimination of radical surprise. The miracle at the Red Sea and the revelation at Sinai were not answers to already known questions."[20] This element of radical surprise in revelation must not be confined to the past for Jewish theology. Fackenheim claimed that the messianic future "must mingle the unexpectable with the expected. Indeed, even from the pre-messianic future radical surprise cannot be eliminated, unless it is prejudged to be a barren sameness of working and waiting. This point may have been academic for most Jewish generations, but not for the generation which has witnessed Auschwitz and the first Jewish state in two thousand years."[21]

The claim that faith must include an experience of radical surprise is due to the fact that, though in relationship with humanity, even in covenant with Jews, God remains a mystery to us. "God's nature is a mystery, and only insofar as He is related to man may faith speak of God; yet even in relation to man God remains a mystery. For God is infinite and man is finite; and a mutual relation between a God who is infinite and men who are finite passes finite understanding. Nevertheless, faith must assert the reality of this relation."[22] In addition to this philosophical notion of the mystery of God, I believe there is another reason why Fackenheim believed that revelation and faith must be a radical surprise to humanity.

According to Fackenheim, after the Holocaust, not only faith in God was questioned, but also faith in humanity was shattered. The already present metaphysical gap between God and humanity had become even wider as a result of the Nazi logic of destruction. If divine revelation responds to the needs of humanity, then God must address the Holocaust. Fackenheim did not wish to limit God to this realm and allow Hitler a victory over the divine by forcing the content of the Jewish faith to be shaped solely by the Holocaust. Though Jewish theology must confront the event of the Holocaust, it must encounter this challenge with the impossible but necessary return to the events of the Exodus and the covenant begun at Sinai.

In his 1970 work, *God's Presence in History*, Fackenheim explored two categories of events of Jewish history—root experiences and epoch-making events. After an examination of two such root experiences, we explore the Holocaust as an epoch-making event that threatens the present accessibility to the root experiences of Judaism.

Fackenheim described the events at both the Red Sea and at Sinai as root experiences. In defining root experience, it seems that he bases his conditions of what makes a root experience on the accounts of these two events. That is, he does not set forth criteria and then measure the Red Sea and Sinai according to them. Instead he uses these two experiences to dictate what the conditions for other potential root experiences would be.

The first condition of a root experience in Judaism is based on a "dialectical relation between present and past." In the instance of the Red Sea, a present-day Jew does not actually witness what the

Israelites saw then, but also *knows* that the Israelites witnessed divine presence and that we do not see the same activity today.[23] In an endnote, Fackenheim asserted that this dialectical relation between present and past is at the core of Jewish faith and is what is so profoundly challenged by the Holocaust. He relates a portion of the Passover Haggadah, "It was not one only who rose against us to annihilate us, but in every generation there are those who rise against us to annihilate us. But the Holy One, blessed be He, saves us from their hand." Fackenheim explained, "Whether, and if so how, the contemporary religious Jew can still include this sentence in the Passover Seder liturgy is the paramount question behind my entire investigation in this book."[24]

By itself, this first condition of a root experience would also necessarily allow personal, individual visions of the divine to be considered root experience. That this is not Fackenheim's intention is made clear by the second condition of root experience. A root experience must be public and historical in character. At the Red Sea, *every* Israelite witnessed God's activity in human history. This activity profoundly impacted those present, and what is more, it radically impacted the course of human history, Jewish history in particular.

Fackenheim concluded his set of conditions with what he deemed to be the most important. The third condition of a root experience, and this is really the follow-up to the first, is that this past experience must be accessible to the present. He explained that the Israelites at the Red Sea witnessed both a historical event *and* the presence of God. Contemporary Jews can recall the event, but they do not actually see what the Israelites saw. At issue in the third condition of a root experience is whether, and if so how, the presence of God then is made accessible to us now. If the divine presence is no longer accessible today, then it cannot be a root experience of Judaism. If the reality of God's presence at the Red Sea is no longer relevant or true for Jews today, then the event loses its truth and, in a sense, God is no longer, and never really was, present. If, on the other hand, God's presence is known and experienced through a connection to the past root experience, then God's presence is a reality for us even today, if only by this sense of accessibility. "Thus the pious Jew remembering the Exodus and the salvation at the Red Sea does not call to mind events now dead and gone. He reenacts these events as a *present reality:* only thus is he assured that the past saving God still saves, and that He will finally bring ultimate salvation." To know that the Israelites witnessed divine activity at the Red Sea or at Sinai we must have access to their vision.[25]

Still, what does it mean to have access to their vision of a natural-historical event of God's presence? "According to the Midrash all generations of Israel were present at Sinai, and the Torah is given whenever a man receives it."[26] The gift of revelation is given anew each time it is received. As claimed above, revelation is complete only when received. Therefore God's revelation to us is completed *each* time it is received.

Fackenheim explained that the reenactment of root experiences is threatened by historical crises, or epoch-making events. Epoch-making events, such as the Maccabean Revolt, the destruction of the Temple, and the Spanish Exile, are historical events that produce despair and doubt about the actuality or even the possibility of the divine-human encounter of the root experiences. These events must not be ignored, nor should they conquer Jewish faith. Fackenheim placed the Holocaust in this category.[27]

Though the Holocaust is categorized as an epoch-making event, Fackenheim asserted that it was a unique and unprecedented evil in Jewish history, and indeed in all history.[28] He cited five facts to support this claim:

1. Fully one-third of the whole Jewish people were murdered; and since this included the most Jewish of Jews—East European Jewry—Jewish survival as a whole is gravely in doubt.
2. This murder was quite literally "extermination"; not a single Jewish man, woman, or child was to survive, or—except for a few that were well-hidden or overlooked—would have survived, had Hitler won the war.
3. This was because Jewish birth was sufficient cause to merit torture and death; whereas the "crime" of Poles and Russians was that there were too many of them, with the possible exception of Gypsies, only Jews had committed the "crime" of existing at all.
4. The "Final Solution" was not a pragmatic project serving such ends as political power or economic greed. Nor was it the negative side of a positive religious or political fanaticism. It was an end in itself. And, at least in the final stage of the dominion of the Third Reich (when Eichmann diverted trains to Auschwitz from the Russian front), it was the only such end that remained.
5. Only a minority of the perpetrators were sadists or perverts. For the most part, they were ordinary jobholders with an extraordinary job. And the tone-setters were ordinary idealists, except that the ideals were torture and murder.[29]

In his claim of the uniqueness of the Holocaust, Fackenheim did not claim that the sufferings of the Holocaust were greater than those of African slavery, Hiroshima, or any other tragedy in history. "All this is by no means to deny the existence of other catastrophes equally unprecedented, and endowed with unique characteristics of their own. But to make this admission is only to say that these other catastrophes, too, must be confronted in their own right. To link Auschwitz with Hiroshima is not to deepen or widen one's concern with humanity and its future. It is to evade the import of Auschwitz and Hiroshima alike."[30] Fackenheim argued that to attempt to generalize and universalize unique events and unique historical communities is to attempt to destroy the particularity that was a primary aspect of the event in the first place. It was not as people in general that Jews were killed; rather it was as Jews that they were killed. To extend the claim, it was not simply *any* city that was bombed, it was Hiroshima.

A second possible aspect to the claim of the uniqueness of the Holocaust is that the event thus necessitates a unique response. Fackenheim claimed that Jewish resistance to the Holocaust world was a unique response in human history. This idea of resistance is be further explored later in the chapter.

Given the unique nature of the Holocaust, Fackenheim asserted that the actions and policies of the Nazis were unique. Fackenheim denied a rational explanation of Nazism. *No* theory can adequately explain the Holocaust. And yet, according to Fackenheim, despite the lack of an adequate explanation, we must continue to explore and express what happened. In this pursuit, Fackenheim denied three views of Nazism. First, we must not view the Nazis as inherently evil people. Second, we must not explain the evil away by taking the opposite view, that all people are sinners, some worse than others. Finally, he denied the banality of evil theory. Fackenheim took up for consideration each of these theories in turn and dismissed them all.

First, in regard to the belief that the Nazis were inherently and uniquely evil, Fackenheim pointed out that they were not simply insane or immoral exceptions to human nature.

> Lest unauthentic refuge be sought in the most obvious place, it must be stressed from the start that the sadists, perverts, madmen—the kind that may be found anywhere and at any time—were least in significance.
>
> More significant were the ordinary men and women who performed their new, extraordinary jobs in much the same manner in which they had once performed—and would soon again perform—their ordinary jobs. However, most significant of all—indeed, setting the tone—were the idealists: these were much like other idealists, except that their ideals were torture and murder. (They did not just "use" torture, but "worshipped" it.)[31]

The point that Fackenheim makes has theological, or more precisely anthropological, ramifications.

Human freedom is ambiguous in that it can be put toward good ends or evil ends. In other words, the worst consequence of our freedom is its potential for evil. Fackenheim's point is that we cannot dismiss the Nazis simply as an exception to the rule of human nature. They were ordinary people who did evil. The severity of their thoughts and actions must not allow us to now think that such an event is impossible today. Human good and human evil are always possible and are often manifest simultaneously within the same community and within the same individual. The perpetrators of the Holocaust were not pure evil; rather, they were people who had choices to make and they put their free will to evil ends. This fact makes the possibility of similar evils that much more horrifying.

Next, Fackenheim explained that just as we should not imagine the Nazis as pure evil in their nature, "we cannot, on the grounds that all men are sinners, dissolve or weaken the distinction between those who *might* have done it and those who *did* it."[32] Fackenheim asserted that this second mistake, often made by Christians, too readily groups these intentions and actions with all other instances and manifestations of sin. Such a move destroys the particularity of the evil.

Finally, Fackenheim referred to the doctrine of the banality of evil as "quite untenable."[33] According to this theory, individual Nazis were not evil, but the deeds they performed were. The Nazis simply performed these deeds because of the momentum of the system in which they found themselves at that particular time. Consequently, responsibility is not to be placed on any person, but on the theory of mass destruction. In response, Fackenheim asserts, "Not only Eichmann but *everyone* was more than a cog in the wheel. The Nazis viewed their 'non-Aryan' victims as less than human. *We* cannot view *them* as less than human—will-less automata: we must view them as human beings like ourselves."[34] The deed cannot be separated from the doer as easily as the doctrine of the banality of evil would have us think. However evil their actions were, these were freely willed actions of humans who could have, but did not, live and act differently.

Shifting the focus away from the perpetrators of the evils in his attempt to find explanations, Fackenheim turned next to those who suffered the horrors. Fackenheim most poignantly described the tragic and unique events of the Holocaust as actually destroying the image of God in many individuals. He explained, "The divine image in man *can* be destroyed." Fackenheim cited Primo Levi's testimony of the *Muselmann*, found in *Survival in Auschwitz*, in support of this claim:

On their entry into the camp, through basic incapacity, or by misfortune, or through some banal incident, they are overcome before they can adapt themselves; they are beaten by time, they do not begin to learn German, to disentangle the infernal knot of laws and prohibitions until their body is already in decay, and nothing can save them from selections or death by exhaustion. Their life is short, but their number is endless; they, the *Muselmaenner*, the drowned, form the backbone of the camp, an anonymous mass, continuously renewed and always identical, of non-men who march and labor in silence, the divine spark dead within them, already too empty to really suffer. One hesitates to call them living; one hesitates to call their death death.[35]

As we see in a later section of this chapter devoted to Jewish resistance, however, "the murder camp did not succeed in destroying the divine image in all its victims."[36] In this response Fackenheim began to take up the religious implications of the Holocaust.

Fackenheim next examined the Jewish understanding of suffering during the Holocaust with traditional Jewish responses of the past and concluded that they were all inadequate to address this new event. Jewish theology had to be reinterpreted if its encounter with the Holocaust were to be genuine. Three traditional interpretations of suffering, for example, include the idea that suffering was the deserved result of wicked behavior, that it was a result of a hiding of the divine Face, or that God suffers with Israel.

First, before the Temple's destruction, the rabbis often understood suffering as deserved punishment, as in the Book of Judges. Job questions this interpretation, but largely on an individual level. Even Jeremiah interprets the destruction of the first Temple as divinely willed punishment. This interpretation is rejected by rabbinical thought in response to the destruction of Temple by Titus in 70 CE and Jerusalem becoming a pagan city under Hadrian in 135 CE. Fackenheim explained, "No rabbi described Titus as God's instrument. No rabbi understood the paganization of Jerusalem as an event which was divinely willed."[37] Likewise, Fackenheim believed that the reality of the Holocaust denies a traditional Jewish response to suffering, that this suffering is a punishment for sin. He explained that the rabbis suspended such a line of thought when Jerusalem was paganized. "For however we twist and turn this doctrine in response to Auschwitz, it becomes a religious absurdity and even a sacrilege."[38] Fackenheim went on to challenge that sin cannot explain this suffering when one considers that at least one million Jewish children died under Nazism. "We too may at most only suspend Biblical doctrine, if only because we, no more than the rabbis, dare either to deny our own sinfulness or to disconnect it from history. Yet, suspend it we must."[39] Fackenheim's appeal to suspend and not to forever deny the doctrine of suffering as punishment for sin exhibits his twin commitments to both the Jewish faith and to the reality and nature of the suffering. The core of this suspension is the absurdity of applying the doctrine to the Holocaust. "All history is full of unjust suffering; this term, when applied to Auschwitz, is hopelessly inadequate."[40] Suffering as punishment for sin generally involves a breaking or at least damaging of Israel's covenant with God. Fackenheim explained:

> As in our torment we turn, as an ultimate resort, to the traditional doctrine that all Israelites of all generations are responsible for each other, we are still totally aghast, for not a single one of the six million died because they had failed to keep the divine-Jewish covenant: they all died because their great-grandparents *had* kept it, if only to the minimum extent of raising Jewish children. Here is the point where we reach radical religious absurdity.[41]

Based on this absurdity, Fackenheim rejected putting the blame for the Holocaust on Jewish sin.

The concept of the hiding of the divine Face, as in the Psalms, was a second alternative used to explain Jewish suffering. Fackenheim explained that this hiding, or any notion of divine self-concealment, "if taken by itself and made absolute, was bound to lead to despair."[42] The understanding of divine self-concealment had implied a temporary concealment in the past. How could one understand the paganization of Jerusalem sixty-five years after the destruction of the Temple? Is God still concealed, or is God simply absent? Where is hope to be found under such circumstances? Why continue to perform the commandments out of obedience to an absent God? Fackenheim wrote that "[n]either the past saving Presence nor the past commanding Presence could have continued to be reenacted. The past saving presence would have been overwhelmed by the present catastrophe. Even the past commanding Presence would have vanished; there would have remained only obedience to commandments performed in God's absence."[43]

From Fackenheim's perspective, the third traditional response to suffering, the notion that God suffers with Israel, is also inadequate. After the destruction of the Second Temple and the paganization of Jerusalem, the rabbis responded by saying that God lamented God's decision to destroy God's Temple and exile God's people. The Presence of God is exiled with the Jews. Likewise when they return, the Presence of God will return with them. God never leaves the Israelites. God suffers and laments with them. "The Jew would be in exile, but not cut off from the divine Presence. He could still hold fast to history, for the God who had been present in history once was present in it still and would in the end bring total redemption."[44]

Fackenheim objected to such a God who still commands and comforts but is not really the "sole Power." Rabbi Joshua ben Levi, in the *Babylonian Talmud*, Tractate Yoma 69b, explained that God's power should be understood to mean that God "controls His anger and is long-suffering to evil-doers."[45] In response to Rabbi Joshua ben Levi's explanation, Fackenheim wrote, "We conclude, then, that the rabbis remained true to the catastrophic historical present, even as they remained faithful to the saving and commanding past. They remained stubborn witnesses to the nations that all history both stands in need of redemption and is destined to receive it."[46]

In addition to finding these three options unsatisfactory, Fackenheim also denied explanations of suffering that appeal to suffering as redemptive and to the concept of martyrdom. Fackenheim also refused to accept a Christian view of suffering as redemptive. Many Christian theologians have chosen to interpret the suffering of Jews during the Holocaust as redemptive. For if suffering, Jewish suffering, is not redemptive, what is the purpose? If suffering serves no greater good, then it is entirely evil. One asks oneself how God could permit suffering that serves no greater good. Can the suffering of Jews during the Holocaust be thought of as redemptive, as serving some greater purpose? Fackenheim answered by contrasting Christian suffering as redemptive with the deaths of the Holocaust:

> First, theirs was not a chosen but a choiceless suffering. Secondly, the sufferers were nonbelievers as well as believers. Thirdly and climatically, being a people, the "people of Christ" included the children. In Auschwitz Jewish babies were thrown into the flames without being killed first. Their screams could be heard in the camp. To find redemption in the suffering of these babies, or of those cursed to hear their screams, is a human impossibility and—so one hopes—a divine one as well.[47]

Thus, suffering as redemptive is denied.

Fackenheim also denied that Jews who died during the Holocaust can be thought of as martyrs. Martyrs choose, perhaps not to die, but what they die for. In the story of Abraham and Isaac, Isaac has been presented by Jewish theology as a potential martyr, not a sacrifice. "Isaac was not a child but rather a grown-up man of thirty-seven years, and he was no unwilling sacrifice but rather a willing martyr." Fackenheim distinguished Isaac from those who died during the Holocaust. He wrote: "Auschwitz was the supreme, most diabolical attempt ever made to murder martyrdom itself and, failing that, to deprive all death, martyrdom included, of its dignity." He went on to ask, "At Auschwitz, however, there was no choice; the young and the old, the faithful and the faithless were slaughtered without discrimination. Can there be martyrdom where there is no choice?"[48] It is not a simple matter to respond to this objection. Fackenheim claimed that if there can be no form of martyrdom when there is no choice, Hitler wins a battle. "Yet we protest against a negative answer, for we protest against allowing Hitler to dictate the terms of our religious life. If not martyrdom, there can be a faithfulness resembling it, when a man has no choice between life and death but only between faith and despair."[49]

According to Fackenheim, the Holocaust shattered all earlier thought and demanded a new creative response that is both revolutionary and loyal to earlier thought. For, in the final analysis, Fackenheim asserted: "Resisting rational explanation, Auschwitz will forever after resist religious explanations as well. No religious meaning will ever be found in Auschwitz, for the very attempt to find it is blasphemy. There remains only the possibility of a religious response; this, however, is inescapable. To find such a response may as yet wholly transcend any Jew's power. Yet his faith, his destiny, his very survival will depend on whether, in the end, he finds it."[50] For Fackenheim, authentic response to the Holocaust is for the Jew to resist despairing of faith in God and humanity and to resist acts of dehumanization and oppression in the name of survival as Jews.[51] Those who chose faith, not despair, during the Holocaust then provide the basis of hope that Jews of today will choose to resist despair through faith now. Again, such resistance is possible today only because it was actual during the Holocaust.

We have seen that, according to Fackenheim's theological method then, Jewish theology and existence after the Holocaust must confront the epoch-making event of the Holocaust, if it is to have access to the root experiences of Judaism, characterized by the divine incursion into human history. Jewish existence confronts the Holocaust through resistance. Fackenheim's theological method is dialectical not so much because he seeks to correlate supernatural revelation events, the root experiences, with natural events of history, including its events of crisis; rather, his method dialectically moves backward from post-Holocaust existence, which significantly includes the emergence of the state of Israel, to the root experiences, confronting the Holocaust, which impedes the journey, but never fully subsumes it. Consequently, the Holocaust is not really a positive theological source, as the black experience is a source for Cone, but rather a shaping event for Jewish experience that cannot be ignored and that has an important theological impact on one's conception of both God and humanity, to say the least. After gaining a fuller understanding of Fackenheim's views of revelation, covenant, faith, and history through an examination of his conceptions of God and humanity, his category of resistance is explored.

Emil Fackenheim on God

Fackenheim asserted that God, though transcendent, is immanent in human history. Paradoxically, the infinite interacts with the finite. Further, divine interaction with the finite is not a relation to humanity in general, but rather to a particular people. The foundation of the Jewish tradition is the claim that God lives in a covenantal relationship with Israel. Fackenheim explained that God is present to Jews in history in both saving and commanding manifestations, with the events of the Exodus and Mount Sinai serving as quintessential examples. Though present in a Commanding Voice, there was no saving divine presence during the Holocaust, Fackenheim claimed. The absence of a saving divine presence at Auschwitz raises the issue of theodicy and the related dynamic of divine power and human freedom. Fackenheim's understandings of divine activity in history, including the covenant, the Holocaust, and the nation of Israel, are presented in this section. Fackenheim's provocative notion of the Commanding Voice of Auschwitz, which articulates the 614th commandment, demands a human response. I believe the concept of this human response could be strengthened even further by a reconceptualization of Fackenheim's account of divine activity and human freedom. Building on the analysis of Fackenheim's concept of God, the subsequent section explores his theological anthropology, especially as related to the Commanding Voice of Auschwitz.

Fackenheim criticized what he termed the modern view of religion in which God is no longer a reality but simply an idea. The social scientific account of religion ignores the claims of the religious adherent that God is real and that one lives in a relationship with God. At least since the Enlightenment,[52] this notion of the reality of God has been challenged as naïve supernaturalism or superstition. The religious claim that God exists cannot be proven and is therefore false, according to this worldview. Fackenheim contrasted this viewpoint with the "biblical and rabbinic tradition." This tradition argues that God not only exists, but also that God exists in relation to humanity and is present and active in human history.[53]

The simultaneous claim of divine transcendence and divine involvement in human history appears to be an irrational paradox.[54] For Fackenheim, however, such a claim is not to be rationalized, but rather lived.[55] It may be said that for Fackenheim, the relationship of God with the world is more important theologically than the character or nature of God within God's self.[56] He asserted that God is intimately related to the world, yet remains infinite, writing "the ultimate principle of Judaism [is]: *the intimacy of the divine infinity.*"[57]

During biblical times, and for a time after, God's present and active force in the world was rarely questioned by the faithful, Fackenheim explained. However, during the Enlightenment, stories of the Bible were rejected as mere myth and human creation. Of course God does not play an active role in the world, these philosophers claimed. The Creation, Flood, and Exodus were simply stories created by people, perhaps inspired, but certainly the product of human imagination.[58] In the wake of the Holocaust, the search for God surely should not look to history for answers. For, according to such a line of thought, God is no longer to be found there.[59] The Holocaust shatters any faith that we may still have had in a God who acts in human history and yet, paradoxically, the same reality grabs us and forces us to return to the faith of those who came before us, according to Fackenheim. If there is to be faith in God after the Holocaust, it must be rooted in the accounts of God's activity in the past, at the Red Sea and at Sinai.

Fackenheim explained that our openness to divine presence now is possible through our connection to the divine presence of the past. He wrote, "The Jewish faith, originating in root experiences of a saving and commanding divine Presence, remains in a state of *immediate openness* to such a Presence as throughout history it reenacts the ancient root experiences—open to the possibility of a divine Presence even in times when the actuality is only a memory and a hope."[60] Despite his openness to the incursion of the divine into history even after the Holocaust, Fackenheim still felt the need to address the philosophical denial of the simultaneity of divine transcendence and divine immanence.

Fackenheim discussed the tension between God's transcendence and God's immanence using Hegelian terms. God transcends the world and humanity. In no way could God be conceived of as becoming incarnate. "*The Jewish religion, unlike the Christian, cannot accept the identity of the human nature and the Divine. When encountering any such teaching, whether in Christianity or elsewhere, it rejects it passionately and emphatically.*"[61] Despite the denial of incarnation and the assertion of transcendence, Fackenheim maintained God is immanent in the world and makes contact with humanity. "Yet a divine-human moving-toward-each-other in Judaism is not merely asserted by us, on the basis of texts culled, possibly arbitrarily, from the sources. It is also the persistent, authoritative, Jewish self-understanding." He cited a *midrash* to express this:

> When God created the world, he decreed that "the heavens are the heavens of the Lord and the earth is for men" (Ps. 115:16). But when He intended to give the Torah He repealed the former decree and said, "The Lower shall ascend to the Upper, and the Upper shall descend to the Lower, and I will make a new beginning," as it is said, "And the Lord came down upon Mt. Sinai, and He said unto Moses, 'Come up unto the Lord.' " (Exod. 19:20)[62]

Fackenheim interpreted the story as articulating "a primordial infinite distance between the divine Creator and the human creature; a 'new beginning' manifest in the meeting of the two; and a 'descent' of the one and 'ascent' of the other, even as both remain other to the other."[63] The fact that each party remains other to the other points to the fragmentary nature of divine presence. Additionally, divine presence is fragmentary because it must be particularized. "Jewish Messianism always requires the particularity of Jewish existence. Its God is universal; but, because His presence is *in* history and does not (or not yet) transfigure history, it can only be a *particularized* presence, and for this if for no other reason, it is a *fragmentary* presence."[64] In other words, God does not relate to humanity as a whole, but to smaller communities of people at a time.

The Jewish covenant is the central manifestation of this intimacy of the infinite.[65] In the covenant God strikes a perfect balance between proximity to the world and a relationship with Israel and this balance transcends any philosophical problem of universalism and particularism according to Fackenheim.[66] Furthermore, this concept of the covenant is based neither on arrogance nor elitism, but rather on responsibility, love, and hope.

Fackenheim stated, "A God that is 'far' and far only, then, is not the God of Judaism. Neither is a God that is 'near' and near alone." While the former danger was the problem with Deism, Fackenheim cautioned modern religious people of the latter danger in particular. The modern religious believer has a tendency, he claimed, to see God's presence in human history and progress. The liberal or utopian view of history naively asserts that human development and progress are inevitable. After the events of the twentieth century, humanity's progress is anything but inevitable. This view is also theologically faulty. Fackenheim explained that when God is too closely identified with human history, "the intimacy *exhausts* the infinity, resulting in the loss of the eternity of the God of Israel . . . since He too is 'near' and near *alone*, He is not the God of Israel."[67] Thus Fackenheim asserted that God must remain the other and transcendent if God is to remain God.

In distinction from a God who is either too far or too near, Fackenheim presents the God of Judaism as a transcendent God of history who enters into covenant with Israel. Even after addressing the issue of transcendence in history, the problem of universalism and particularism remains. How can the one eternal, undivided God of all humanity enter into a particular relation with one community?

Like Christianity and Islam, Judaism lays claim to universal truth. Unlike these other traditions, however, it does not actively proselytize. Fackenheim refuted the theory, popular in the nineteenth century, that forms of religion evolved in history, moving from a particularist tribalism to universalism. Citing God's covenant with Noah, the belief that the righteous of all nations will have a share in the world to come, Fackenheim asserted that if Judaism is particularistic, no arrogant supersessionist theory of religious evolution explains it. Besides, he said, Christianity claims a false universalism in the light of its claim that salvation is possible only through faith in Jesus as the Christ and through the Christian Church.[68] That is, though Christianity claims universal access to salvation, in fact, it allows this access for only a particular group.

Fackenheim explained that the covenant and the concept of the chosen people exhibit particularistic as well as universalistic elements. He wrote, "A purely universal God would not choose this or that people, for He would not choose at all: His concern with mankind, if such there be, would be with humanity in general. Neither would a purely tribal or particular god choose: Such a god would be bound up with his tribe or people, as if saying 'right or wrong, my people.' "[69] For God to relate to humanity, it must be in the form of a particular relationship with a particular people.

The claim that God acts in history begs the question of how God does so. Fackenheim cited a fascinating *midrash* that explores the tensions of divine involvement in human history. In the story of the exodus of the Israelites out of Egypt, through the Red Sea, even if one believes that God's hand was evident in Israel's salvation, one still wonders what the deaths of the pursuing Egyptians says about God's benevolence and power. Fackenheim wrote, "A much-quoted Midrash relates that when the ministering angels beheld the destruction of the Egyptians at the Red Sea they wanted to break out into song. God, however, reproved them, saying, 'My children lie drowned in the Red Sea, and you would sing' (*Bab. Talmud*, Tractate Megillah 10b)." Fackenheim interpreted the *midrash* to mean *"Even in the supreme but pre-Messianic moment of His saving presence God cannot save Israelites without killing Egyptians."*[70]

I believe this *midrash* indicates at least three points. First, God does act in history, or at least did so at one time. Second, when God enters into human history, God's actions bear the same ambiguity that human actions do. Any act in history sets into motion a chain, or more precisely, a nexus of events, that were not foreseen in the intention of the original act. Even if the effects of a certain action could be foreseen, we often still do not act with the best interests of all people, or even ourselves, in mind. Similarly, when God acts in history, that action has repercussions, whether intended or not, good or bad. When God parts the Red Sea to save the Israelites, the Egyptians are destroyed. In other words, following political realism, even God acts with "dirty hands."

Fackenheim dismissed using this *midrash* in support of any notion of universal benevolence; however, the *midrash* does in fact point to God's love as well as God's power. God cares about the Egyptians who die as a result of God's own activity. God calls them, "My children." The chosen nature of the Israelites, in distinction from the created nature of all other peoples is discussed in the pages that follow. For now, and this is the third point I take from the story, it must be stated that this particular *midrash*, at the very least, hints at some concept of universal divine love.

Fackenheim returned to the philosophical question that a covenant between the infinite and the finite poses. How can this relation exist?

As we see in his treatment of resistance during the Holocaust, Fackenheim responded to the philosophical paradox with an existential and historical statement of fact. "Yet the question, though seemingly unanswerable, again and again finds a positive answer as the Divine-human covenant is reconfirmed, renewed, extended."[71] In other words, the impossible is possible because it is actual.[72]

The claim to a special covenantal status for Israel is one of the most commonly challenged ideas of the Jewish tradition.[73] Fackenheim himself referred to the biblical concept of the Jews as the chosen people of God as "that most uncomfortable of all Jewish teachings."[74] Fackenheim explained that it is uncomfortable because it seems elitist. However, he understood that Israel is not chosen to enter into covenant with God because of some special merit on its part. Instead Israel is chosen to bear a yoke of responsibility. Before the revelation at Sinai, God tells the Israelites, "You have seen what I did to the Egyptians, and how I bore you on eagle's wings and brought you unto Myself. Now therefore, if ye will hearken to My voice indeed, and keep My covenant, then ye shall be Mine own treasure from among all peoples, for all the earth is mine; and ye shall be unto Me a kingdom of priests and a holy nation."[75] Election is thus a responsibility and a privilege.

Israel bears the burden and the joy of performing the 613 commandments and acting as "a kingdom of priests and a holy nation." Fackenheim explained that rabbinic commentary understands the term priest as both prince and servant.[76] The covenant requires no superhuman task, but exemplary conduct and faithful loyalty.[77]

Fackenheim cited Martin Buber's commentary on the above passage from Exodus to further elucidate its meaning. Fackenheim related Buber's suggestion that "the image is of an eagle carrying its young until they can 'dare the flight' themselves and 'follow the father.' It contains 'all in one' three activities, 'election, deliverance and education.' "[78] I believe Buber's comment is insightful and intriguing.

Fackenheim expanded on his claim that God is present to Israel in a covenantal relationship by explaining that God is present in different ways at different times. Fackenheim distinguished between the saving presence of God and the commanding presence of God. In the Exodus story, God saves the Israelites from the pursuing Egyptians by parting the Red Sea. God's saving presence is encountered by the miraculous parting of the Sea; God is the primary actor when relating to the Israelites as saving presence. However, the Israelites are saved not simply by the parting of the Sea, but also by proceeding through the opening made for them by God. They complete God's saving act. Fackenheim clarified, "*Salvation itself is not complete until the Voice is heeded.*"[79] God tells the Israelites to go through the opening God has created for them and they follow the order. Here we begin to see God as commanding presence.

Fackenheim wrote, "A saving divine Presence may require only human recognition; a commanding divine Presence requires human action. The saving Presence may conceivably (if only momentarily) overwhelm human freedom. The commanding Presence cannot do likewise without becoming an intrinsic impossibility."[80] Fackenheim referred to commanding presence as paradoxical. He explained, "For, being *commanding*, it *addresses human freedom*. And being *sole Power*, it *destroys* that freedom because it is only human. Yet the freedom destroyed is also required."[81] Fackenheim explained that divine power simultaneously destroys and requires human freedom because, in that it is sole power, divine presence negates human selfhood. However, in that human response to divine Power is needed for it to be true power, human freedom is necessary. At Sinai, God's commanding Presence is fulfilled only in human action according to the commandments given.[82]

These concepts of God's activity and presence in human history raise the question of the dynamic of God's power and human freedom.[83] For, if divine power is truly omnipotent, it cannot but overwhelm human freedom; if humans are truly free, then certain events remain beyond the reach of God's intervention. The tension between divine power and human freedom remains a paradox. In the Jewish tradition, this paradox is lived rather than rationalized. Time and again Fackenheim attempted to "solve" a philosophical problem through thought and showed how religious faith resists rationalization. In this way, "religion" and "life" sit beyond the limits of philosophy and thought.[84] Paradox of this sort, however, is not avoided in the Jewish tradition, but rather it is viewed as an opportunity for insight.

Fackenheim explained that the rabbinical tradition of *midrash* expresses the tension between divine power and human freedom through the use of symbol, metaphor, story, and parable.[85] For example, one symbolic treatment of how God's power is both dependent and independent of humanity is found in *midrash*. Fackenheim cited the *midrash*: "*Ye are My witnesses, saith the Lord, and I am God* (Isa. 43:12). That is, when ye are My witnesses, I am God, and when ye are not My witnesses, I am, as it were, not God (Midr. Ps. on Ps. 123:1).

When the Israelites do God's will, they add to the power of God on high. When the Israelites do not do God's will, they, as it were, weaken the great power of God (Lam. R. I, 33, on Lam. 1:6)."[86] Fackenheim elucidated that these are symbolic metaphors. Furthermore, he asserted, "The paradox in these statements is fully intended, and the term '*as it were*' has the full rank of a technical term in rabbinic theology, indicating the symbolic character of the statement it qualifies."[87] Thus the paradoxical relation between divine power and human freedom remains.

One modern attempt to resolve the tension between divine power and human freedom is developed by process theology.[88] According to process theology, God essentially and necessarily shares power with creation and develops in relation to it. However, Fackenheim rejected the God of process theology. Concerning the process God Fackenheim wrote:

> The God of Jewish tradition could be present, in the here and now. He could single out persons and peoples, and be sought out by them according to the need of time and place. A transcendent First Cause or immanent Cosmic Process, in contrast, is a timeless principle; and it can inspire to action, not by acts of singling out, but only as an eternal ideal. For a First Cause is indifferent to the particular; and while a Process contains all particulars, it embraces them as a homogenizing Whole. Moreover, neither God can be sought out by men in the here and now. He is accessible, if at all, only by thought rising to timelessness. In short, if the radical rationalist reformers are right, then the here and now, once of the essence of Jewish religious belief and life, reduces itself to a mere unessential accident.[89]

Fackenheim believed that the God of process theology negates the essential particularity of the divine-human relationship of covenant.[90]

Fackenheim believed any attempt to limit divine power in the name of human freedom would eventually deteriorate into humanism.[91] That is, in a zero-sum understanding of power, if humans have more power, God necessarily has less. He also rejected this God on practical terms, in as much as saying that one could not really pray to the God of process theology. Here Fackenheim insisted on a more personal notion of God and a personal relationship between God and Israel.

In my opinion, Fackenheim rejected the process God without fully considering the possibility that, just as with the biblical God, universal qualities may be held in dialectical tension with particular qualities in the process conception of God. God, as process, is a universal force but encounters and is experienced by humans in particular times and places. In addition to this balance of universal and particular, the God of process theology is also simultaneously transcendent and immanent, and changeless in the fact that this force is ever changing.

Perhaps the barrier between Jewish theology and process theology is due to differing understandings of power.[92] I believe that one may respond to Fackenheim's robust notion of divine power with the claim that the term "power" must be reinterpreted. Omnipotence need not be discarded as a divine characteristic, if power is understood as persuasive power rather than as dominating power, as Melissa Raphael asserts.

Nevertheless, the horrific reality of the Holocaust challenges *any* attempt to explain divine presence or power. It is one thing to claim that God was present in the past, in biblical events; it is another to argue that God is still present to us. More importantly, was God present during the Holocaust? In his *God's Presence in History*, Fackenheim argued that God was certainly not a saving presence at Auschwitz. Though not a saving presence, God may be described as a commanding presence, even at Auschwitz.[93] Fackenheim asserted that the Commanding Voice of Auschwitz proclaimed that "the authentic Jew of today is forbidden to hand Hitler yet another posthumous victory."[94] The authentic Jew of today[95] does this by continuing to exist as a Jew and by despairing of neither God nor humanity.[96] It is to his theory of humanity that I turn now, with more detailed examination of his category of resistance to follow.

Emil Fackenheim on Humanity

As with the above examination of James Cone's theological anthropology, this analysis of Fackenheim's concept of humanity explores his ideas of human nature, creation, sin, and freedom. Fackenheim's theological anthropology differs from Cone's in that Fackenheim seldom dealt with "man"[97] in general, particularly after 1967 when the Holocaust and the state of Israel became his focus, preferring instead to deal with Jews in particular. That is, in his work of the last thirty-odd years of his life, it is difficult to find a statement that addresses the human condition in general, in terms of sin, freedom, or other traditional categories of theological anthropology. Instead, one encounters assertions on the Jewish human condition in the wake of these two realities. Consequently, the major part of this section presents Fackenheim's understanding of the Jewish human condition in the light of the Holocaust, looking particularly at Jewish resistance *during* the Holocaust. It is only with these acts of resistance in mind that one may speak authentically about human nature. For, according to Fackenheim, it is this resistance during the event that makes resistance today possible.

According to Judaism, humans are created as free beings. There is no doctrine of original sin, as it is found in Christian doctrine. Instead, humans have both an inclination for good (*yetzer ha-tov*) and an inclination for evil (*yetzer ha-ra*). Thus we maintain free will despite the Fall. Though there is no original sin in Judaism, there is recognition of the human propensity for sin. Fackenheim approvingly cited Abraham Heschel's claim that "sin, for Judaism, may not be original; but it is, nevertheless, universal."[98] Sharing similarities with Reinhold Niebuhr,[99] Fackenheim's theological anthropology views humans as capable of both greatness and depravity, as both spiritual beings and animals. These are the very tensions that define us as humans. Despite a general balance of good and evil within human nature, we do, for whatever reason, tend toward sin. However, redemption is available through divine grace and human efforts.

As was evident in the above section on Fackenheim's view of God, his understanding of humanity was developed in opposition to the prevailing modern view that humanity can perfect itself without God's help. Again, this is due to the human inclination toward sin and the simple facts that we are finite and imperfect creatures. Fackenheim steadfastly maintained human redemption and the messianic age are possible only with divine aid. The Christian historical focus on determining the balance of human power and divine grace necessary for redemption is not present in Fackenheim's deceptively simple claim that God and humanity together bring it about.[100]

Fackenheim explained that the coming of the messianic redemption is an event for which we must both wait and work toward. Only God knows when it will occur and, in a sense, only God can bring it to fruition. Nevertheless, while we wait for God, we wholeheartedly must pursue this goal. He wrote, "A Messianic future simply incommensurate with all historical human action would retroactively destroy the historical meaning which it was intended to consummate; yet if Jewish faith has come to expect this future at all, it is precisely because meaning, however fragmentary, is nevertheless actual in pre-Messianic history."[101]

Redemption is ultimately in God's hands, but this does not turn humanity into puppets. Fackenheim explained, "God will redeem man, but not by making him either less or more human; either assertion would make human existence meaningless—a tragic contradiction to no purpose. God redeems man by preserving the contradictory elements that constitute his humanity, yet by transforming them in such a way as to take the sting out of the contradiction."[102] In other words, in one of Fackenheim's most densely meaningful statements, he says, "Men must act as though all depended on them; and wait and pray as though all depended on God."[103]

Biblically, the emphasis on a divine-human partnership is most profoundly expressed in the idea of the covenant. After destroying almost all of creation in the Flood, God promises Noah that such a divine act will never again occur. According to Judaism, God makes a covenant with Noah,[104] and thus all humanity (since Noah and his family are the entire world's population at this point), whereby Noah and his descendants are given seven commandments to follow. This may be seen as a general covenant. Despite this covenant with God, humanity continues to sin. In response, God elects one man, Abraham, and his descendants with whom to enter into covenant.

At Sinai God and Israel enter into a special covenant, an agreement of loyalty and obligation. The nature of this covenant as philosophically paradoxical and yet actual in the lives of Jews has been discussed already. The relevant aspect of the covenant in this discussion is that it demands Jewish obedience to the 613 commandments. Within these commandments is the divine grace necessary to fulfill them—for God would not make these impossible demands on Israel. In performing these commandments, Israel acts to redeem all humanity.

We have seen how the Holocaust challenges faith in God, but it also tests faith in humanity. Surely the Holocaust destroys any simple, unequivocal claims to human goodness or human ideals. Fackenheim believed that the modern assertion about the goodness of humanity and about its utopian potential was naïve and misguided before the Holocaust, but nothing if not obscene after Auschwitz. To illustrate and support this claim, Fackenheim looked to horrific examples from the events of the Holocaust.

The Nazi "logic" of destruction attempted to make the Jew destroy his own dignity, humanity, and self-worth through several techniques. Quoting a survivor's experience, Fackenheim stated, "This found no clearer or more systematic expression than what is called—this too rightly—'excremental assault.' "[105]

A survivor writes:

> Imagine what it would be like to be forbidden to go to the toilet; imagine also that you were suffering from an increasingly severe dysentery, caused and aggravated by a diet of cabbage soup as well as by the constant cold. Naturally, you would try to go anyway. Sometimes you might succeed. But your absences would be noticed and you would be beaten, knocked down, and trampled on. By now, you would know what the risks were, but urgency would oblige you to repeat the attempt, cost what it may . . . . I soon learned to deal with the dysentery by tying strings around the lower end of my drawers.[106]

Fackenheim continued, "Clearly, excremental assault was designed to produce in the victim a 'self-disgust' to the point of wanting death or even committing suicide. And this—nothing less—was the essential goal. The Nazi logic of destruction was aimed, ultimately, at the victim's self-destruction."[107] The "ideal" for the Nazis would be Jewish suicide preceded by Jewish self-hatred and dehumanization. However, Fackenheim claimed, when suicide did occur, it was out of self-respect rather than self-hatred.[108]

Another example of human evil is drawn from Fackenheim's own experiences at Sachsenhausen. Along with others, he was forced to march to and from the factory in which he worked. Fackenheim employed the testimony of Dr. K. J. Ball Kaduri, fellow camp prisoner: "In this spurious march *the fiction is maintained* that each row must keep in step, that no one must fall behind. The moment disorder occurs, either when those in the back fall behind, or those in front are too far ahead, the stormtroopers hit the offenders with their rifle butts, and someone is an offender even if his heavy breathing shows that he finds it difficult to keep up (Italics added)." Fackenheim explained that it was in the realization that the march was a farce that the Jews were able to marshal strength. The realization of the senselessness of the march led them to "form inner defenses against it." He explains, "We *knew* that this system had no purpose. Hence we also knew that its only purpose could be torture for torture's sake—to break us down. *And, aware of this purpose, we resisted it.*"[109]

Whence this will to resist? Again, certainly God may no longer be encountered as saving or redeeming presence during the Holocaust. For, if God could save, surely God would have saved then. But what of God's commanding presence? God may not have been present as a saving force at Auschwitz, but it may be possible to speak of God's commanding presence, even at Auschwitz, because of Jewish response to it.[110] Fackenheim asserted, "Jewish opposition to Auschwitz cannot be grasped in terms of humanly created ideals but only as an *imposed commandment*. And the Jewish secularist, no less than the believer, is *absolutely singled out* by a Voice as truly *other* than man-made ideals—an imperative as truly *given*—as was the Voice of Sinai."[111] The importance of the otherness of this command is that it must convey the notion of radical surprise that is characteristic of divine incursion into human history. If the Commanding Voice were based on human ideals, it too, like faith in human goodness, would be fundamentally challenged by the Holocaust.[112] Understood as divine commandment, the Voice contains within it the grace necessary to carry out its initiative. Finally, Fackenheim explained, "There must be *commandment* where there is hope."[113] He contended provocatively that the command must precede hope itself, not vice versa.

Fackenheim called the voice the commanding Voice of Auschwitz. On what basis does Fackenheim formulate this notion of the commanding Voice of Auschwitz? Fackenheim looked to the thoughts of Holocaust survivor Pelagia Lewinska upon the realization that the Nazis wished to destroy not only Jewish lives but also Jewish dignity and self-respect. Lewinska describes the effect such a realization had on her. "But from the instant that I grasped the motivating principle . . . it was as if I had been awakened from a dream . . . . I felt under orders to live . . . . And if I did die in Auschwitz, it would be as a human being. I would hold on to my dignity. I was not going to become the contemptible, disgusting brute my enemy wished me to be."[114]

Fackenheim went on to ask of Lewinska's testimony, "Whose orders? Why did she wish to obey? And—this above all—where did she get the strength? We answer the last question by discovering that it is unanswerable. Once again 'willpower' and 'natural desire' are both inadequate. Once again we have touched an Ultimate."[115] Though, as Fackenheim says, Lewinska herself does not say who provided her the orders, other Jewish accounts do not withhold the identity of the commander. Fackenheim called the source of the orders that Lewinska and others heard the Commanding Voice of Auschwitz.[116]

Fackenheim asked:

What does the Voice of Auschwitz command?

Jews are forbidden to hand Hitler posthumous victories. They are commanded to survive as Jews, lest the Jewish people perish. They are commanded to remember the victims of Auschwitz lest their memory perish. They are forbidden to despair of man and his world, and to escape into either cynicism or otherworldliness, lest they cooperate in delivering the world over to the forces of Auschwitz. Finally, they are forbidden to despair of the God of Israel, lest Judaism perish. A secularist cannot make himself believe by a mere act of will, nor can he be commanded to do so . . . . And a religious Jew who has stayed with God may be forced into new, possibly revolutionary relationships with Him. One possibility, however, is unthinkable. A Jew may not respond to Hitler's attempt to destroy Judaism by himself cooperating in its destruction. In ancient times, the unthinkable Jewish sin was idolatry. Today, it is to respond to Hitler by doing his work.[117]

In his 1970 work *God's Presence in History*, Fackenheim went on to assert, "The Voice of Auschwitz commands Jews not to go mad. It commands them to accept their singled out condition, face up to its contradictions, and endure them. Moreover, it gives the power of endurance, the power of sanity. The Jew today can endure because he must endure, and he must endure because he is commanded to endure."[118] In his 1982 work, *To Mend the World*, Fackenheim called this statement "radically inadequate." There he referred to his Kantian (we can do what we ought to do) or neo-orthodox (grace both commands and provides the freedom to act) response as too optimistic, given the "world of the Holocaust." Fackenheim explained, "All brave talk today, *after* the Holocaust, such as 'never again' or 'we can do what we ought' or 'faith is indestructible' either knows not what it says or else is haunted by the fear that, were it then and there rather than here and now, its god and man, hope and will, faith and thought would all be indiscriminately prey to the Nazi logic of destruction."[119]

Such talk of an active response to the Nazi logic of destruction is possible, Fackenheim believed, because it was once actual[120] and it was actual during the Holocaust in the form of resistance.[121] He wrote:

Only in this midnight of dark despair does post-Holocaust thought come upon a shining light. The Nazi logic of destruction was irresistible: *it was, nevertheless, being resisted.* This logic is a *novum* in human history, the source of an unprecedented, abiding horror: but resistance to it on the part of the most radically exposed, too, is a *novum* in history, and it is the source of an unprecedented, abiding wonder. *To hear and obey the commanding Voice of Auschwitz is an "ontological" possibility, here and now, because the hearing and obeying was already an "ontic" reality, then and there.*[122]

Fackenheim explored the definition of resistance. Does resistance mean an armed violent battle against Nazism? Could resistance include active nonviolence or even passive nonviolence? Should instances, though seemingly simple from a view removed from the Holocaust world, of dignity, self-respect, love, and prayer be thought of as resistance in some way? Fackenheim believed so and I must also. Resistance must be understood as taking on all of these forms.

According to Fackenheim,

> For Jews (and semi-, quarter-, or honorary Jews) caught by the full force of the Nazi logic of destruction, resistance was a way of *being*. The Warsaw Ghetto "secularist" fighter expressed this way with revolvers and Molotov cocktails. The "religious," unarmed, unmilitary Hasidim with their *tefillin* expressed it with prayer, dancing, and song. The two ways were no longer antagonistic or even wholly distinct. Here at last we have reached the Ultimate that holds together and unites all these forms of resisting, all these ways of being.[123]

Resistance, which may take various forms, is an assertion of one's humanity in the face of dehumanizing forces. On an existential level, resistance struggles against despair. On a sociohistorical level, resistance struggles against oppression. Either struggle may take the form of thought, action, or, more often than not, both.

Discussing a more overt, active form of resistance, Fackenheim wrote that the Jews performed "small acts of sabotage. We never fooled ourselves into thinking that we did or could do any noticeable harm to the Nazis. Still, even small acts of sabotage maintained our morale."[124] One of the leaders of the Warsaw Ghetto Uprising, Itzak Cukierman, cited by Fackenheim, wrote:

> By following guerilla warfare theory, we saved lives, added to our supply of arms and—most important—*proved to ourselves that the German was but flesh and blood, as any man. And prior to this we had not been aware of this amazing truth! If one lone German appeared in the Ghetto, the Jews would flee en masse, as would Poles on the Aryan side.* Now it became clear that the armed Jew had the advantage over the German . . . something for which to fight. And now the German— once cocky and bent on murder and plunder—felt insecure, knowing that he might not emerge alive from a Jewish house or cellar; and he ceased harassing Jews (italics added).

Fackenheim asserted that "this insight must be considered as nothing short of revelation."[125]

Discussing the Treblinka revolt during which Jewish inmates destroyed gas chambers, Fackenheim claimed that "[t]he astounding fact about the Treblinka revolt is not that the gas chambers were quickly rebuilt; it is that the inmates, who can have had no illusions on this score, nevertheless attempted to destroy them, and succeeded."[126] In other words, true resistance is that which is taken up without regard for the result—it is the means not the end that should be the focus.

Armed Jewish resistance to Nazism, though certainly present, was not pervasive, it seems. It is this dearth of explicitly violent resistance that has led some scholars to claim that Jews went passively to their deaths. Not only is this a narrow and unimaginative concept of resistance, but it also reveals much about one's understanding of what successful resistance should look like. Those who claim that Jewish resistance was nonexistent or very rare believe that resistance must be measured in military concepts of wounded, killed, and property destruction. If, however, one comes to measure the success of resistance by one's survival, dignity, self-respect, and love for fellow human beings under the most unimaginable and horrifying of conditions, resistance is clearly evident throughout Jewish accounts of the Holocaust. The true measure of the success of Jewish resistance to the Holocaust was the fact that it happened at all.

Though resistance may take the form of thought, it is vital, according to Fackenheim, for it to move into the sphere of action. He explained that thought itself must resist despair and escapism.[127] Fackenheim asserted, "Having reached a limit, *resisting thought must point beyond the sphere of thought altogether, to a resistance which is not in 'mere' thought but rather in overt, flesh-and-blood action and life.*"[128] Resistance must not be limited to philosophical resistance, however important. It must take the form of action even today for it to be genuine.[129]

The category of resistance, then, is vital to Fackenheim's understanding of humanity. For resistance is based on the assertion that human life is worthwhile. One resists the forces that seek to murder, or otherwise destroy one's existence; it is an act of survival taken against dehumanization. Resistance is also an act of hope based on love, faith, and trust in fellow human beings. According to Fackenheim, after the Holocaust we are commanded to resist dehumanization and despair; we are commanded to survive and to hope—impossible but necessary demands.[130]

Importantly, Fackenheim maintained that, though the Holocaust may transcend meaning, there must be a Jewish response to the event.

The response Fackenheim proposed is resistance. Resistance to murder, to oppression, to dehumanization, and to despair is the most meaningful response to the Holocaust a Jew can make. In resistance the Jew asserts his right to exist, as a Jew, in all his particularity, complexity, and ambiguity. Resistance is not a "solution" to the "problem" of the Holocaust; it is an affirmation and declaration of Jewish humanity.

Resistance is possible today only because it was actual then, during the Holocaust. Fackenheim refused to make claims that would not withstand the scrutiny of the Holocaust victims, resisters, and survivors. He felt that he could make assertions, such as those on the Commanding Voice, only because they were made before him. These are not abstract philosophical and theological thoughts for Fackenheim, for whom theology is formed and lived on earth by those who have the least reason to believe in God, the victims, sufferers, resisters, and survivors of terror. It is to these people that Fackenheim looked for his understanding of resistance today, after the Holocaust.

Fackenheim explained, "The Jew after Auschwitz is a witness to endurance. He is singled out by contradictions which, in our post-holocaust world, are worldwide contradictions. He bears witness that without endurance we shall all perish. He bears witness that we can endure because we must endure; and that we must endure because we are commanded to endure."[131] Resistance today is possible because it was actual then. Also today, just as then, resistance is carried out in response to the commanding presence of God. I examine three examples of contemporary resistance that Fackenheim developed: mad *midrash*, the struggle for the existence of the state of Israel, and the effort to bring about the mending of the world, or *tikkun olam*.

Emil Fackenheim on Resistance

Three examples of resistance developed in the theology of Emil Fackenheim are life lived in *midrashic* existence, the emergence of the state of Israel, and *tikkun olam*, or mending of the world.[132] Each of the three, either in thought or in deed, resists despair of God or humanity and resists forces of dehumanization and oppression, especially when these forces attempt to destroy Jewish existence or faith. Though distinct in certain ways, these three categories potentially overlap. For example, a Jew living in Israel and striving toward redemption lives a *midrashic* existence. Further, Fackenheim himself seemed to understand the importance of Israel as an act of *tikkun olam*. However, each of the three notions does have unique characteristics. *Midrashic* existence is largely an emotional, mental, creative expression of paradox, whereas Israel is a religious and political form of resistance. Whereas *midrashic* existence and the state of Israel are largely open to Jews alone, *tikkun olam* seems to be a category available to Jews and non-Jews alike.[133] The three categories share a conceptual origin in specifically Jewish traditional thought; they also may be interpreted as responses to the Holocaust and to the Commanding Voice of Auschwitz in that each resists despair and dehumanization. Each insists on remaining faithful to both God and humanity despite the horrors of Auschwitz, on actively fighting for the survival of Jewish existence, and on maintaining hope that through divine-human activity, an impossible, yet necessary mending will take place.

Though Fackenheim placed a premium on action above thought with respect to his concept of resistance, resistance is not limited to the sphere of action. Thought itself must resist despair and escapism. An example of the type of thought that resists despair and escapism is evident in *midrash*, the copious exegetical material on the Bible developed between the fourth and twelfth centuries. In 1976 Fackenheim described what he termed "*midrashic* existence." The central characteristic of *midrashic* existence, according to Fackenheim, is a life lived in tension between extremes and a consciousness of these tensions.

One of the greatest tensions faced by *midrashic* existence exists between divine omnibenevolence and omnipotence and the ambiguities of the world, including evil. Philosophy may demand us to choose between belief in a good and powerful God and the world, which at times seems to contradict God's perfections in its finiteness and failures. *Midrashic* existence is lived between these two options and it encompasses both. For example, in regard to the tension between divine omnipotence and human freedom, *midrashic* existence points out a paradox: "*Midrashic* existence acts as though all depended on man and prays as though all depended on God."[134]

The paradoxical nature of revelation and of faith in this incursion of the infinite into history is embraced by *midrash*. The contradictions of faith, genuine or only apparent, are addressed, but not necessarily resolved by *midrash*. The tradition of *midrash* is a central source for Fackenheim's theological enterprise. Fackenheim wrote that *midrash* reflects upon root experiences, is aware of the contradictions inherent to these experiences, but nevertheless remains stubbornly committed to the truth of these experiences. *Midrashic* reflection does not resolve the contradictions of root experiences, but only "expresses" them. Fackenheim claimed that *midrashic* "expression (a) is fully conscious of the contradictions expressed; (b) is fully deliberate in leaving them unresolved; (c) for both reasons combined, is consciously fragmentary; and (d) is insistent that this fragmentariness is both ultimate for human thought and yet destined to an ultimate resolution. *Midrashic thought, therefore, is both fragmentary and whole.*"[135] Finally, another trait of *midrash* is that it is presented in the forms of story, parable, and metaphor, which reflects the nature of the root experience as both fragmentary and whole.

Midrashic existence is best explained and explored through stories. "The *midrashic* Word is story. It *remains* story because it both points to and articulates a life *lived with* problems and paradox—the problems and paradox of a divine-human relation. This life is *midrashic* existence."[136] Story is able to transcend the limitations of rationality and reality, and yet maintain its own type of rationale and understanding of reality.

Fackenheim asserted that the Holocaust challenges even the world of *midrash*. Just as the Holocaust is unique in history, "mad *midrash*" created in its aftermath is unique. Fackenheim called this *midrash* mad, not because it is insane, though. He explained his choice of terms. "What is this madness? Not insanity, if 'insanity' is 'flight from reality.' It is just because it dare not flee from *its* reality that this *midrash* is mad. This madness is obliged—condemned?—to be sane."[137] This madness is also not irrationality, nor is it a flight to mysticism. Instead, the madness Fackenheim described must become an opportunity for transformation and mending.[138]

Mad *midrash* must resist the "anti-world" in which despair, destruction, and death are the only choices. Fackenheim asserted, "For midrashic madness points to *an existence in which the madness is transfigured.* Midrashic madness is the Word spoken in the anti-world which ought not to be but is. The existence it points to acts to restore a world which ought to be but is not, committed to the faith that what ought to be must and will be, and this is *its* madness. After Planet Auschwitz there can be no health without *this* madness, no joy, no life. Without this madness a Jew cannot do—with God or without him—what a Voice from Sinai bids him do: choose life."[139] Mad *midrash* chooses to fully encounter the absurdity and perversity of existence lived after Auschwitz and, not to transcend these obstacles, but to transfigure them.

For now, I would like to present three compelling examples of *midrash* that are related by Fackenheim that attempt to express some aspect of the Holocaust universe. I cite all three in their entirety for their profundity and for their exemplary importance in Fackenheim's own theology. The first comes from Elie Wiesel's *Night:*[140]

One day when we came back from work, we saw three gallows rearing up in the assembly place, three black crows. Roll call. SS all round us, machine guns trained: the traditional ceremony. Three victims in chains—and one of them, the little servant, the sad-eyed angel. The SS seemed more preoccupied, more disturbed than usual. To hang a young boy in front of thousands of spectators was no light matter. The head of the camp read the verdict. All eyes were on the child. He was lividly pale, almost calm, biting his lips. The gallows threw its shadow over him . . . . The three victims mounted together onto the chairs. The three necks were placed at the same moment within the nooses. "Long live liberty!," cried the two adults. But the child was silent. "Where is God? Where is He?" someone behind me asked. At a sign from the head of the camp, the three chairs tipped over . . . I heard a voice within me answer . . . : "Where is He? Here He is—He is hanging on this gallows . . ."

Fackenheim added,

I heard my second and third stories in 1970, when together with my wife, I went with a group of survivors on a pilgrimage to the murder camp of Bergen-Belsen—and then to Jerusalem. When we arrived at Hannover, the city nearest to Belsen, it rained. The leader of our group told us: "We have revisited this place of our suffering many times. It always rains. God weeps. He weeps for the sins he has committed against his people Israel." And then, by a mere brief airplane ride, we leaped over the eternities that separate Bergen-Belsen from Jerusalem. There, a friend told us how one day at six a. m. he went to the Western Wall, and there, at the most sacred place of the Jewish people, he met an old Jew, who greeted the stranger, saying, "My friend, I have a *simhah*, a celebration! Celebrate with me! Have some schnapps and some cookies!" Having accepted the invitation, our friend some days later returned to the Wall at the same time, only to be greeted by the same old man in the same way. And so it went three or four times. Finally, our friend could no longer restrain his curiosity and asked the old man: "My friend, what kind of celebration is this? A wedding? A Bar-mitzvah? What *simhah* can last for weeks upon weeks?" The old man replied, "I am a survivor of Auschwitz. Also, I am a Cohen, descendent of priests and, as you may know, a Cohen has the duty, privilege, and joy of invoking the blessing of God on his people but a few times a year. In Jerusalem, however, he may bless the people every single day. And since I must be at work in my kibbutz at eight a. m., I come here every day at six a. m. to fulfill my duty and my privilege. This is my *simhah*, my celebration. It will last as long as I live."[141]

In these three stories one encounters a protest against injustice, dehumanization, and a God who would stand by while it happens. One reads of a relationship between God and humanity that is so close that they weep together. Finally one sees an affirmation of life lived in a world that makes little sense. This simultaneous protest against God and love for God exist only in rich and complex faithfulness and commitment to both God and humanity. Despair and escapism are resisted in each of these instances. *Midrashic* existence maintains the paradoxes of life, while mad *midrash* points toward an impossible transformation that must be actualized.

One way in which Fackenheim saw this impossible transformation being actualized is in the emergence of the state of Israel. Fackenheim rejected the explanation and justification of Israel through the Holocaust, saying,

> Israel needs no justification through a link with the Holocaust. What the link does is make the Jewish state at once a moral necessity and an ontological near-impossibility. Israel is a moral necessity: the bimillenial, unholy combination of Jew-hatred and Jewish powerlessness, always intolerable, is now *absolutely* so. Israel is also an ontological near-impossibility: the faith and the courage needed for founding, maintaining, building *this* state, enormous in any circumstances, begs the understanding in *these* circumstances—after a catastrophe calculated to destroy all faith and all courage, not only among the cousins of the victims, but wherever the news reaches and is understood. And since the faith and the courage are nevertheless actual, Israel is nothing less than an orienting reality for all Jewish and indeed all post-Holocaust thought.[142]

Israel's existence is not a gift or payment for the Holocaust, from either the world community or God. Fackenheim explained: "Jerusalem, while no 'answer' to the Holocaust, is a response; and every Israeli lives that response."[143] Fackenheim found hope for redemption in the daily endurance of Israelis and in the philosophy of Zionism. He contended that "Zionism—the commitment to the safety and genuine sovereignty of the State of Israel—is not negotiable."[144] It is not negotiable because the resistance to another Holocaust is not negotiable. This reality leads to the importance of the survival and flourishing of Israel, as well as resistance to oppression and suffering, including within Israeli borders.

The centrality of the state of Israel in Fackenheim's theological system has been evident throughout his writings.[145] But after the Six Day War of 1967, Fackenheim began to draw direct connections between the Holocaust and Israel and between the Voice of Auschwitz and Israeli resistance and survival. In 1970 Fackenheim asserted that "[t]he commanding Voice of Auschwitz singles Jews out; Jewish survival is a commandment which brooks no compromise. It was this Voice which was heard by the Jews of Israel in May and June of 1967 when they refused to lie down and be slaughtered."[146] In 1974, he drew a direct line of relation between the Holocaust and Israel. "*Yet it is necessary, not only to perceive a bond between the two events* (the Holocaust and the founding of the state of Israel) *but also so to act as to make it unbreakable.*"[147] He made a strong assertion when he stated "the heart of every *authentic* response to the Holocaust—religious and secularist, Jewish and non-Jewish—is a commitment to the autonomy and security of the state of Israel."[148] Fackenheim's concepts of resistance and *tikkun* find their *telos* in Israel.

One of my criticisms of Fackenheim's theology, which is explored in more depth in chapter 5, is that the centrality of Israel to his thought is potentially idolatrous. The role of Israel in Fackenheim's theology is in danger of being so central for him that a belief in the importance of Israel as a form of Jewish resistance to the Holocaust may slip toward an uncritical support of the policies of the political entity of Israel. This possibility reveals the potential for a form of triumphalism. Furthermore, unquestioning support of Israel betrays Fackenheim's honorable belief in the importance of social justice. Though resistance to Jewish oppression and despair should be and is characteristic of Fackenheim's thought, it need not be so at the cost of becoming oppressive.[149]

I believe this potential danger results from two problems in Fackenheim's thought: first, there is a direct link made between the original decree of the Commanding Voice of Auschwitz to resist and survive and the political entity of the state of Israel; second, one encounters difficulty in applying Fackenheim's notion of resistance in events other than the Holocaust. With regard to the first, Fackenheim began by asserting that the Commanding Voice of Auschwitz is an externally imposed order from God that demands Jewish resistance to the Nazi logic of destruction. Fackenheim later came to believe that this Voice of Auschwitz was heard again by Israelis during the 1967

Six Day War. What had been an existential demand for resistance has become a political demand for the defense of Israel. In other words, the Voice of Auschwitz had become the Voice of Jerusalem. This shift exposes the fact that the Commanding Voice is as human as it is divine. If a human aspect to the command may be acknowledged, then actions carried out in obedience to it must be subject to the same ethical criteria that apply to any other sociopolitical actions. Thus, the existence and endurance of the state of Israel may be understood to be a valid human response to the Commanding Voice of Auschwitz. However, it must be remembered that this is a *human* action, not divine. It is therefore potentially fallible and incomplete.

The second problem, or more precisely limitation, in Fackenheim's thought becomes evident when one attempts to apply his category of resistance to events other than the Holocaust. Although such an application may never have been intended, I believe Fackenheim's concept of resistance may be a powerfully creative idea that has the potential to be utilized in other instances. The problem is that Fackenheim never offered a clear definition of resistance. In other words, we are simply to know resistance when we see it. Certainly, for example, an abused child taking action against her perpetrator would be an instance of resistance. But how does one interpret an antiabortion protester bombing an abortion clinic? Could he not believe that he, following divine orders, is resisting forces acting toward the murder of a child? How do we define resistance? I do not have a simple answer to this question. However, I believe that this is an issue that must be resolved before the theological category of resistance may be developed further. Perhaps, somewhat paradoxically, this apparent shortcoming is actually an important characteristic of the notion of resistance. In allowing for a broad, flexible understanding of resistance, there is a recognition that resistance involves particular human actions in history that seldom allow for universals or absolutes. The attempt to offer a universal definition of resistance implies the belief that the force or event being resisted is itself universal. Such a move mitigates the very particular nature of oppression and evil and consequently softens the resulting notion of resistance.

For Fackenheim resistance is not only a resistance against something, but also a resistance for something. Resistance, though initially in opposition to evil or despair turns into a productive building toward an end. That end, for Fackenheim, is redemption, which is only possible through a mending of the world, or *tikkun olam*, the third expression of resistance explored here.

Fackenheim's notion of *tikkun olam* finds its source in Lurianic kabbalistic metaphysics. According to a complex Lurianic belief, part of the process of creation involves the emanation of divine light into vessels or bowls. When the vessels could no longer contain the light, they broke. *Tikkun*, then, involves a restoration of these vessels, of creation itself.[150]

Tikkun is both a metaphysical and a historical concept. The mending of the world involves both divine and human efforts in history. Fackenheim explained:

> The "exile of the Shekhina" and the "fracture of the vessels" refers [*sic*] to cosmic, as well as historical realities: it is *that* rupture that our *Tikkun* is to mend. But how is this possible when *we ourselves* share in the cosmic condition of brokenness? Yet just in response to this problematic the kabbalistic *Tikkun* shows its profoundest energy. It is precisely if the rupture, or the threat of it, is total, that all powers must be summoned for a mending. If the threat is to man, there is need to invoke divine as will as human power. If the threat is to God—the "exile" is "an element in God Himself"—then human power must aid the divine. And if this can be said without blasphemy, it is because the human aid is *itself* aided by the Divine. "The impulse below calls forth an impulse above."[151]

Thus, humanity plays a vital role in the process of *tikkun*. How can humanity bring about redemption?

Once again we return to the apparent tension between God's power and human freedom. Fackenheim responded by turning to his dialectical understanding of human freedom and divine activity, and the concept of *teshuva*. "God will redeem man, but not by making him either less or more human; either assertion would make human existence meaningless—a tragic contradiction to no purpose. God redeems man by preserving the contradictory elements that constitute his humanity, yet by transforming them in such a way as to take the sting out of the contradiction."[152] The contradiction is transcended in *teshuva*. "*Teshuva* in Judaism is a many-sided experience. Its core, however, is a divine-human turning-toward-each-other, despite and indeed because of their persistent and unmitigated incommensurability."[153] In *teshuva* not only does God turn toward humanity, but humanity also turns toward God. The human turning toward God involves both divine aid and human free will. Here, the dynamic of divine and human simultaneously moving toward one another, at once both independently and yet impossibly without each other, transcends the issue of who follows whom.

Redemption is ultimately in God's hands, but this does not turn humanity into puppets. "In a history in which revelation is possible the individual is, potentially, singled out; his actions and existence may become a unique fulfillment. To be sure, they cannot become completely redemptive, but neither need they be of a merely repetitive character: they may become unique contributions toward redemption."[154]

According to kabbalistic belief, humanity contributes to the processes of *tikkun* and redemption by following the commandments and offering prayers to God. Human efforts have both practical and mystical aspects. There was an understanding that God and humanity were intimately related and could bring redemption by working together. The event of the Holocaust changed all this.

Fackenheim stated that after the rupture of the Holocaust no *tikkun* is possible. Nevertheless, "the impossible *Tikkun* is also necessary." Once again Fackenheim turned to the victims and survivors of the Holocaust for assistance, saying "*A* Tikkun, *here and now, is mandatory for a* Tikkun, *then and there, was actual*. It is true that because a *Tikkun* of *that* rupture is impossible we cannot live, after the Holocaust, as men and women have lived before. However, if the impossible *Tikkun* were not also necessary, and hence possible, we could not live at all."[155] The focus on acts of resistance and *tikkun* during the Holocaust and the notion that some fragmentary saving divine presence *is* available despite the Holocaust characterize an important development found in Fackenheim's *To Mend the World*. It is in this work that he articulated the previously impossible hope for a mending of the rupture of the Holocaust.[156]

As always, Fackenheim dared to speak of possibility now only because it was evident during the Holocaust. "The Tikkun which for the post-Holocaust Jew is a moral necessity is a possibility because during the Holocaust itself a Jewish Tikkun was already actual."[157] Given the horrific realities of the Holocaust how could Fackenheim have believed that tikkun was actual even during that time? He pointed to the seriousness of this tension:

> The dilemma is as follows. If (as we must) we hold fast to the children, the mothers, the *Muselmanner*, to the whole murdered people and its innocence, then we must surely despair of any possible *Tikkun;* but then we neglect or ignore the few and select—those with the opportunity to resist, the will and strength to resist, deriving the will and strength we know not whence—whose *Tikkun* (as we have seen) precedes and makes mandatory our own. And if (as we must) we hold fast to just

these select and their *Tikkun*, then *our Tikkun, made* possible by *theirs,* neglects and ignores all those who performed no heroic or saintly deeds such as to merit holiness and who yet, murdered as they were in utter innocence, must be considered holy . . . . However, post-Holocaust thought—it includes theological concerns but is not confined to them— must dwell, however painfully and precariously, between the extremes, and seek a *Tikkun* as it endures the tension.[158]

Tikkun is carried out by those who follow the commandments and offer prayers to God, as had been the case in the kabbalistic understanding. *Tikkun* is also sought after in acts of resistance against forces of dehumanization and for human dignity and fulfillment. It is evident in the very existence of Jews as Jews. After the Holocaust, Jewish existence, faith, and resistance against processes that wish to destroy are all acts of *tikkun*.

It is the honest and full confrontation of the Holocaust that prevented Fackenheim from purporting any triumphalistic conception of what redemption will be. "Hence in our search for a post-Holocaust *Tikkun* we must accept from the start that at most only a fragmentary *Tikkun* is possible."[159] Fackenheim envisioned *tikkun* as comprising three aspects: "(a) a recovery of the Jewish tradition . . . ; (b) a recovery in the quite different sense of recuperation from an illness; and (c) a fragmentariness attaching to these two recoveries that makes them both ever-incomplete and ever-laden with risk."[160] Not only is any *tikkun* fragmentary, but we must also be cognizant of this fact and yet, nevertheless, act towards complete and total healing.

This approach to fulfillment shares certain aspects with liberation theology including the belief that redemption brought about by humanity will be fragmentary and a genuine concern about and even focus on *this* world and its social, political, and spiritual realities. Fackenheim prophetically stated that humanity must act for social justice and against oppression. He recognized, however, that history has shown human efforts in this direction to be ambiguous and fragmentary at best. He wrote:

It is one thing to be forced to compromise in the struggle against war, oppression, discrimination and poverty, and to accept such compromises temporarily and with an aching heart. It is another thing entirely to mistake what are at best incomplete achievements finally and self-righteously, as if they were perfect. This believing attitude can never forget that so long as the divine image is violated even in one single human being, the Kingdom of God on earth is incomplete.[161]

This passage combines the acknowledgment that there is a limit to what we can do with the assertion that we must nevertheless do all we can.

Throughout his work, Emil Fackenheim struggled with the question of how it is possible to exist, believe, and flourish as a Jew after the Holocaust. It may be possible to do these things only because they were being done even in the midst of the Holocaust. During and after the Holocaust, Jewish existence, faith, and thriving are acts of resistance. They are acts of resistance against the Nazi logic of destruction and against any forces of dehumanization and oppression. These acts of resistance, evident in mad *midrash*, the existence of the state of Israel, and *tikkun olam*, represent human efforts to mend the world that has been nearly destroyed. In the end, human resistance has the potential to lead to redemption. Chapter 5 explores critiques of Emil Fackenheim's theology by Richard L. Rubenstein, Marc Ellis, Melissa Raphael, and Michael L. Morgan. Bringing these voices into discussion with Fackenheim once again raises the issues of method, God, humanity, and resistance developed in this chapter.

5

After the Holocaust: The Destruction of the God of History, of Chosenness, and of Patriarchy; Critiques and Affirmations of Emil Fackenheim

This chapter explores four Jewish theological voices that address the thought of Emil Fackenheim. Paralleling chapter 3 of this work, we examine a figure who is a pioneering critic and interlocutor of Fackenheim's, a more recent thinker who pushes this critique even further, a feminist critic of the foundations of much of post-Holocaust theology, and finally a theologian who takes up and refines Fackenheim's system for the present.

First, I examine the Holocaust theologian, Richard L. Rubenstein, who argues that Auschwitz destroys any faith in a good and active God of history and the notion of a divine covenant with Israel. Rubenstein claims that we must turn to a God of nature, or Holy Nothingness, and stresses the sociological and psychological role of religion in his advocacy of the primacy of ritual. Further, Rubenstein takes issue with Fackenheim's 614th commandment because it deems as sinful the understandable and valid stance of the Jew who, after Auschwitz, believes neither in God nor in remaining a Jew.

Next, I look at the controversial and provocative Marc Ellis, who takes Jewish theology to task on the notion of Jewish chosenness and on the theological importance of Israel. Ellis challenges Fackenheim's support of the state of Israel as a fundamental aspect of Jewish identity, faith, and empowerment. Ellis also provides a fertile basis for comparison between black theology of liberation and Jewish theology of liberation.

Following Ellis is an examination of Melissa Raphael, who develops a feminist Jewish post-Holocaust theology. Raphael argues that male post-Holocaust theologians, including Fackenheim, attempted to confront the event of the Holocaust with traditional models of God as patriarchal and dominating in mind. If divine power and presence are reinterpreted along feminist lines, the Holocaust remains an event of horrific stature, and yet many of the theodicy problems are reformulated and considered in a perhaps more satisfying way.

Finally, paralleling Hopkins' relation to Cone, Michael L. Morgan is studied as a contemporary theologian who further develops Fackenheim's thought. Morgan's work is used to illuminate Fackenheim's ideas of revelation, history, and redemption for the twenty-first century.

Richard L. Rubenstein: Death of the God of History

Unlike the other critics of both Cone and Fackenheim presented here, Rubenstein is unique in the fact that his first work on the Holocaust preceded Fackenheim's. Along with Ignaz Maybaum's *The Face of God after Auschwitz* (1965), Rubenstein's *After Auschwitz: Radical Theology and Contemporary Judaism* (1966) was published a few years before Fackenheim's *God's Presence in History* (1970).[1] Thus, Rubenstein offers less a critique of Fackenheim than a competing alternative view of theology in the light of the Holocaust.[2]

Rubenstein, whose work has been largely seen as a betrayal of traditional Jewish theologies that stressed faith in the God of history and the divine covenant with Israel,[3] began to focus on more psychological, sociological, and historical aspects of the Holocaust in the 1970s and 1980s.[4] Though compellingly fascinating, this work is not analyzed directly here. This section instead looks at Rubenstein's particularly theological writings, especially the first and second editions of *After Auschwitz*, for a comparison with Fackenheim. Specifically, Fackenheim's articulation of divine presence and human faith after the Holocaust is challenged by Rubenstein's assertion that, after the Holocaust, we live in the time of the death of God, and thus, no covenant between a good and active God in history and a faithful, elected Israel exists.

Rubenstein pointed to a conversation he had with Heinrich Gruber in 1961 as a major turning point in his reflections on the theological implications of the Holocaust. Gruber, Dean of the Evangelical Church in Berlin, was the only German who testified against Adolf Eichmann in his Jerusalem trial and had a long record of resistance against Nazism, to the point of his internment in Dachau. During this meeting, Gruber explained his faith that God had willed the destruction of Jews during the Holocaust as his elect martyrs. As Nebuchadnezzar had been used as a "rod of God's anger," so Hitler was another instrument of God's punishing will, according to Gruber's logic.

The incredible Christian claim that Jews are punished even today for killing Christ is certainly not unique to Gruber. Nevertheless, Rubenstein was struck by two aspects of Gruber's statements. First, this was a Christian who was committed to fighting Nazism and helping Jews during World War II and after. Second, and more profoundly, Gruber was simply carrying out the implications of *Jewish* understandings of covenant, election, and divine providence to their seemingly logical conclusions. For, if God is omnipotent, acts in history, and has a special relationship with Israel, then any suffering or oppression of Jews must be a result of the will of God. Rubenstein writes, "Can we really blame the Christian community for viewing us through the prism of a mythology of history when we were the first to assert this history ourselves? As long as we continue to hold to the doctrine of the election of Israel, we will leave ourselves open to the theology expressed by Dean Gruber, that the Jews are God's Chosen People, God wanted Hitler to punish them."[5] To avoid this obscene conclusion, Rubenstein asserts that traditional Jewish notions of divine activity and of election must be radically reinterpreted or dropped altogether.

Rubenstein argues that, after the Holocaust, we live in the time of the death of God; however, he does not claim that God is actually dead. He explains, "When I say we live in the time of the death of God, I mean that the thread uniting God and man, heaven and earth, has been broken. We stand in a cold, silent, unfeeling cosmos, unaided by any purposeful power beyond our own resources. After Auschwitz, what else can a Jew say about God?"[6] Thus, in our time, God is not active in history; there is no special relationship between God and anyone, Jews included, according to Rubenstein.[7]

Despite these radical claims, Rubenstein does not believe that Judaism ceases to exist. He writes, "Though I believe that a void stands where once we experienced God's presence, I do not think Judaism has lost its meaning or its power. I do not believe that a theistic God is necessary for Jewish religious life . . . . I have suggested that Judaism is the way in which we share the decisive times and crises of life through the traditions of our inherited community."[8] Thus, though Rubenstein cannot support traditional Jewish beliefs, he does maintain the functional role of Judaism in its practices and forms.

In the first edition of *After Auschwitz*, Rubenstein asserted Judaism must focus on its more ritualistic forms and suggested there would be a return to a nature-centered paganism in Israel. He pointed to Israeli folk music and kibbutz life as expressions of this "return to the archaic earth-religion of Israel." Rubenstein predicted "earth's fruitfulness, its vicissitudes, and its engendering power will once again become the central spiritual realities of Jewish life, at least in Israel."[9] He explains, in contrast with the religion of history,

> [i]n the religion of nature, all generations are essentially the same; they grow, they unfold in ecstatic creativity, they ripen, and finally they return, becoming the substance of other individuations which will repeat the cycle. Nature and man are one; nature is man's true being and strength; man is nature's self-reflective expression.

This religion of nature implies a new understanding of the divine as well.

The God of the religion of nature is immanent in the world, within nature, and shares in the life of humanity. Rubenstein explains this God will not be understood as polytheistic; rather "God will be seen as one, but He will be understood to participate in nature's vicissitudes and necessities rather than to create them outside of His solitary perfection."[10] Finally, this interpretation of the divine means that like humanity, God shares the tragic and demonic aspects of the world. *"To say that God and nature are at one with each other, that they are alive and life-engendering, is to affirm the demonic side not alone in us but in divinity as well."*[11] Though Rubenstein maintains some of its elements, his development of the religion of nature is modified in the second edition of *After Auschwitz*.

In the second edition of Rubenstein's essays, he admits that his prediction of a return to Jewish paganism has not come to pass and, further, it would carry inherent dangers if it were to do so. He explains, "[T]oo rigid a commitment to *all of the land of Israel,* especially when combined with apocalyptic messianism, can lead the State of Israel into unnecessarily dangerous confrontations with its

Arab neighbors and with international Islam."[12] Though he softens his interpretation of the importance of land, place, and space in the religion of nature for practical and political reasons, Rubenstein maintains his critique of the God of history, preferring to name God as Holy Nothingness.

Rubenstein's naming of God as Holy Nothingness, a concept initially suggested in the first edition of *After Auschwitz*, is more developed in the second edition. God as Holy Nothingness is identical to the God of the religion of nature, who is immanent in humanity and nature. The language is developed from understandings of the divine or the ultimate sacred in Eastern and Western mysticism and in feminism. Rubenstein explains, "God, thus designated, is regarded as the Ground and Source of all existence. To speak, admittedly in inadequate language, of God as the 'Nothingness' is not to suggest that God is a void; on the contrary, the Holy Nothingness is a *plenum* so rich that all existence derives therefrom. God as the 'Nothing' is not absence of being, but a superfluity of being."[13] In other words, "*the infinite God is not a thing; the infinite God is no-thing.*"[14]

To explain his concept of God as Holy Nothingness Rubenstein uses the mystical metaphor of the ocean and its waves; God is the ocean and we are the waves. The ocean represents all-encompassing reality, including the waves. Yet the wave has a genuine individual reality as a wave, simultaneously distinct from *and* identical to the ocean. This understanding of God as immanent in the very dynamism of humanity and in all creation is influenced by Lurianic Kabbalism, Meister Eckhart, Hegel, Tillich, and Buddhism.

As with his earlier description of the God of the religion of nature, God as Holy Nothingness is most aptly understood as a maternal force. In contrast with the biblical God of history, designated as father, king, and judge, God as Holy Nothingness "creates as does a mother, in and through her very substance. As ground of being, God participates in all the joys and sorrows of the drama of creation, which is, at the same time, the deepest expression of the divine life. God's unchanging unitary life and that of the cosmos's ever-changing, dynamic multiplicity ultimately reflect a single unitary reality."[15]

In both his denial of the traditional God of history and the election of Israel as a result of the lack of supporting empirical evidence and in his claim that, after the ethnic suffering evident in history, religion may best be understood as nontheistic, Rubenstein shares much in common with William R. Jones. Also, just as the humanism of Jones and Anthony Pinn was shown to dismiss rather than "solve" the problem of theodicy, so does Rubenstein's God as Holy Nothingness place the responsibility for evil effectively on human shoulders. Admittedly, God as ground of all being shares in our experiences and is, in this way, also both guilty and responsible for suffering and evil. However, practically speaking, humans bear the burden of evil in both systems. Just as Jones served as one of Cone's most ardent and creative critics, Rubenstein has challenged the thought of Emil Fackenheim since their earliest written encounters with the Holocaust and its implications.

Like Fackenheim, Rubenstein asserted the centrality of both the Holocaust and the modern state of Israel for contemporary Jewish theology. Also as Fackenheim had, Rubenstein claimed that the Holocaust was a unique event of suffering and evil. For him, the uniqueness of the Holocaust stems from the theological import of its realities for both Jews and Christians. He explains, "No other contemporary event is so inextricably linked to the classical interpretation of God's action in history for humanity's salvation in both traditions."[16] Though both agree that the Holocaust is unique and central to any subsequent Jewish theology, Rubenstein differs radically from Fackenheim in his interpretation of divine presence during the Holocaust and the proper human, specifically Jewish, response to this divine presence or absence.

Fackenheim asserted that God is evident to Jewish believers during and after the Holocaust as Commanding Presence. The Commanding Voice of Auschwitz issues the 614th commandment, essentially saying that Jews are not to allow Hitler any posthumous victories.[17] Rubenstein responded to Fackenheim's claims by arguing that God had not been present during the Holocaust, that his own formulation of God as Holy Nothingness is actually consistent with the Jewish mystical tradition, and that Fackenheim's categorizing of Jews who despair of God and/or humanity after the Holocaust as Hitler's allies is a "bitter cruelty."

Rubenstein's logic in denying both the presence of the traditional biblical God of history and the covenantal relationship between God and Israel has been discussed above. The ample horrific empirical evidence of Jewish suffering and the lack of any redeeming worth of the Holocaust universe are more than enough for Rubenstein to reject the presence of God and of the covenant. He complains that Fackenheim refuses to let these facts fundamentally alter his theological claims. He writes, "Fackenheim thus forecloses debate on the fundamental question of theology before he begins. He rejects the evidence of history as an argument against God's loving action in history; he rejects psychological, sociological, and anthropological attempts to comprehend the Divine Presence in their own terms." In other words, Fackenheim asserts the presence of God based solely on irrefutable faith, according to Rubenstein.[18]

Rubenstein believes that, for Fackenheim, there are essentially only two possible religious responses to the Holocaust. The first, which Fackenheim chooses, is to remain faithful to God and the covenant by following the 614th commandment. The second, which Rubenstein believes Fackenheim dismissed his theology as, is atheism, nihilism, and despair. Rubenstein argues that there is a fuller spectrum of possible responses, including his own interpretation of God as Holy Nothingness. In fact, Rubenstein argues, this theological interpretation of the divine in the aftermath of suffering has precedent within the Jewish tradition. "Traditionally, both rabbinic Judaism and Christianity have tended to regard Jewish misfortune as evidence of God's punitive chastisement of his erring people. Within Judaism in previous periods only the mystics denigrated by Fackenheim sought an alternative response to catastrophe and found it in the doctrine of the cosmic exile of the *Shekhinah* from the Divine Ground or *En Sof*." In other words, Fackenheim dismissed as idolatrous Rubenstein's turn to a mystical and pagan theological interpretation in which God's immanence in creation and humanity is stressed in response to human suffering.[19]

For Fackenheim, it is the radical otherness of the divine that makes God's Commanding Presence possible. The result of any ontological overlap or identification between God and humanity would be the end of the covenant, commandment, and redemption, according to Fackenheim. These three aspects of the Jewish tradition require a dialectical relationship of otherness for them to exist. Though I find Rubenstein's God as Holy Nothingness to be a theologically creative position, for me Fackenheim's development of resistance as ethical response is much more compelling and courageous than Rubenstein's pessimistic nihilism. Though Rubenstein's position is philosophically sound, I do not think it encourages acts of social justice or a metaphysical mending of the world.

Fackenheim's articulation of the 614th commandment does seem to deem any Jew who despairs of God or humanity after the Holocaust to be Hitler's ally, as Rubenstein argues. However, I fervently do not believe this to have been Fackenheim's intent. His notions of

Commanding Voice of Auschwitz and the resulting 614th commandment are not meant to categorize and denigrate; they are, on the contrary, meant to inspire a courageous, hopeful, and meaningful response to a terrible event in history. Though he certainly never went as far as considering a theology of radical immanence or panentheism, interestingly in his later work, Fackenheim's ethical use of the Lurianic category of *tikkun* implies a divine immanence in human activities. This point is introduced, but not fully explored in Fackenheim's writings. Perhaps it would be interesting to examine whether Fackenheim's ethical notion of resistance might be a possible corollary of his unexplored understanding of the theological implications of *tikkun*. For me, Rubenstein's articulation of God as Holy Nothingness encourages such an exploration of the idea of divine immanence as saving presence in the efforts to mend the world.

Marc Ellis: Chosenness and Justice

Just as Richard Rubenstein challenged Emil Fackenheim's definition of an authentic Jew as one who does not provide Hitler posthumous victory through despairing of God or humanity after the Holocaust, Marc H. Ellis questions Fackenheim's assertion of the correlation between the Holocaust and Jewish political empowerment in the form of the state of Israel. Ellis believes that Holocaust theologians,[20] including Fackenheim and Rubenstein, understand the lesson of the Holocaust, if that designation is not obscene, to be the need for Jewish empowerment so that a second Jewish Holocaust becomes an impossibility. Ellis agrees, but also asserts that Jews must help create a world in which *no* community suffers the hatred and oppression that led to the Jewish Holocaust. In other words, Ellis argues that the misuse of Jewish power against the Palestinians betrays the memory of Jewish suffering and oppression, as Jews, no longer the victim, become the abuser. Ellis raises important objections to Fackenheim's notions of God, Judaism, *tikkun*, and resistance. In addition, Ellis makes a courageous effort to link post-Holocaust Jewish thought with liberation theologies, including Cone's black theology of liberation.

Presented with the radical challenge of the Holocaust, Jewish theologians and thinkers such as Elie Wiesel, Emil Fackenheim, Richard Rubenstein, and Irving Greenberg sought a radical and new theological understanding of God and the Jewish community. With the emergence of the state of Israel in 1948 and especially during and after the Israeli victory in the Six Day War of 1967, the dialectic of the Holocaust and empowerment appears, Ellis explains. He asserts that with increasing Jewish empowerment these Holocaust theologians were faced with a unique challenge in the history of Jewish thought. He writes, "Suffice it to say here that Holocaust theology emerged out of a situation of powerlessness that demanded a mobilization of psychic energy and material activity toward empowerment; the dialectic of Holocaust and empowerment acted as a counterbalance and a critique of weakness and empire. However, it did not have within it a way of analyzing power once achieved."[21] According to Ellis, the powerlessness that provided the foundation for Holocaust theology demanded Jewish empowerment, but this theology did not know what to do with power once achieved. He makes a further point in his description of the state of Holocaust theology today: "A strange paradox ensued . . . : a theology which poses the most radical religious and ethical questions functions politically in a neo-conservative manner."[22]

In these characterizations Ellis is not entirely accurate. Holocaust theologians, including Fackenheim, do in fact have a way of analyzing Jewish power. The assertion of the need for continuing Jewish empowerment is not identical to the absence of political analysis; rather it is an analysis with which Ellis disagrees. Nevertheless, Ellis' critique of Holocaust theology is strongest when he emphasizes the need for the acceptance and consideration of a wider spectrum of political views with regard to Israel. Ellis explains, "An underlying strain in Holocaust theology sees the world as hostile to Jewish interests and survival. Therefore any public criticism of Jewish empowerment endangers the survival of the Jewish people."[23] There is an inherent danger in the possibility that unquestioning support for Israeli political and military policy is demanded for authentic Jewish identity. Here Ellis' point echoes Rubenstein's argument that Fackenheim's formulation of the 614th commandment excludes other valid Jewish viewpoints.

According to Ellis, authentic Jewish identity includes not only the recognition of the need for Jewish empowerment after the Holocaust, but also the commitment to help create a world in which no other powerless community suffers or is oppressed, particularly by Jewish powers. Ellis asserts, "A Jewish theology of liberation must insist that the issue of anti-Semitism survives and be confronted at every opportunity. At the same time, however, it must refuse to use anti-Semitism as an ideological weapon to instill fear and counter legitimate criticism. The slogan 'Never Again' too often becomes the rationale for refusing to trust and to risk."[24] He continues, "A Jewish theology of liberation affirms empowerment with the proviso that one must affirm the empowerment of others as well. Israel, as an autonomous and powerful presence in the Middle East, is firmly established. What is needed, however, is the story of Israel's empowerment, a story that includes the injustices inflicted on the Palestinian people."[25]

It is admirable and courageous to assert that empowerment must include all those who are suffering and oppressed. However, to state that the existence of Israel is "firmly established" ignores Palestinian and other calls for its destruction as well as efforts to carry out such calls. Furthermore, the story of Israel's empowerment does indeed include acts of injustice perpetrated upon Palestinians. It also includes the dogged determination and precarious military victories of Israelis made necessary by Arab acts of aggression against Israel through the years. As Ellis asserts, it is far too simplistic for anyone to emphasize one side of the story at the expense of ignoring the other. To my understanding, though at differing ends of the political spectrum, neither Fackenheim nor Ellis is really guilty of this simplistic perspective. I believe Ellis is aware of the complexities involved here, and takes the position he does in large part as a counterbalance to the tendencies of Fackenheim's generation.

Ellis' advocacy of Palestinian human rights is an expression of his commitment to the social justice movements associated with liberation theologies.[26] Ellis creatively develops his Jewish theology of liberation by linking Holocaust theology and liberation theology, taking the voices of Palestinians as a central source.[27] As Ellis admits, tensions between Jewish thought and liberation theologies exist. Jewish thinkers have not embraced liberation theology for at least three reasons. First, politically, some Jewish thinkers may be wary of liberation theology's third world perspective, which attacks imperialism and neocolonialism and is often seen as an anti-Semitic threat. Israel is often grouped with the United States as the target of the political analysis of liberation theologies. Second, theologically, liberation theology's claim that God acts in history for the oppressed seems to be another form of Christian triumphalism that ignores the Jewish suffering and destruction during the Holocaust. Ellis explains this point: "On the one hand, the Exodus—God who rescues the people from bondage—is contradicted by the Holocaust event; on the other hand, the need for empowerment renders prophetic voices naïve and even dangerous."[28] Finally, liberation theologians ignore the existence of Jews in the contemporary world. Ellis states:

> In most liberation theologies the Jewish Exodus is used as a paradigm of revolution, but contemporary Jews as nowhere to be found in the writings of the theologians. This continues an age-old Christian tradition of seeing the Jewish people as bequeathing the "Old Testament" and Jesus and then disappearing from history, their mission accomplished. The use of the Jewish story is coupled with our historical invisibility. Thus, liberation theologians often miss an element crucial to the Exodus story itself: that it has a history of interpretation by the people who lived the story and who live today.[29]

One way in which to move constructively within these tensions, as Ellis puts it, is to look to similarities of the experience between Jews during the Holocaust and the oppressed of modern society.[30] Ellis explains that such a comparison does not seek to "mitigate the unique quality of historical events, nor does it encourage a superficial universalism." To illustrate his linking of the events of oppression during the Holocaust and modern day Latin America, Ellis compellingly juxtaposes accounts from a Jewish mother provided during the 1961 Eichmann trial and from a pastoral worker in Guatemala in the 1980s. He also compares descriptions of resistance movements from both communities, in this case Warsaw Ghetto fighters and Nicaraguan peasants.[31] Though too long to cite here, Ellis' use of these stories is exemplary of his efforts to point out similarities between the histories of these various communities. The paralleling of the accounts effectively joins the stories of oppression, despair, and resistance by overcoming the genuine differences between the situations through an appeal to human dignity and freedom. One cannot read these individual accounts without realizing the likenesses and the potential for solidarity. Ellis' point is to show that Jewish suffering during the Holocaust is comparable to the contemporary suffering of Latin Americans, African Americans, and Palestinians.

This effective comparison demands Jewish-Christian dialogue and solidarity in the name of justice, according to Ellis. He asserts that a Jewish encounter with Christian liberation theology would serve to remind Jews of their historical commitment to social justice and to enrich their identity in a way that does not perpetuate systems of oppression and suffering. Ellis writes, "If Holocaust theology placed the essential question of Christian life before the Christian community, that is, what does it mean to be a Christian after Auschwitz, Christian liberation theology placed the essential question of Jewish life before the Jewish community, that is, what does it mean to be Jewish after Auschwitz and within empowerment?"[32] Ellis calls for a new Jewish theology in the light of contemporary suffering and oppression.

Ellis outlines six features of his new Jewish theology of liberation. First, there is a "tension between particularity and universality as a self-critical voice that comes from the depths of the Jewish tradition and seeks to serve the world." Second, it must engage historical realities and events and not seek to too easily transcend the world. Third, this theology must be inclusive of differing voices, including women, secular Jews, and those who critique Israeli social and political policies. Fourth, "Jewish theology has no choice but to balance the survival of the Jewish people with the preservation of its message of community." Fifth, "Jewish theology requires the recovery of Jewish witness against idolatry as testimony to life in its private and public dimensions, as the essential bond of Jews everywhere, and as the fundamental link to religious and humanist communities of good will around the globe." Finally, this theology must serve as a "call to *teshuvah*: commitment and solidarity in all their pain and possibility, as well as a critical understanding of the history we are creating and the courage it takes to change the course of that history."[33]

Like Fackenheim, Ellis asserts that the Holocaust and Jewish empowerment call into question traditional understandings of Jewish identity. The attempt to include secular Jews in their definitions is remarkable. They differ of course in the basis for this inclusivity. For Fackenheim, authentic Jewish identity has been seen to be based theoretically on the commitment to not to grant Hitler posthumous victories by despairing of God or humanity and practically on the refusal to negotiate the character of Israel. For Ellis, Judaism must not be equated with Zionism. According to Ellis, a Jewish theology of liberation must be cognizant of the dangers of Jewish empowerment in both Israel and in the United States. For Ellis, authentic Jewish identity involves solidarity with the oppressed of the land, whether they are Jews during the Holocaust or the Latin American poor and the Palestinians of today. Ellis asserts that Jews today must not repeat the oppression that was suffered during the Holocaust by their own continuing acts of oppression today in the name of empowerment.

For Fackenheim, the Holocaust was a unique event and incomparable with other forms of oppression and suffering, including the situation of Palestinians today. Fackenheim would not be so quick to view Jewish suffering as relegated to only the past. As he would see it, the precarious situation of Israel in the midst of its Arab neighbors continues to raise the specter of Jewish destruction even now. It is the Jews of today, not just during the Holocaust who are under constant threat of annihilation, according to this view. In contrast, Ellis asserts a dialectic of suffering Jews during the Holocaust and empowered Jews today in Israel. No longer suffering and oppressed, Jews today are called to solidarity with those who are powerless and down-trodden. The sufferings of the Holocaust are not wholly unique, Ellis claims. There are links among various forms and events of oppression. As a community that has suffered oppression for thousands of years, Jews are in a unique position to end the cycles of oppression and death.[34]

Though the linking of Holocaust theology and liberation theology sets a helpful precedent for this work, I find that I disagree with aspects of Ellis' perspective. Just as it is foolish not to recognize modern Jews as empowered oppressors of other communities (Palestinians, South Africans under apartheid), as Ellis asserts,[35] it is shortsighted to interpret Israel and modern Jews as identical to other situations of empowered oppressors (eg., the United States). The substantial contemporary power of the Jewish community is unlike that of any other if in no other regard than the fact that the Holocaust raised the possibility of the end of Jewish existence and the potential for any type of Jewish empowerment. As Fackenheim explained, Israel, though no answer to the Holocaust, is a response. Viewed in this light, Israel is subject to the same political and ethical criticisms as any other nation is. However, one must also recognize the importance and need of the existence of Israel as a safe haven for worldwide Jewry and as a political expression of Jewish empowerment in a world that has attempted, and nearly succeeded, in destroying Jewish existence.

While Fackenheim refused to accept the comparison between the Holocaust and contemporary acts of oppression, Ellis compellingly links Jewish suffering then with Latin American, African American, and Palestinian suffering today. Though there are important differences among these communities, there are important similarities too. For example, the notion of resistance to dehumanization and the demand for the recognition of the full dignity and humanity of each individual and each community, though always distinctive and particular, link the situations. The important contributions of Ellis' work include the comparison of these forms of suffering and resistance and the hope that the Israeli expression of political empowerment would also include a courageous effort at ensuring justice and mercy for all.

Like Ellis, Melissa Raphael challenges the theological dominance of Fackenheim, Rubenstein, and others in an effort to improve upon and diversify Jewish interpretations of the Holocaust. In the next section, Raphael's critique of patriarchal notions of God and her own assertion of divine presence during the Holocaust in the form of mutually caring relationships among women is explored.

Melissa Raphael: A Feminist Jewish Post-Holocaust Theology

Emil Fackenheim, Richard Rubenstein, and other post-Holocaust theologians encountered a theological crisis in their experiences of God's absence, impotence, or even death during the Holocaust. For many, the horrors of Auschwitz denied the existence of God or at least demanded a rethinking of God, humanity, and Israel. For Fackenheim, God was present during the Holocaust as the Commanding Voice of Auschwitz; Rubenstein declared the death of the God of history and the covenant and the vitality of God as Holy Nothingness. Though certainly viewing the Holocaust as no less a theological crisis, Melissa Raphael asserts that Fackenheim, Rubenstein, and other male post-Holocaust theologians were struggling with how to reconcile the Holocaust with a particular understanding of God, a God of patriarchy. Raphael argues that the thought of this previous generation of thinkers does not resonate with her because these thinkers have largely ignored the experiences of Jewish women during and since the Holocaust. The cost of this failure is the inability to conceive of God as fully present to Israel both during and after the Holocaust in relationships of mutual care. Employing women's Holocaust memoir literature, Raphael develops a theology of *Shekhinah* (the female aspect of divine presence) that focuses on the caring relationships among women exhibited in acts such as the washing of the face and body of another person, and in acts of mending and sewing. Like Fackenheim, Raphael builds on the Lurianic kabbalistic category of *tikkun*; she argues that these seemingly ordinary acts are in fact simultaneously evidence of divine presence and evocative of the presence of the divine even in Auschwitz, making possible a mending of the ruptures in history, humanity, and within God. Rather than offering a full-out challenge to Fackenheim's theology, Raphael supplements his theology with the range of experiences and acts of resistance of Jews during the Holocaust. When these experiences are explored theologically, Raphael's resulting model of God allows for a creative and exciting way in which to understand the divine-human relationship and acts of resistance as restoring creation and the divine, as well as providing an ethical demand for care of the other.

Melissa Raphael challenges Fackenheim and other male post-Holocaust theologians, because they have developed their reconsiderations of God and Israel with little or no attempt to take into account the experiences of Jewish women during and since the Holocaust. Much like Delores Williams' simultaneous critiques of male black theology and white feminist theology, Raphael felt her own consideration of the Holocaust from a feminist perspective filled a void in the sense that Holocaust thinkers had ignored feminism and Jewish feminist theologians had largely ignored the Holocaust.[36]

Raphael asserts that male post-Holocaust thought is patriarchal in at least five ways.[37] First, Holocaust theology has conceived of God as standing over history so that "its function is to secure the sovereignty of God's name." Second, it is patriarchal to claim the political and military strength of the state of Israel to be a sign of divine providence. Third, the positing of the centrality of autonomy and free will to the conception of human nature as a defense for the lack of divine response to human suffering is characteristic of patriarchal thought. Fourth, post-Holocaust thought is "markedly androcentric in its model of God and its historical focus." Fifth and finally, in its "protesting God's failure to be patriarchal *enough*," post-Holocaust theology indicates both the hope that God would have entered history to decisively save Jews during the Holocaust, or at least punish the abusers, and a disappointment and an anger that this did not come to pass.[38]

To unpack these general claims about male post-Holocaust theologians, Raphael treats several of these thinkers, including Fackenheim, individually. Raphael's central criticism of Fackenheim's theology is that, because he failed to fully consider the experiences of Jewish women during the Holocaust, his formulation and articulation of the Commanding Voice of Auschwitz seem to be another effort to conceive of God as a powerful entity who barks orders to his audience. The form of divine presence as commanding presence further grinds Jewish personhood to the ground and tries to beat Hitler at his own game. Raphael explains:

[C]onsidering the mode and possibility of divine presence in Auschwitz from a relational perspective, did its inmates want, and do we now want, to hear another commanding voice in or from Auschwitz, where women and men were continuously berated, shouted and sworn at by their *Kommandant* and those who did his bidding? Does a Jew want to feel that she is still under orders, subjected to another overbearing masculine will? Fackenheim styles his God the "Commanding Voice of Auschwitz," but the Jewish people were surely subject to enough raucous commands in that place. The commanding voices of its atrocious hierarchy were infinitely more than enough. A German *Kommandant* who knew and watched suffering and did nothing to stop it bears too close a resemblance for comfort to a God who commands Jewry to remain Jewish but does not command Germany to call a halt to the agonies it has commanded . . . . Jewry was caught in a deafening cross-fire of command and countermand—the one bearing a disquieting formal similarity to the other.[39]

In addition to objecting to the form of divine presence and its implications, Raphael also raises the particular issue of how Jewish women are to understand and respond to Fackenheim's Commanding Voice of Auschwitz.

Echoing the insights of Judith Plaskow and Rachel Adler when they question Jewish women's identity and obligation to the covenant, given their restricted access to the male community of Israel and thus to divine revelation and presence at Sinai, Raphael asks, "What does it mean for a woman to hear and obey God's commandment in the second Sinai of Auschwitz when she was not there to receive the revelation of Torah at first?" The fact that Fackenheim ignored the restriction of Jewish women from normative Jewish life, including understandings of prayer, study, and worship, is belied in his choice to conceive of divine presence during the Holocaust as commanding presence. Raphael asserts, "Only where the Jewish God is also called by her female names and pronoun will her voice be heard by all Jews because a God made exclusively in the masculine image is always calling over women's shoulder to someone else."[40]

Related to Raphael's central critique of Fackenheim's failure to include the experiences of Jewish women during the Holocaust in his conception of divine presence as commanding is her support of Marc Ellis' problematizing of Fackenheim's support for the state of Israel. Raphael writes, "In their different ways, most post-Holocaust thinkers—whether conservative or liberal—have offered the establishment of a Jewish state as (effectively) a substantial compensation for the Holocaust." She goes on, "Even if Jewish feminism supports at least the principle of Israel as a homeland for Jews, it would not, particularly from an early twenty-first century perspective, invoke territorial acquisition and the conflict and suffering it has spawned as a providential sign, compensating for the depthless suffering of the Holocaust or redeeming God from unbelief." In addition to Ellis' concern over Palestinian rights, Raphael adds that the state of Israel has "perpetuated gender and intra-ethnic inequalities."[41] Though not unique to Israeli culture, Raphael's point is that such injustices prevent even tentative claims to contemporary Israeli society as above reproach.

Though valid in her assessment of remaining gender and ethnic injustices, Raphael misreads Fackenheim's understanding of the state of Israel. Fackenheim saw Israel as a human, Jewish *response* to the 614th commandment, certainly not as "compensation" for the Holocaust. For Fackenheim, the notion of compensation for the Holocaust is inadequate and obscene. God is present in Israel as commanding presence; Jews are to respond to this presence in their efforts to prevent a second Holocaust. In his later work, Fackenheim moved toward the notion that God is also evident as saving presence in human acts of *tikkun*. Though perhaps other male post-Holocaust thinkers are subject to Raphael's criticism, Fackenheim is not. If Raphael's critique of Fackenheim's theology bears weight, it is in the respect that Fackenheim does not specifically develop his foundational notion of divine presence with both Jewish men *and* women in mind.

Raphael's argument that post-Holocaust theology has neglected Jewish women is persuasive and fascinatingly full of new theological possibilities. Her own constructive theology is built on the memoirs of Jewish women during the Holocaust. It is in these writings that Raphael finds evidence for her notion of divine presence in women's relationships of mutual care.[42] In these relationships, in which women cared for one another through kind and selfless activities such as washing of the face and mending of garments, God's presence as *Shekhinah* became manifest. Within the Talmudic and later kabbalistic traditions, *Shekhinah* is used to refer to divine presence, particularly in its feminine characteristics. Raphael explains, "The Shekhinah traditionally marks Judaism's faith in God's immanence. As the attribute of presence, Shekhinah's does not make God identical with the world. God's transcendence ensures that the divine will and purpose are unconditioned by human evil, while God's immanence ensures that humanity can become God's partner (*shuttaf*) in bringing God's purposes to fulfillment in the immanent realm."[43] Thus the question, where was God during the Holocaust? is rephrased as *who* was God?

Raphael's answer is that the divine was present as *Shekhinah*, sustaining caring human relationships and simultaneously being restored by these human activities.

Raphael draws on the same Lurianic principles of divine-human relationship and *tikkun* as Fackenheim had done earlier.[44] Raphael explains, "Later Jewish mysticism is founded upon doctrines of creation and redemption where at creation God empties God-self of God so as to enter into a relationship with the world which will not absorb it into the totality of Godhead. And this God's creation will only be redeemed by the mutuality of divine and human labor; the world is mended not solely from above but also from below."[45] The importance of human activity for the process of redemption is evident in Fackenheim's theology as we have seen earlier. It is the *type* of activity that distinguishes Raphael's understanding of *tikkun* from Fackenheim's. Whereas for Fackenheim, maintenance of Jewish identity, resistance to despair, and support for Israel are acts of restoration, for Raphael, interpersonal relationships between women served a redemptive purpose.

Raphael suggests, "If God is, as it were, completed by the creation of humanity in God's image and restored by the human recreation of humanity in God's image, perhaps, for some, it was less a question of how God might have been present to Jewry in the Holocaust, but how Jewry might have been present to God."[46] Patterned after the divine-human relationship of mutuality in redemptive efforts, it is in mutually caring relationships among humans that Raphael finds that Jewry was present to God even during the Holocaust. She persuasively argues, "It seems possible to discern a causal relationship between the holiness of women's relational acts in Auschwitz and God's self-manifestation or presence."[47] In a context in which Nazism sought to destroy human dignity, family and nonfamily relationships, and notions of purity through "excremental assault," the refusal to allow one's personhood or that of others to be diminished, the efforts to forge caring relationships with individuals sentenced to likely death, and the attempt to maintain a psychological and physical sense of cleanliness are all incredibly courageous acts of resistance, Raphael asserts.

Through the use of Jewish women's memoirs, Raphael relates some of the methods the Nazis employed to prevent the formation and sustenance of relationships among concentration camp inmates. She explains, "Genocide is the murder of a people not only by killing but by breaking its solidarities, erasing its past and terminating its future."[48] An ethic of every person for herself was instilled in inmates as food, water, and supplies were stingily distributed. Families were separated by gender; the elderly, sick, children, and mothers of young children were regularly killed immediately upon arrival at a camp. Raphael cites, "A woman simply standing next to a child, or looking after someone else's child could be sent to the gas. In short, although mothers, daughters, and sisters within an approximate age range could enter Auschwitz together, a woman whose death was postponed by her selection for labour was intended to be a woman already divested of dependent relationships."[49] The torture and murder of family members, the tattooing of a number on one's arm as identification, the loss of otherwise simple personal items including photographs, and the terror of the unknown made caring interpersonal relationships among Jews in the camp seemingly impossible. That such relationships did exist in the face of such conditions indicates nothing less than divine presence, according to Raphael.

One example of such a relationship presented by Raphael is the *Zehnerschaft* ("group of ten"). This group, formed in the Plaszow labor camp in 1943, was made up of mostly young Orthodox women. Raphael describes, "Significantly, the women of the *Zehnerschaft* did not limit their assistance to members of their own circle but, during the two years they were together, endangered their own lives to help other women by sharing food, a broken lice comb and other precious commodities, regardless of whether these other women were observant Jews."[50] Though implicitly limited to *Jewish* women in Raphael's account, this example nevertheless may begin to provide support for a notion of resistance carried out by individuals who are not typically found in solidarity with one another.[51]

Along with the many other stories of selfless and compassionate group solidarity that Raphael relates, this example may validly be interpreted as having theological significance. Citing Judith Tydor Baumel, Raphael claims, "Care was not merely expedient, nor wholly a product of oppressive gender ideology, but was integral to the whole of Jewish religious, political and cultural life, as underpinned by the values of *hesed* (kindness)."[52] Raphael goes on to explain how these acts of kindness are acts of resistance and restoration: "*Hesed* was a way of seeing and recreating a woman's full humanity. As such, it was an act of resistance: a faithfulness to the image of God in her suffering face and a judgment on the gross inhumanity that sought to make any person less than human. *Hesed* presented God by holding up the image of God in the restored image of the human."[53] Similar to Fackenheim's understanding of divine command and human response, Raphael's notion of divine presence both depends on and also grounds human acts of mutual care. She writes, "In Auschwitz, the revelation of the human(e) *as presence to the other* was entirely dependent upon the real presence of God as that to which the human other was agonizingly transparent. For the same reasons, the presence of God was entirely dependent on our showing ourselves to have been human(e)."[54] One particular act of kindness Raphael interprets in this way is the washing of another's body and face.

Raphael asserts that activities carried out to maintain a semblance of normalcy or to sustain one's personhood may be interpreted as ways to maintain the image of God among persons and to conjure divine presence. The Jewish men Fackenheim highlighted maintained and asserted their Jewish identity through Torah study and prayer, typically male manifestations, given the gender divisions of traditional Judaism. Jewish women, however, did not practice the religion in the same ways. Therefore, Raphael asserts, we must look for ways in which Jewish women had always manifested their religious identities, through the purification and sanctification of the family and home. She explains, "Wherever women maintained the even notional purity of Israel before God by relationship or the cleaning that is a function of relationship, they sanctified Auschwitz and carried on Israel's covenantal task of making the world fit for the indwelling of God."[55] According to this understanding, when women cared for other people by cleaning them, they struggled to remain holy, pure, and in this sense, fully human. Raphael writes, "In the holocaustal context, washing should not only be understood as the physical act of wiping away material dirt in the rare instances that that was possible; rather it could be an act of *seeing through* Nazism and seeing through the effects of Nazism to the divine image reflected in the darkened mirror of the suffering human face."[56] In the act of washing another's face, the Jewish women from whom Raphael draws theological insight resisted the fate of Levi's *Muselmanner* and the onslaughts of the "excremental assault"; they manifested their own full humanity *and* that of the other; they helped make manifest the very presence of God.

Through acts of resistance these women struggled toward redemption. For it is through mutually caring relationships that, in a sense, we are re-created in God's image. Where full humanity is manifested, God as *Shekhinah* is present and redemption is possible even during and after the Holocaust. Raphael explains:

> The sanctification of the world through the redemption and restoration
> of the divine image from the pit of holocaustal impurity is a revelation

of God's face/presence that is also a revelation of the human face/presence because when humankind is truly human, God is known as God: the very essence of the eschaton. The face/presence of God is also the face/presence of our redeemed humanity, knowable in the world. The revelation of the human being as a divinely created person, not an object or means, reunites the creatures and the creator, closing the circle between creation and redemption.[57]

As Fackenheim had, Raphael employs the Lurianic concept of *tikkun olam*. Human acts of care, love, purity, mending, and resistance to despair and dehumanization draw forth divine presence and in the process help build a mending or restoration of the world and the divine. Unlike Fackenheim however, Raphael finds the primary examples of acts of *tikkun* in the midst of Jewish *women's* experiences during the Holocaust.

Raphael's theology both challenges and complements Fackenheim's thought. She asserts that Fackenheim and his generation of theologians continued their use of patriarchal notions of humanity and divinity and ignored the experiences of women during the Holocaust. As a result, theirs was a God who was not patriarchal enough; in other words, God understood as all-powerful, dominating presence has always been a model of God that failed to reflect women's experiences of the divine as caring, relational, and subtle sustaining presence. Fackenheim's assertion of God as Commanding Voice of Auschwitz is replaced with God as *Shekhinah*, present primarily in and through human acts of care, love, and mending. Like Fackenheim then, for Raphael divine presence is evident through human acts of resistance and *tikkun*, but it is a different conception of presence being made manifest through different acts of resistance and *tikkun*.[58]

Michael L. Morgan: Jewish Theology in the Twenty-First Century

Now that we have examined three critiques of Emil Fackenheim's thought, we turn our attention to a contemporary proponent and student of his, Michael L. Morgan. Paralleling Dwight Hopkins' relationship to James Cone, Morgan serves the purpose of developing original Jewish theology from the foundation provided by Fackenheim. Largely following Fackenheim's work, Morgan explores the state of

Jewish thought in the twenty-first century. Like Fackenheim, one of Morgan's central concerns is whether it is possible to formulate a theology and ethics that remains faithful to historical realities, especially the Holocaust while simultaneously appealing to a transcendent source. Morgan analyzes Fackenheim's thoughts on this issue and explores how developments in Fackenheim's work over time make such a theology possible and necessary. Building particularly on shifts evident between Fackenheim's writings of the late 1960s and his *To Mend the World* (1982), Morgan too asks whether an authentic Jewish response to the Holocaust is possible and if it is, what grounds such a response. Morgan's "interim Judaism" no longer finds the pre-Holocaust Jewish conceptions of God, human nature, revelation, or covenant to be adequate, nor new understandings of these categories to be satisfactory as of now. After an examination of Morgan's interpretation of aspects of Fackenheim's work, we briefly look at the content and direction of Morgan's own constructive work. As was the section on Hopkins above, this section is not so much as a critique of Fackenheim's work as a way of showing the nature and content of one trajectory of Fackenheim's thought.

Though Morgan has written several essays and articles on modern Jewish thought and on major modern thinkers, including Spinoza, Mendelssohn, and Buber, among others,[59] his primary focus has been on post-Holocaust Jewish thought, Emil Fackenheim in particular.[60] Morgan describes Fackenheim's "crucial shift" from before 1967 when he understood Jewish faith to be irrefutable in regard to historical contingencies to after 1967 when Fackenheim "came to realize that nothing in Judaism is immune to historical alteration and even refutation." He continues, "In 1967, [Fackenheim] came to speak of the Midrashic framework as being open to historical modification and of Jewish faith as exposed to history, and especially to the extremities of human possibility. Once this openness is admitted, only then can the atrocities, the horror, the radical evil of the Nazi Holocaust be honestly and seriously confronted."[61] Morgan helpfully interprets Fackenheim's writings on the Holocaust to be in three stages after 1967. The first stage includes Fackenheim's initial writings on the Holocaust, including *Quest for Past and Future* (1968) and *God's Presence in History* (1970). Stage two includes Fackenheim's interpretations of modern philosophy in the light of the Holocaust in his *Encounters between Judaism and Modern Philosophy* (1973) and the collected essays on his further reflections on the Holocaust in *The Jewish Return into History* (1978). Finally, the third stage, which is evident in his *To Mend the World* (1982), is characterized by the rethinking and re-forming of his previous work. Since the present work is most concerned with Morgan's most complete statement on the Holocaust and his writing, I focus here on his understanding of the developments in Fackenheim's thought as they are expressed in this third stage.

In the first stage of his reflections on the Holocaust, Fackenheim had taken for granted that there could be a Jewish response to the horrors of Auschwitz, argues Morgan. The question for Fackenheim at that point was not whether a response was possible, but rather how such a response could be actual.

As Morgan points out, Fackenheim's earlier conception of the commanding Voice of Auschwitz was largely unfounded. In other words, Morgan asks of the early Fackenheim, what grounds the imperative to respond through resistance? For, if thought itself is ruptured in the encounter with the Holocaust, "what we want to know of Fackenheim's obligations is how secure their grounding is, the grounds that is for the obligation to oppose this evil, the conditions that make such opposition possible and the results that flow from it."[62] For Fackenheim, in his early writings, resistance must be based on a non-human, externally imposed commandment. However, Morgan writes, Fackenheim "reaches his conclusions too hastily, both the fact that the imperative is imposed and that it is a commandment."[63] In other words, faith must precede this imposed commandment, and yet the commandment itself is the very basis of faith, which along with thought has been ruptured by this epoch-making event.

Morgan explains:

Indeed, perhaps even the claim that opposition requires an imperative is already too hasty. Why not a reaction to threat? Or a repugnance to a storied ugliness or hatred? In part, Fackenheim's problem arises because he directs thought, once stopped in its tracks, to turn to subsequent Jewish life in order to seek guidance about a response. Such life is not clearly a response, nor is it based on more than defiance or revulsion or conformity, at least not consciously and intentionally. But in part the problem is deeper, for even once an imperative of opposition is identified, its *ground* is not so easily got. It may be clear that in order to pick out its subjects and in order not to be conditioned by human will it must be *imposed* from the outside and also enabled from the outside. But if faith is not yet assumed, what grounds its status as imposed? What, in different terms, makes it both possible and necessary? What gives opposition its realism and authority?[64]

Morgan points out that by his *To Mend the World*, Fackenheim found that his prior understanding, relying on either a Kantian imperative or a neo-orthodox understanding of commandment, was "glib and insensitive."[65] By the late 1970s and early 1980s, Fackenheim had come to question whether authentic Jewish response to the Holocaust was at all possible.

In *To Mend the World* Fackenheim, drawing on Primo Levi's description of the *musselmanner*, those neither living nor dead, questioned whether human response to the Holocaust is possible when there is no human to respond. As Morgan describes, "This is not merely a question about freedom; it is about the resources for dignity, a sense of selfhood, of value, of importance, of strength, and of courage."[66] If these resources and senses are absent, from what may a person draw to respond? The Holocaust universe sought self-dehumanization of Jews to the point that there could be no response, let alone resistance, because there would be no person. To speak of post-Holocaust response today without response during the event would be groundless and false. As stated in chapter 4, post-Holocaust response is possible today only because it was actual during the Holocaust itself.

At the limits of thought, Fackenheim turned to the actual, concrete lives of Holocaust victims and survivors. For, it is in the experiences of these people that any theory must find its foundation. Morgan writes, "Post-Holocaust Jewish thought is authentic only if it is realized in post-Holocaust resistance to the horrors of Auschwitz, and this is possible only because both resisting thought and active resistance as responses to a grasp of the event and to a sense of an imperative to resist, were actual in the midst of the event itself."[67] In this way, Fackenheim now based both the imperative to resist and the possibility of resistance on the fact that response in the form of resistance actually occurred.

Fackenheim's claim that Jewish resistance as response to the Holocaust is possible today because it actually happened during the event provides the basis for Michael Morgan's own constructive enterprise. With Fackenheim's work lending a framework, Morgan explores the nature and content of Jewish thought and life in the twenty-first century. Just as Fackenheim had understood, Morgan argues that Judaism must continually reflect on its transcendent and historical past as well as correlate this tradition with contemporary social and historical realities.

Morgan names contemporary Jewish life as "interim Judaism." Judaism in the interim lies between a certainty of the past, when faith in God as transcendent and in covenant with Israel could be accepted as a given, and a simultaneous doubt in and hope for the present and future, when such faith is challenged if not ruptured by the Holocaust. Morgan explains that an interim Judaism

> is not one consolidated around a "grand theory" or some single, comprehensive understanding of the central Jewish themes of revelation and redemption. In a sense, it is a Jewish life "without clear concepts of revelation and redemption," but not because Judaism can do without these notions permanently but rather because Judaism today must continue for the moment without them. In this sense, the Judaism I have in mind is pragmatic, independent of theory, and interim.[68]

Morgan analyzes three particular aspects of interim Judaism: the problem of objectivity, the search for transcendence, and messianism and politics. These three issues are not unique to the twenty-first century, and in fact much of Morgan's *Interim Judaism* (2001) is focused on the early twentieth-century intellectual world. Morgan simply makes the claim that these issues are still relevant today, and must be reexamined in the light of the Holocaust and contemporary developments such as postmodernism.

Morgan understands the problem of objectivity and the search for transcendence to be characteristic of interim Judaism.[69] Given the events of the two World Wars, the Holocaust, and other political and social realities, there is a general sense that society has lost its bearings. There is no adequate account of unity, purpose, or meaning, according to this way of thinking. The horrors and vicissitudes of history have destroyed any ground of objectivity, any basis for transcendent truth claims, or any hope of redemption. Morgan writes, "Redemption of this kind is a matter of orientation, the goal of a life that has some directedness. Such orientation, by its very nature must be objective. If it were not, then that which gives our lives direction and meaning would change and thus the direction would change, thereby condemning it to instability; or the ground of orientation would depend upon varying or diverse conditions, which would make it insecure and unreliable; or the ground of orientation would be different for different individuals or groups and thus would involve competing claims to direction."[70] This characteristically modern problem of a lack of objectivity is heightened for Judaism in the light of the Holocaust.

For after the Holocaust what could possibly be the basis for faith in God, humankind, covenant, or redemption? In Morgan's words, "After the Holocaust, objectivity is both more dubious and more necessary than it had seemed before . . . . [T]he old problematic of objectivity and relativism, as we have called it, is now deepened and dramatized. After Auschwitz, no principles can be unconditional, and yet some must be. This paradox is the new crisis of objectivity that faces us."[71] Following Fackenheim's argument in *To Mend the World*, Morgan also turns to lived experience when thought reaches a limiting paradox.

Based on thought alone, it may seem paradoxical or impossible to locate an objective ground for reality and for faith in God, humanity, and redemption after the Holocaust. However, it is in the lives of Jews who maintain faith in God, hope for humanity, and expectation of redemption, that Morgan finds the ground of objectivity today. Morgan asserts, "The goal is to understand what the Jew's relationship to the Jewish past is and should be, what the relationship to Jewish texts, tradition, and learning is, what the relationship is to communities, and ultimately to God. As for what objectivity means to people and where its grounds lie—these things are not abstract intellectual problems. Rather, they will arise out of lived experience with communities, texts, traditions, rituals, and indeed with God."[72] That the basis of objectivity and the possibility of access to the Jewish past are founded on the activities of those who simply carry out these processes despite the lack of a theory for doing so makes this approach to the problem of objectivity only an interim position. Morgan looks toward a future in which a return to the Jewish past and tradition and a rediscovery of transcendence will not be antithetical to an honest facing of historical realities, primarily the Holocaust.

In addition to the problem of objectivity and the search for transcendence, another aspect of interim Judaism Morgan explicates is the relationship between messianism and politics. At issue here is the relationship between human social and political movements and ultimate, eternal realities and processes. Just as historical events such as the two World Wars and the Holocaust raise the problem of objectivity and make the search for transcendence difficult, they also undermine any utopian social movements or programs that claim the reality and inevitability of the perfection of human society. The Holocaust challenges one's faith not only in God, but also in humanity. After the Holocaust, Morgan asks, how are we to understand the role of human efforts aimed at redemption? Further, what is the role of the state of Israel in this process? Morgan is interested here in the dialectic involved in the traditional Jewish understanding of the role of human activity in bringing about the messianic age. It is said, by some, that the messiah will come when humans have bettered the world as much as possible, and by others, that the messiah will come when humans have done as much evil as society can bear.

After reviewing several modern Jewish understandings of the relationship between politics and redemption, including Buber, Rosenzweig, and Fackenheim, Morgan asserts that human history does in some way contribute to social and cosmic redemption. He makes such a claim despite the revelations of the Holocaust that humanity may not be a good or strong enough foundation on which to place redemptive hopes. He explains, "After Auschwitz, it may be difficult to have faith in human capacity, but at the same time, as these thinkers might argue, it is equally difficult to abandon human capacity altogether. Whatever trust in God remains, it is certainly no stronger than our faith in humankind; while we struggle to regain the former, we must at least, as a temporary strategy, accept to some degree the latter."[73] Morgan appeals once again here, not to theory, but to the lives of Jews who struggle toward redemption regardless of whether humanity or God can bring it about in the end.

This commitment to the struggle for redemption without the assurance of its success is characteristic of interim Judaism. Morgan suggests that "American Jewish life might take the shape of an interim activism, a commitment to worldly acts that seek to repair what is broken but that are performed independently of any messianic expectations."[74] Thus, following Fackenheim, Morgan advocates that Jews act to mend the world, knowing that it will be a fragmentary mending at best, and hoping that such activity will elicit a divine response.

Morgan's characterization of an interim Jewish ethics serves as an important element in the following constructive portion of the present work. With my own temporal and existential separation from the impact of the Holocaust on all subsequent theology, I may be tempted to construct a theology that too easily maintains faith in God and humanity without a thorough recognition of what impact the Holocaust must have on these categories. With Morgan's pragmatic and interim Judaism in mind, it is understood that theology today must not try to be too grandiose and complete. His acceptance and articulation of a religious tradition that must be understood as interim in fundamental ways is courageous and admirable.

A Consideration of Humanocentric Theism, Resistance, and Redemption

This chapter, and the work as a whole really, attempts to draw resources from two primary schools of thought, post-Holocaust Jewish theology and African American liberation theology. To be sure, as we have seen in the preceding chapters, each of these theological groupings is dynamic and varied. Though, strictly speaking, this work is not an interreligious dialogue between a Jew and a Christian, it does certainly bring Jewish and Christian theologies and ethics first into parallel encounter and now into more direct conversation. Before moving into such a conversation, it is helpful and necessary to give at least brief attention to challenges involved in both black-Jewish relations and in Jewish-Christian encounters historically and today. Though there have certainly been episodes of tension between African Americans and Jews, there have also been periods of great solidarity and cooperation. Below I give some attention to periods of alliances and then also discuss some of the contentious issues. Then, after acknowledging the problematic history of the relations between Jews and Christians and the subsequent limitations and dangers of that encounter today, I explore some of the opportunities that emerge in the midst of Jewish-Christian dialogue. Though clearly any effort at multiethnic or interreligious encounter must be aware of limitations, dangers, and concerns for each side, I believe a theology that draws inspiration and ideas from these traditions can be creative and enriched as a result of such an encounter. In the second half of this chapter, I hope to draw out creative theological and ethical ideas by putting select thinkers from these traditions into conversation. The primary theologians that are utilized here include James Cone,

Emil Fackenheim, William R. Jones, Melissa Raphael, and Dwight Hopkins. In this final portion of the book I offer the theological perspective of humanocentric theism and its ethical corollary, resistance as my contribution to the entire discussion.

African American-Jewish Relations

The relationship between African Americans and Jews has been a complicated one, to say the least. At times the encounter has been fruitful and positive, at others strained and ugly. There is no single unambiguous manner in which to characterize how these two communities have interacted with one another. Further, of course, neither African Americans nor Jews constitute a monolithic, homogenous group. Even when the general tide is more positive or negative, there have always been exceptional views and thinkers involved in the conversation. Throughout their encounter there were differing views within each community about the way in which to relate to the broader American context in general and about the way in which to deal with other racial, ethnic, and religious communities in particular. There certainly were, and still are, grounds for solidarity in that both groups shared many of the concerns and interests. Both communities were often oppressed and marginalized, though in differing ways. In addition, the two groups also disagreed with one another at various points ideologically and practically in their goals as well as tactics and methods to achieve these goals. Furthermore, broader cultural, political, and historical forces could at times foster greater solidarity between blacks and Jews, and at other times exacerbate divisions. These forces include Communism, the Great Depression, Nazism, World War II, the cold war, and Israel, among others. Here, I explore some of the areas of solidarity and also raise some of the contentious issues between blacks and Jews in twentieth- and twenty-first century America.

To state the obvious, both blacks and Jews have been oppressed and marginalized, both beyond and within American borders. Eric Sundquist explains:

> By virtue of sharing the shifting margins of American life, Jews and blacks have shared perspectives on the rewards and dangers of assimilation, the vicissitudes of intermarriage and passing, and the meaning of citizenship in the face of discrimination and racist violence.

Both peoples have conceived of themselves as "chosen" and found themselves wandering "in strange lands," their primary identities derived from belonging not to a particular nation-state but instead to a religio-cultural diasporic "nation" with an identifiable set of relations to sacred texts and a lost homeland.[1]

Of course, even though both groups were "strangers in the land of America," in Sundquist's phrase, they experienced oppression and marginalization in distinctive ways. "By virtue of being or becoming 'white,' Jews, even recent immigrants, might more quickly be accepted 'as one born among' other Americans, but Judaism and Jewishness would still set them apart. By virtue of being usually Christian and often generations-long residents, blacks might lay stronger claim to being 'as one born among' other Americans, but their beginnings in slavery and their blackness would still set them apart."[2] Some of these distinctions would later be manifested in differing perspectives on subjects such as identity, integration, separatism, and assimilation.

On different, yet analogous paths for a time, it was in the early to middle parts of the twentieth century in the United States that blacks and Jews began to interact more directly with each other. At this point, there was into America an influx of Jewish immigrants leaving Europe in the wake of the rise of Nazism and an almost simultaneous, but unrelated, migration of blacks northward into urban areas.[3] Encountering Jews fleeing Nazi persecution, African Americans expressed empathy and frequently identified their own experiences in America with those of the ancient Israelites and modern Jews. Stretching back to the antebellum period, the black use of Jewish themes such as slavery, exodus, chosenness, exile, and Zion, was now again in evidence in the experiences of Jewish immigrants in ways that many blacks could readily identify.[4] Also, some African Americans saw in the Nazi Holocaust just how terrifyingly far racialized oppression and violence could be carried. Finally, in the light of such destruction as well as their own experiences in America, blacks recognized the necessity of a geographical homeland, and were often very sympathetic to Zionism at this time.[5]

On the other side, Jews were in a unique position to understand the severity of black oppression and the need for political resistance against it. In American racism, oppression, and violence, Jews could recognize their own experiences over time, and especially during the

Holocaust. In regard to Jewish American identity, Eric Sundquist explains, "Hewing between the poles of colored and white, race and its absence, Jews were driven to a stronger identification with whiteness by the lingering pressures of anti-semitism but at the same time were lured, often for the same reason, toward affinity with blacks—not only with their suffering, but also with their uncompromising demand for political power, their artistic invention, their supposed sensuality, or their hipness."[6]

In the wake of the Holocaust both Jews and blacks recognized the wisdom and the practical necessity of solidarity with the other community. While blacks saw in Nazism the potential for such destruction by the white power structure in America; Jews learned that it would be wise to be in solidarity with non-Jews, if only for the sake of greater numbers. Both groups now saw the need for political action and alliances of all sorts, particularly with one another.[7]

Though evident from around the 1920s or so onward, it was especially during the civil rights movement that black-Jewish alliances flourished. Remembered by many as the "Golden Age" of black-Jewish relations, the motivations for each community during this period could be characterized as a mix of altruism and self-interest.[8] Cheryl Lynn Greenberg writes:

> For liberal and progressive black and Jewish leaders, previous positive experiences of cooperation that created greater familiarity and sympathy fostered coalition as well. They helped convince both communities that civil rights issues were interconnected and that safeguarding the rights of others strengthened one's own security. This encouraged both black and Jewish groups to expand their collaboration to embrace issues of only indirect interest to themselves.[9]

During this period there were collaborative efforts to secure rights in the areas of housing, employment, and education.[10]

Despite the very genuine manifestations of black-Jewish solidarity in such spheres, there were also points of tension between the two groups from the beginning. For example, "Contemplation of the holocaust might make possible deeper empathy between Jews and blacks, but it proved, over time, just as likely to confuse their alliance and drag them into arguments over comparative victimization."[11] Such arguments could quickly turn into shouting matches in which neither side truly listens to the other and certainly in which neither side "wins." There were also racial/ethnic and socioeconomic class divisions between the two communities. While Jews could, and many of them did, blend more easily into whiteness, African Americans would remain black. In addition, from very early on in their encounter, Jews and blacks encountered one another on an unequal economic playing field.

> Economic interactions far outpaced political ones; because of proximity, black suffering in the Depression had a Jewish dimension. African Americans, who so often moved into previously Jewish neighborhoods, encountered Jewish merchants, landlords, and rental agents . . . . Black domestics seeking day work stood on street corners in the Bronx; many of the housewives who picked them up were Jews. Black musicians, whose pay scales and work opportunities both declined during the Depression, continued to rely on Jewish club owners, agents, and middle-men.[12]

Especially by the 1960s and 1970s, in part because of the realities and legacy of these distinctions in race and class, some blacks began to question Jewish support for black civil rights. Several African Americans posited that Jews were using blacks as a shield to protect themselves from white, Christian oppression and questioned why Jews advocated black integration but not Jewish assimilation.[13]

Frustrations with the perceived lack of real economic and political gains of the civil rights movement led many blacks within the movement to question the nonviolent and integrationist philosophies advocated by Martin Luther King, Jr. and others. For example, groups such as the Student Nonviolent Coordinating Committee (SNCC) considered the possible advantages of the use of force and called for black self-reliance and separation from whites. From this new militant perspective, black separatism was a result of the failure of American liberalism and the sense of betrayal in still being shut out of the American political and economic structure.[14]

In addition to the black power movement, the Six Day War of 1967 and differing black and Jewish responses to it both contributed to and were indicative of the virtual crumbling of black-Jewish relations during this time. Up to this period, and especially during the civil rights movement, both blacks and Jews largely advocated a liberal position. By the late 1960s though, one can see a black move further toward the left and a Jewish turn toward the center and even right; each of these broad political and social shifts is certainly understandable in its context.

In the threats of the Arab world, led by Egypt's Gamal Abdel Nasser, and the buildup of Egyptian troops before the war, Jews feared the possibility of another Holocaust and the destruction of the state of Israel. During and after Israel's overwhelming victories over its Arab neighbors in the Six Day War, Jews recognized the necessity for Israel to exist; they also realized how precarious and fragile its existence was. Eric Sundquist explains the consequent shift:

> Despite their activism on behalf of desegregation, however, the national backlash against communism, their own distrust of black militancy, and increasing attention to Israel, especially after the Six-Day War in 1967, gradually fortified a centrist position among American Jews, a seeming retrenchment that may simply have confirmed the inherent limits of their liberalism but in any case prompted a shift from a universalist focus on social action to a more particularist focus on Jewish "reawakening" and renewal of community.[15]

When the Jews were already feeling confused and betrayed by black calls for separatism and greater focus on the economic and political well-being of the black community than on opportunities for individuals, the Six Day War pushed many of them away from liberalism toward the center and right and also toward greater assimilation to whiteness. The war simultaneously showed the fragility of Israel's existence and, in Israel's military dominance, provided the foundation for a robust Jewish and Israeli pride.

Though in earlier decades blacks had largely supported Israel,[16] this perspective began to change for many of them in the wake of Black Power and the Six Day War. Eric Sundquist writes, "In the anticolonial inversion of Exodus adopted by Black Power, especially after the Six-Day War in 1967, blacks were (still) slaves in the Egypt of America, while the Egypt of Africa, often imaginatively allied not only with Ethiopia but also more generally with pre-1948 Palestine, was said to be their spiritual homeland—a nation at war with Israel and, by extension, with Jews in America."[17] With the movement toward the left, many African Americans identified more with the Arab World, supported by communist Russia, and less with Israel, supported by the very white American power structure that still oppressed them. Furthermore, Sundquist asserts:

> This shift in allegiances grew as much from Black Power's domestic agenda as from its response to America's support for Israel, but it also had an abstract psychological dimension. Insofar as a heritage of bondage and powerlessness was part of the foundation of black nationalism and its liberationist ethos, the very existence of the state

of Israel, which ended Jewish exile, diminished its value as a model. The demonstration that Jews were no longer powerless—indeed were a military power allied with and armed by the United States—diminished it further still.[18]

Throughout this time, black anti-Semitism was based on and articulated in primarily economic rather than theological terms.[19]

Though anti-Semitism still existed, in general Jews were successfully accepted in American society and could "pass" as white in ways that blacks never would be able to. Gains made in limiting racial and ethnic restrictions in employment and housing illustrate the difference.

> Once employers agreed not to solicit racial or religious information, Jewish groups considered the problem largely solved; without knowing an applicant's background, employers would now hire on the basis of merit. And for many Jews, at least those without identifiable Jewish surnames, this was indeed the case . . . . But for African Americans writing one's race on a form is usually superfluous and most continued to be denied employment, housing, loans, and accommodations. For black organizations, unlike Jewish ones, theoretical race blindness was not enough.[20]

Thus for many blacks, attention to racial and religious identity and to individual opportunities was not enough. Instead, the focus had to be on class and structural matters, which in turn exposed more of the differences between blacks and Jews.

> Jews had largely embraced the status quo. To their black colleagues Jewish leaders recommended patience, moderation. This was not condescension or withdrawal from their political commitments. Rather, Jews' faith in liberalism and their blindness (along with that of most other whites) to what scholars call white skin privilege, the often invisible benefits that being white provides in American society, allowed them to believe they had risen on their own merits; they felt confident black people were capable of doing the same.[21]

It is from this perspective then that many Jews from the 1970s to the present oppose affirmative action programs supported by many African Americans. "Not only were affirmative action programs that involved set-asides or quotas reminders of many colleges' earlier Jewish quotas, they were wrong for the same reason: such programs violated the spirit of the race-blind liberalism Jews endorsed."[22] In short, Jews believed in the system and felt that blacks were trying to cheat it, while blacks believed the system itself was flawed because it still allowed racism to exist in covert, and thus more dangerous, form.

Eventually, "A dialogue had become an acrimonious argument, then shouted epithets, then sullen silence, and finally somber reminiscence, in tribute and regret."[23] There are differing scholarly assessments of the likelihood and potential character of any black-Jewish solidarity today, but many would say that any sustained and serious alliance is unlikely in the present climate. In Eric Sundquist's view, "Today the very notion of a coalition seems quaint."[24]

From a potentially more positive perspective, Cheryl Lynn Greenberg approvingly cites Clayborne Carson's contention that the split was less between Jews and blacks than between liberals and leftists.[25] Greenberg thus details multiple examples of black-Jewish solidarity throughout the 1970s up to the present, among either those of the left or those still in the liberal sphere.[26] She asserts, "Rumors of the death of black-Jewish relations have been greatly exaggerated. If the pattern between blacks and Jews in the first two-thirds of the twentieth century was one of growing cooperation with an undertone of persistent conflict, the pattern in the last third of the century might be characterized as one of growing conflict that did not erase the possibilities of cooperation."[27] Following Greenberg, I believe the realities of the situation call for awareness of tensions between the two communities and caution against any facile appropriation of themes from either community's traditions, but they do not close the doors to fruitful insights and theological conversation that may emerge in the crosscurrents of this fascinating and complex encounter.

Jewish-Christian Relations

Like black-Jewish relations, the Jewish-Christian encounter is also complicated and often strained. While an outsider to both the African American and Jewish communities, I am a Christian who advocates liberation theology as a significant and powerful theological movement and I seek to draw resources from Jewish theology to challenge, develop, and enrich my own theology. Because of the traditional Christian position of supersessionism in regard to Judaism, the idea of a Christian seeking to simply take Jewish ideas and claim them as his/her own is problematic. To clarify, I do not intend to "steal" ideas from Judaism and then simply express them in a Christian way.

Not only would such a method be arrogant and insensitive, but it would also defeat one of the principles of interreligious dialogue, which is awareness of and respect for genuine differences that should remain differences. Krister Stendahl expresses the futility of such an approach:

> I have come to think that a truly healthy relationship between religions presupposes a capacity to see in the other some things that are beautiful, even and especially things that tell you something about God, but are not part of your own tradition. That is more than tolerance, even more than respect. I call it "holy envy," for it is not yours. It would be cut flowers in your home, so let it stand and grow as you marvel.[28]

From a pluralistic standpoint, which I explain below, I am looking to particular Jewish claims and ideas so that my own Christian views may be complemented and enriched. I hope to exhibit some measure of wisdom in discerning how this encounter can be fruitful yet can still respect the integrity of the genuine differences between these two religious traditions.

Challenges

Obviously there are challenges involved in Jewish-Christian relations in general and theological dialogue in particular. The history of Christian domination and oppression of Jews has been well documented and discussed. Ironically it is in part because of the similarities between the two traditions that a sibling rivalry of a sort has developed. The early Christian community triumphantly defined itself as the people of the new and true covenant. From this perspective Jews had ignored God's will and had refused to recognize Jesus as the messiah. Christianity had superseded, if not outright replaced, Judaism. Jews in turn asserted that Christians had erroneously and blasphemously claimed Jesus as the messiah. Irving Greenberg explains:

> Each religion paid a price in dismissing the other. Christianity skewed toward dualism, minimizing the religious significance of carnal matters, the law, and the body. Judaism slid into denigrating political and military power, and narrowed its concern vis-à-vis non-Jews. Both faiths

stepped away from history as a meaningful theater of operations for God and humanity, at great cost to their inner spiritual strength, to their constituencies, and to the world around them. Additionally, Christianity was led to terrible excesses vis-à-vis the Jewish faith and people.[29]

The Christian attitude of superiority, position of supersessionism, and claim that Jews had committed deicide were used to justify Christian violence against Jews throughout the Middle Ages and into the modern era.

After the Holocaust Jewish-Christian dialogue becomes more necessary than ever, but also more complicated in some ways. Since the Holocaust there have been more sincere Christian efforts at reconciliation with Jews and with Christianity's own Jewish roots. These still fragmentary responses and considerations have in turn been answered by Jewish considerations of Christianity and the possibilities and limitations of Jewish-Christian encounters after the Holocaust.[30] For example, Irving Greenberg maintains, "New patterns of understanding are possible alongside the finality of Christ or the absoluteness of the Jewish covenant. After the Holocaust, the relationship of Judaism and Christianity should enable one to affirm the fullness of the faith claims of the other, to affirm the profound inner relationship between the two, and to recognize and admit how much closer they are to each other than either has been able to say."[31]

Though there has been a marked improvement in the ways in which Christians view and approach Judaism, there is still a tension between this greater respect and the drive to proselytize. For example, some Jews may understandably interpret Christian interest in dialogue, however courteous and respectful, to be motivated by a missionary impulse. Also, the valid Jewish fear of assimilation and dwindling numbers within its community is heightened in the aftermath of an event in which one-third of Jews were murdered. The Roman Catholic Church's Vatican II document on Christian relations with non-Christians, *Nostra Aetate*, is indicative of this tension. On the one hand, it affirms God's still-standing covenant with Jews and argues that Jews should not be charged with deicide. On the other hand though, Christians are still called to practice and proclaim the one true religion and try to convert non-Christians, including Jews.[32] Further, certainly the "Great Commission" of Christianity is not unique to Roman Catholics either. My own sense is that it is very common among most Christian communities to allow that non-Christian traditions contain some truth, yet nevertheless maintain the belief that Christianity is the superior, most true religion.

Diana Eck's framework is very helpful in distinguishing among three approaches to religious traditions other than one's own. Exclusivism involves the claim that one's tradition is the only true, valid path to God and that all others are false. Inclusivism acknowledges some partial truths in other traditions while maintaining that one's religion is still better than that of others. An example of this inclusivistic perspective is expressed by the Roman Catholic Church in *Nostra Aetate*: there are true and admirable aspects to Judaism, yet Christianity provides the complete Truth. Religious adherents of other traditions are to be respected, but, in the end, should be converted, in other words. I believe both of these positions of exclusivism and inclusivism make genuine interreligious dialogue difficult.

Opportunities

In contrast with either exclusivism or inclusivism, I advocate a pluralistic understanding of religions, maintaining that the various world religious traditions are each valid and true. From this view for example, I may say that Christianity is the best religion for me, while Judaism is the best religion for a Jew. Further, I maintain that a pluralist perspective genuinely recognizes differences among religious traditions and resists the temptation to blur the real diversity that exists. I feel this important characteristic is applicable to black-Jewish relations as well. As explained by Diana Eck, pluralism recognizes and embraces differences among religious traditions. For it is through an encounter and exploration of similarities but more importantly differences that we may develop in positive ways.

Eck clarifies the pluralist position through five statements. She asserts: "*Pluralism is not the sheer fact of plurality alone, but is active engagement with plurality* .... I have to *participate* in pluralism. I can't just stand by and watch."[33] Pluralism entails actually grappling with different religious traditions, contemplating various beliefs and practices, and actively encountering the myriad manifestations of religiosity in our society.

Second, Eck explains that "*pluralism is not simply tolerance, but also the seeking of understanding.*"[34] Though "mere" tolerance is not to be underestimated in this context, pluralism involves more than this. Eck posits that toleration implies the temporary acceptance of the other that may at any time be removed if one so wishes. In contrast, pluralism is not simply accepting the fact of the other's existence, something with which one must deal, in other words, but rather the appreciation of and desire to pursue deeper relationship.

Eck's third explanatory statement on the pluralist positions is that *"pluralism is not simply relativism, but assumes real commitment . . . .* Relativism assumes a stance of openness; pluralism assumes both openness *and* commitment."[35] Her fourth assertion in regard to the pluralist position is that *"pluralism is not syncretism, but is based on respect for differences."*

Eck's final, and in many respects most important, element of the pluralist position is that *"pluralism is based on interreligious dialogue."* She describes dialogue as "an opportunity to deepen our knowledge and understanding of the one we call God. It is an occasion for truth seeking dialogue—to offer our own testimony, to hear the testimonies of others in their own terms, to wrestle with the meaning of one another's terms, and to risk mutual transformation."[36] From the pluralist perspective then, the goal of dialogue is not simply the cognitive one of learning facts about another tradition, but more centrally the spiritual one of seeking the truth.

In his essay "Events and Pseudo-Events" in a collection of writings, *Faith and Violence*, Thomas Merton explains the notion of pseudoreality, the idea that we construct and perpetuate, often unconsciously, a false sense of self and the world to make ourselves feel good about our selves, our world, and our place in it. He uses the Latin word *simulacrum*, usually translated as idols, to describe our masks, self-deceptions, or false versions of reality. Merton writes, "We make simulacra and we hypnotize ourselves with our skill in creating these mental movies that do not appear to be idols because they are so alive!"[37] Through contemplation, Merton explains, we may begin to see this construct as false; we may see through the façade and begin to encounter genuine reality, genuine self.

I understand interreligious dialogue potentially to serve an analogous role to Merton's practice of contemplation. Dialogue can serve as a lens through which we can see "genuine reality." Through dialogue we can begin to move out of our self-imposed vacuums and get a greater sense of reality, a greater sense of our genuine selves. Two aspects of genuine reality that Diana Eck highlights at the end of *Encountering God* that I understand as virtues that may be gained through interreligious dialogue, including dialogue between

Jews and Christians, are a sense of interdependence and a wider sense of "we."

We must come to see that we are all interdependent on one another politically, culturally, economically, environmentally, *and* religiously. Drawing from Gandhi and Martin Luther King, Jr., Eck asserts that the notion of "we" must include the entire global village, especially the poor of the world. She quotes King, saying

> [I]n a real sense, all life is interrelated. The agony of the poor impoverishes the rich; the betterment of the poor enriches the rich. We are inevitably our brother's keeper because we are our brother's brother. Whatever affects one directly affects all indirectly. To imagine such a household will require what King called "a revolution of values." A genuine revolution of values means in the final analysis that our loyalties must become ecumenical rather than sectional. Every nation must now develop an overriding loyalty to mankind as a whole in order to preserve the best in their individual societies.

Eck continues in her own words, saying,

> Part of the revolution of values is a revolution of attitudes, a revolution of theological attitudes being foremost among them. A household cannot function on the underlying premise of exclusivity, though each community within the household may be exclusive in some things, such as its central rituals. A household cannot finally function on the underlying foundation of inclusivism either, for it will have to be *our* household as human beings, not ours as Christians, Muslims, or Buddhists, to which everyone else is welcome. No one community can set the terms for the whole. The underlying foundation of the world household will finally have to be pluralism.[38]

In other words, a genuine, wider sense of "we" emerges only through dialogue and especially through pluralism.

Furthermore, "we" must be understood to include especially the poor of the world. Religious people in general, and Christians in particular, must come to understand the centrality of the "preferential option for the poor" that is evident within the world's great religious traditions. After a shift of consciousness we are called upon to act differently to live our lives differently. Once one sees reality, then one should be compelled to act on this to bring about true peace and social justice.[39]

For anyone involved, then, whether exclusivist, inclusivist, or pluralist, a few benefits of interreligious dialogue include a more accurate understanding of others (textbook knowledge of beliefs, practices, history of religious traditions, awareness of diversity within traditions); a fuller, more nuanced understanding of oneself and; potentially positive social and political implications of greater understanding of fellow human beings and communities.

Finally, two further virtues that may be gained through dialogue, especially possible for pluralists I believe, are a greater appreciation of genuine differences and the humility and excitement that often result in the discovery of other, equally valid paths to truth. Pluralism should not mean the belief that all religions are the same. One's initial contact may be through a discovery of similarities, but pushing beyond these similarities is most challenging and rewarding. If one is in fact better off because of the differences and, if they enrich one's self and one's world, then dialogue is both desirable and necessary.

Humanocentric Theism and Resistance

In the remainder of the book, I explore the potential for a constructive theological and ethical perspective that builds on the foundations laid by James H. Cone and Emil L. Fackenheim in the hope of developing an understanding of God and humanity that both recognizes the reality of suffering and evil and provides a standpoint from which it is possible to respond effectively to suffering, evil, economic, social, and political oppression, and existential despair. I examine questions of God's relation to the world and humanity, God's activity in history, and the nature of human freedom.

Here I articulate a conception of God that I call humanocentric theism. Though this conception is fundamentally based on the theologies of Cone and Fackenheim, it also diverges from their views in important ways. The critiques of William R. Jones, from whom I take the term humanocentric theism, of Melissa Raphael, and of Dwight Hopkins are central to my own reformulations of some aspects of Cone and Fackenheim's theologies.

After this discussion of God, our attention is turned to theological anthropology. In that section I wish to develop the categories of human freedom and resistance. My understanding of humanity that follows from the foundational conception of God is not very different from that of Cone or Fackenheim in content. Where I differ from Cone and Fackenheim is in the theological basis for my understandings of freedom and resistance and in the implications this has for redemption.

God: Humanocentric Theism

This section on God explores three related theological issues: (1) how social and historical context shapes theological content; (2) divine-human relation in the Christian and Jewish traditions; and (3) divine presence and power. These issues are central to both Cone and Fackenheim and provide a fertile basis for placing them in dialogue. After exploring Cone's and Fackenheim's views, I utilize William R. Jones and Melissa Raphael, as well as Dwight Hopkins, to suggest possible directions for a revised humanocentric theism.

Cone and Fackenheim

On the first issue of how social and historical context shapes theology, Cone and Fackenheim hold very similar positions. Cone argues that the Bible and the entire Christian tradition must be interpreted from the perspective of the African American experience. He claims that this is the proper perspective because it is the truest to the activity of God in the Bible, from the Exodus, through the prophets, and especially in the life, death, and resurrection of Jesus Christ. That is, the Bible tells the story of a God who sides with the oppressed, most compellingly so in Jesus Christ. The ministry of Jesus during his life and the fact of the resurrection mean that God acted as liberator of the oppressed in the past and continues to do so today. Cone points to the black experience itself as proof that God acts as liberator of the oppressed. Therefore, according to Cone, the message of Christianity for today is black liberation. The black experience of oppression and liberation is both shaped by and in turn shapes Cone's theological claims.

Likewise for Fackenheim, the Jewish experiences of history deeply shape what valid theological truth claims may look like. Jewish theology has always been profoundly historical, asserted Fackenheim. Understandings of God necessarily shifted after each Temple destruction, exile, and the Emancipation. This fact is even more so after the Holocaust and the reemergence of the state of Israel. All previous theological claims must be reinterpreted in the light of these two enormous events. Fackenheim questioned whether a return to the Jewish tradition of the past is even possible after the Holocaust. For Judaism to still be meaningful after the Holocaust, the event must be taken with the utmost seriousness and relevance. The social and historical events of the twentieth century must shape the content of Jewish theology.

Though Cone and Fackenheim differ in their specific theological claims and their selection of social and historical events that they regard as important, each thinker denies that theology may be formed in a historical vacuum. Such a postmodern claim is common in contemporary theology, yet one gets the sense that for both such an argument is both profoundly central to and problematic for their respective theologies. Both Cone and Fackenheim reacted to a conservative theological context in which universality and objectivity were understood to be necessary for meaningful theological assertions. Yet neither theologian could ignore the importance of his own community's experiences in the twentieth century. Both Cone and Fackenheim attempt to maintain a faithfulness to the universal truth claims of their own religious tradition while simultaneously responding to the profound events of their times.

Cone and Fackenheim assert that all readings of texts and traditions are contextual and subjective. There is no universal and purely objective reading of texts, traditions, or histories. The only way to a universal truth claim, which they both wish to maintain, is through the particular social, cultural, and historical experiences of a community. God does not relate to all peoples the same way; God maintains special and distinct relationships with communities of people throughout history, both Cone and Fackenheim argue. In Cone's Christianity, universality is available only through the particularity of God's relationship with the oppressed, most profoundly expressed through the life, death, and resurrection of Jesus. In Fackenheim's Judaism, universality is accessible only through the particularity of God's relationship with Israel, most profoundly expressed in the covenant. For Cone, God sides with the oppressed of society; for Fackenheim, God maintains a covenantal relationship with Israel. Cone and Fackenheim differ from both conservative theological interpretations and postmodern analysis in that they claim that their perspectives, because they are particular and contextual, offer a path to the universal. In this way they remain true to both their respective religious traditions and to their respective ethnic community's contemporary experiences and history.

I concur with the assertion that one's social, cultural, and historical context shapes the content and form of one's theological claims. Though largely unacknowledged in the history of religious traditions, this has always been the case. The fact that theology is shaped by context is not unique to contemporary theology; the acknowledgment of this fact and the self-awareness it creates are relatively recent developments. That theology and religious traditions in general are historical and contextual does not mean that universal truth claims can no longer be made. It simply means that there must be an understanding that simultaneous and differing truth claims may validly exist side by side. This is the profound lesson of cultural and religious pluralism.

In addition to the issue of how social context shapes theological content, the topic of divine-human relationship is central to the work of both Cone and Fackenheim. Unlike in their claim that context shapes content, in the issue of divine-human relation Cone and Fackenheim hold divergent views. This point of difference is in part a manifestation of their respective religious traditions.

Cone maintains that God acts in history as liberator of the oppressed, most compellingly so in the incarnation, crucifixion, and resurrection of Jesus Christ. The quintessential conception of the divine in Christian theology is incarnational. Certainly, Cone's naming of God as liberator is founded on the stories of the Exodus and the prophets of the Hebrew Bible. However, it is the fact that God decisively enters into history as Jesus Christ that most profoundly indicates God's relationship to humanity of simultaneous love for the oppressed and justice for the oppressor. Because of the resurrection of Jesus, God acts in such a way always, argues Cone. Liberation is already, but not yet accomplished for the oppressed in Jesus Christ. Granted, economic, social, and political oppression still exist, yet, liberation is assured because of the activity of Jesus Christ. Humans play a role in the struggle for liberation in utilizing the freedom granted to them by the already won victory in Christ. In the face of continuing black oppression, Cone can maintain faith in an inevitable liberation because he understands the life, death, and resurrection of Jesus to be the central act of liberation in history.

Such assured confidence in God's benevolence and providence did not come so easily for Fackenheim. His understanding of the divine-human relationship, like Cone's, is based initially on the stories of the Hebrew Bible. As for Cone, for Fackenheim also, God enters into a special relationship with a particular community of people, not all people in general. Whereas for Cone this community is the community of the oppressed, for Fackenheim God enters into a covenantal relationship with Israel. This covenantal relationship obliges Israel's allegiance and obedience with no guarantees of inevitable benevolence. God is present as both saving and commanding force in the root experiences of Judaism, the Exodus and Sinai. This divine presence and the nature of the covenant are brought into question if not entirely destroyed by the Holocaust. Fackenheim argued that the Holocaust creates a rupture in the possibility of a return to the root experiences of the past. Unlike for Cone then, for Fackenheim, contemporary Jewish suffering and despair profoundly bring into question the nature and reality of the divine-human relationship of covenant. There is no already accomplished victory to which Fackenheim may appeal to point to inevitable redemption or to a still vital covenant. During and after the Holocaust, Fackenheim suggested, God is present as commanding voice. God commands that Jews not give Hitler posthumous victories by despairing of either God of humanity. Fackenheim's later work suggests that divine saving presence may be hinted at in human acts of *tikkun olam*, or mending of the world.

The nature of divine-human relation for Cone and Fackenheim then is shaped by the central faith claims of their respective traditions. For Cone, this relationship is expressed most profoundly in the incarnation, death, and resurrection of Jesus Christ. God's siding with the oppressed throughout the Hebrew Bible is intensified in God's siding with the oppressed to such a degree that God becomes incarnate as an oppressed Jew, living among and ministering to other oppressed people. His resurrection, according to Cone, indicates that this liberating relationship characterizes God's relation to the oppressed of all times. For Fackenheim, the divine-human relationship is expressed in God's covenant with a particular people, Israel. This is a relationship of both love and obligation. The Hebrew Bible is full of stories of Israel straying from and returning to God and of God's responsive love and justice toward Israel. Jewish suffering during this time is explained by the claim that it is deserved as a result of the sins of Israel. Such an explanation for suffering becomes obscene in the face of the murder of one million Jewish children during the Holocaust. Here, Jewish suffering cannot be understood as divine punishment for straying from the covenant. During the Holocaust, it seems, it is God who strays from the covenant with Israel. Fackenheim asserted that, for now at least, after the Holocaust God must be understood as commanding presence only, with no assurance of salvation, given the realities and horrors of the Holocaust. These sufferings of history for Fackenheim do bring into question the nature of the covenantal relationship with Israel in a way that black suffering challenges Cone's notion of God as liberator of the oppressed, but never destroys it entirely.

The third related issue of divine power and presence must also be addressed here. Both Cone and Fackenheim allow for a robust understanding of human freedom, but place a far greater emphasis on the divine omnipotence. If the issue of presence must be understood as an either/or situation, in which God is ultimately understood as either transcendent to humanity or immanent within, both Cone and Fackenheim would describe God's relation to humanity as transcendent. Though certainly immanent in human history and within humanity itself at times in vitally important ways, God in both Cone and Fackenheim's theologies is transcendent to the failures and frailties of human history. Both thinkers exhibit the Barthian/Kierkegaardian tendency of emphasizing the ultimate qualitative distinction and hierarchy between God and humanity. I disagree with their inclination to stress divine omnipotence and transcendence as a response to historical suffering of moral evils. In distinction I suggest a model of God in which God exhibits power primarily through human freedom and is immanent within humanity.

As described above, Cone attempts to critique the falsely claimed close alliance that he saw between white racist theologies and the will of God, while simultaneously wanting to align divine will and preference with the black experience. In his attack on racist theology, Cone argues for God's transcendence over human culture and society, saying that white Christianity was not truly Christian. On the contrary, Cone believes that God's immanence was evident in black culture and Christianity. He believes that this divine preference for and immanence in the black experience was not simply a racial matter, but rather an issue of which type of Christianity best understood and expressed the liberative will of God that, for Cone, was so obviously the message of the Bible and the mission of Christ. Cone, however, pushes the notion of divine immanence within black culture only so far. Though in different ways, just as whites could sin, so could blacks. Black sin, understood as not seeing through racist ideology and struggling for one's freedom alongside God, could result in the failure of the liberation struggle if there were no divine transcendence.

God's transcendence and omnipotence assure the virtual inevitable liberation of the oppressed, according to Cone. These divine traits are the basis for black hope and faith. When humanity falls short of social justice and liberation, which commonly occurs as the history of racism in the United States attests to, God's transcendence and omnipotence mean that God does not let us down in the end. Cone admits that divine power does not mean that God can do whatever God wants to do. He advocates a strong notion of human freedom, but always understands this freedom within the context of divine power.

Cone does not appeal to human freedom, however, when dealing with the problem of why there is black suffering if God acts as omnipotent liberator. Rather, he responds to the theodicy problem by appealing to the lived faith of Christian African Americans. Cone backs away from a philosophical response to black suffering, claiming that such an approach would be too abstract and alien to black faith. He feels that the lived faith of black Christians overcomes the apparent paradox of continued suffering by maintaining a simultaneous human drive for liberation and an assured faith that God is liberator. In other words, given his conception of divine transcendence and omnipotence, there is no real theodicy problem for Cone.

Like Cone, Fackenheim argued against either extreme of a God who is too far or too near. The God of the Jewish tradition is a personal God who enters into a covenant with Israel, but remains always Other to Israel. Fackenheim called this the principle of the intimacy of the divine infinity. Arguing against modern secularism, Fackenheim asserted that God is deeply and intimately involved in Israel's affairs. The divine and the human move toward one another as it were. Israel's history and welfare affect God's very being in a sense here. Although at times Fackenheim maintained a balance between this divine intimacy with Israel and divine transcendence, he focused primarily on divine transcendence and omnipotence.

Fackenheim emphasized divine transcendence and omnipotence to oppose what he viewed as at least three dangerous alternatives. First, he felt that the Christian doctrine of incarnation was impossible for Judaism because he interpreted this to mean to identify the divine with human nature. There could be no mixing of divinity and humanity. If the two did not remain ultimately separate, the Jewish covenant would cease to exist. There could be no covenantal relationship if there were only one party.

The second tendency Fackenheim sought to reject was the God of process theology. Whereas he opposed the Christian doctrine of incarnation because it was not consistent with his understanding of divine transcendence, he rejected process theology because it did not adequately account for divine power. Fackenheim felt that a God who was understood as a general cosmic force, always becoming, and lacking ultimate power could not address Jewish theological needs and standards. This God would be too universalistic, thus mitigating the particular relationship between the divine and Israel. Further, such a God who could not actively control human history would not be worth praying to. Finally, Fackenheim rejected process tendencies because he felt that this view too closely aligned human culture with divine will.

In other words, Fackenheim refused to see God's presence within human history and progress.

After the events of the twentieth century, it is difficult if not impossible to hold a utopian view of human historical progress. Thus, Fackenheim opposed what he believed were too naïve and optimistic conceptions of divine presence and power in modern thought because they ignored the realities of the Holocaust. A God who is too closely identified with humanity, a God who is immanent in human activity, must be understood as dying along with a naively optimistic view of human nature, much as Elie Wiesel described God's presence with the boy hanging from the gallows in his *Night*. Whether or not God was present during the Holocaust, Fackenheim argued, God must be understood as ultimately transcending the horrors of human history if God is to be God at all.

Fackenheim offered the view that God was present during the Holocaust as Commanding Voice. As stated earlier, his later work suggests a not fully developed element of his theology in which God may be understood to be present as saving force in the activity of resisting Jews. Though he does not explore this understanding, I believe it hints at his willingness to entertain the notion that, after the Holocaust, divine power may best be understood as manifesting itself through human acts of resistance.

Cone and Fackenheim reject the notion of an exact identity between God and human culture and history. An equation of divine will with human society has led to Ku Klux Klan and Nazi claims that their respective racist ideologies were the will of God. Any person or group can claim divine support for their cause, and this has occurred throughout religious history. As humans we can never fully know God's will or whether God is present at certain places or times. In addition, both argue that as creator and sustainer of the universe and humanity along with it, God is ultimately distinct from and transcendent over humanity.

Jones, Raphael, and Hopkins

At this point I wish to build on the theological foundations laid by Cone and Fackenheim, but by way of drawing from voices critical to particular aspects of their thought. As discussed in chapter three, William R. Jones criticizes Cone and other first-generation black liberation theologians for presupposing divine goodness, given what he feels is a lack of any evidence that God has acted as liberator of those suffering from economic, social, and political oppression. This critique is primarily relevant in regard to Cone rather than Fackenheim. Below, I attempt to address Jones' concerns and show that, if divine goodness can in fact be established, his critique encourages a reinterpretation of divine power rather than a full assault on divine goodness. It is in this sense that his thought can also speak to Fackenheim's position.

Whereas Jones questions Cone's claims of divine benevolence, Melissa Raphael asserts that male Holocaust thinkers, including Fackenheim, problematically utilized classical and patriarchal understandings of divine power in their formulations. She insightfully claims that if one conceives of power as relational and persuasive, some of the theological problems and existential dilemmas expressed by male Holocaust theologians may be mitigated. In this way, Raphael's call for a new understanding of divine power is relevant to Cone, Fackenheim, and Jones.

Advancing on this trajectory from Jones and Raphael then, I suggest that a revised version of Jones' category of humanocentric theism might offer a creative possibility for responding to suffering and moral evil. This revised notion of humanocentric theism draws from both a reinterpretation of divine power as persuasive and from black liberation theology's claim of a divine preferential option for the oppressed. With Jones, this humanocentric theism refuses to view ethnic suffering as positive or redemptive. However, in distinction from Jones, the version of humanocentric theism suggested here asserts divine goodness, but bases this understanding on Jones' own norm of the functional ultimacy of humanity. According to this understanding of humanocentric theism, the divine will for the liberation of the oppressed is conveyed through subtle forms of persuasive power. Human efforts to carry out this liberative will are then understood as manifestations of divine power. My revised humanocentric theism shares many key theological aspects with Raphael's *Shekhinah* and Dwight Hopkins' Spirit of Total Liberation in Us. It is suggested that this revised humanocentric theism may provide a meaningful way to understand human liberation efforts and also demand human resistance against economic, social, and political suffering and oppression.

Again, one of Jones' primary points of contention with Cone is that Jones asserts there has been no liberation event for African Americans. Jones essentially argues that if there is no such liberation "event," then there is no evidence of divine goodness; thus, why would one reasonably assume such goodness? If God is liberator, as Cones claims, why has there been no liberation event? Jones asks. As I read it, here Jones assumes God is omnipotent in this question. In his critique of Cone's "assumption" of divine goodness for example, Jones is still operating with classical notions of divine omnipotence. In effect he is saying, "I will not believe God is good until I see proof of God's power, manifested in unequivocal power and efficacy on behalf of the oppressed." God could do something positive, but chooses not to, and thus we cannot presuppose goodness. For me, this involves an understanding of divine power as overt and dominating, not as persuasive.

Trying an alternative approach in formulating humanocentric theism, Jones begins to open up to a notion of divine power as persuasive and subtle, rather than overt and dominating. From his perspective, this new understanding of power still does not allow one to assume divine goodness anymore than a classical notion of power would. That is, Jones concedes that God persuades humanity but is not explicit about what God persuades us to do. Theoretically, God could still persuade some of us toward evil.[40] Still primarily relying on a traditional interpretation that divine power must be dominating if it is to be efficacious, Jones demands a specific divine act of liberation in human history before any claim of a preferential option may be made. However, what is it that God persuades us to do if not commit ourselves to the struggle against forces of dehumanization and despair? Jones somehow understands divine neutrality to follow from the idea of divine power as persuasive.

Central to this issue of divine neutrality or preferential option is how divine goodness is understood and what "proof" of divine goodness may be offered. Jones essentially asserts that no theology should really presuppose divine goodness without evidence to support such a claim. To do so may result in a theology with a questionable economic, social, and political liberation potential. Many theists might respond that for God to be God, though divine power may be reinterpreted, divine goodness is not negotiable. For example, Howard Burkle argues the notion that God may be evil is "inherently inconsistent and therefore not a possibility at all. God cannot be demonic because 'God' means 'absolute perfection.' If the dominant universal power is not *perfectly* good, there is no God."[41] In response, Jones argues that "the superiority [Burkle] assigns to the option of benevolence rests on the question-begging foundation of a stipulative definition."[42] Though I agree with Burkle's conclusion that God is in fact good, I believe Jones offers a valid critique of simply presupposing or asserting divine goodness a priori.

As an alternative, I suggest the very norm of Jones' humanocentric theism, the functional ultimacy of humanity, as, if not proof of divine goodness, at least an indication of such. I do this to make an internal criticism of Jones. Jones demands that one cannot believe in divine goodness and in suffering as redemptive without an exaltation-liberation event in history. One might point toward the Exodus and the life, death, and resurrection of Jesus as "proof" of divine goodness, as Cone does. However, as Jones asserts, I am not sure this indicates divine goodness specifically in regard to African Americans. An additional option, which does speak to an exaltation-liberation event specifically for blacks, would be to point to the abolition of slavery in the United States and the gains of the civil rights movement of the twentieth century. In fact, Dwight Hopkins makes this very move. Again these examples may also be understood multievidentially, as Jones claims. In other words, why were conditions for blacks so bad in the first place that emancipation and a civil rights movement were necessary at all?

Instead, I believe Jones himself offers an alternative path toward the claim of divine goodness. Jones writes:

> To avoid collapsing humanocentric theism into humanism, it is important to note that the human has the exalted status of co-determining power by virtue of God's gracious endowment. Moreover, the ground for this endowment is the self-limitation of God's overruling authority in human history. Thus, the misuse of human freedom clears up the mystery of oppression and removes God's responsibility for the crimes of human history.[43]

Here, Jones seems to point to the claim that the source of and sustaining presence beneath the functional ultimacy of humanity are divine grace. In other words, as Jones indicates, humanocentric theism should not begin by simply presupposing divine goodness, but rather understand divine goodness as indicative of a context or system that explains human freedom. The fact that we are functionally ultimate or free is itself evidence of divine goodness.[44]

However, this evaluation of human freedom as unequivocally good is problematic for Jones. He explains, "Granting freedom to humans for example, is logically and theologically multievidential. Ultimately, this divine 'grace' tells us nothing about whose side God is on or about the divine intent for the future of the human species and its oppressed communities."[45] Thus, for Jones, God's sharing of power with humanity does not indicate divine goodness. At this point then, one has to wonder whether Jones' alternative would be a God who is *neither* all-good nor all-powerful, or perhaps no God at all.

It seems more reasonable to me to understand human freedom, or the "functional ultimacy" of humanity, as indicative of divine goodness, and then to conceive of divine power as persuasive. Divine goodness, presence, and power are evident in granting freedom to humanity in general, and in God's preferential option for the power in particular, witnessed to in the Hebrew Bible, in the life of Jesus Christ, and, for many theists, throughout multiple events in human history. In this way, my revised humanocentric theism draws significantly from Cone. The demand for an exaltation-liberation event is also mitigated if one understands divine power as persuasive and human action as functionally ultimate. We would not then expect an overwhelming, coercive divine act in history unless God is actually conceived of as omnipotent.

Part of what is at stake here is Jones' first standard for any adequate black theodicy. He claimed that "suffering must not be ultimately blamed on God."[46] To do so, Jones believes, would be to define such suffering as positive in some sense and this would lead to quietism and the call to endure or even embrace such suffering as potentially redemptive. I agree with Jones' critique of understanding any form of ethnic suffering as anything but negative and with the consequent demand to resist it. However, I believe the revised notion of humanocentric theism suggested here adequately addresses Jones' concern. God *is* indirectly to "blame" for suffering, if we understand God to be "blamed" for the reality of the functional ultimacy of humanity, as Jones characterizes this concept. Again, he writes, "The human has the exalted status of co-determining power by virtue of God's gracious endowment."[47] Thus, God is not guilty for ethnic suffering, but God is responsible for it.[48] God is responsible then not only in terms of explaining the origins of evil, but also in considering ways in which ethnic suffering and moral evil should be resisted today. If divine power is persuasive and truly shared, in this sense, with humanity, then both God and humanity should share the credit and the blame. If we can acknowledge that the functional ultimacy of humanity is good and is based on divine grace, then it follows that God persuades us toward the good, and God does in a sense take sides with the oppressed.

According to my interpretation of humanocentric theism, God may still be understood as liberator, but one must look to acts of resistance carried out by *human beings*, who may be understood as carrying out God's liberative will. So, if we wish to learn about God, we must look at the activity and presence of God in human acts of resistance carried out by members of oppressed communities. Admittedly there is a danger of arrogance or triumphalism when the claim is made that we can look to human events to witness the activity of God. However, God as persuasive power in human history makes little sense, if we cannot identify, at least in broad terms, what it is that God persuades us to do. I believe Jones' denial of a God who takes sides indicates his admitted preference for a position of humanism rather than the humanocentric theism.

Like Jones, Emil Fackenheim also questioned divine goodness in his encounter with the Holocaust. In part, as Melissa Raphael asserts, this is because Fackenheim was operating with classical notions of power. As we saw in chapter 5, Raphael claimed male Holocaust thinkers, including Fackenheim, neglected the experiences of Jewish women during the Holocaust and assumed a patriarchal perspective of God. Thus, they were essentially "protesting God's failure to be patriarchal enough." Though no saving divine presence was evident during the Holocaust for Fackenheim, Jews did hear and respond to the Commanding Voice of Auschwitz. According to Raphael, in expressing this concept, Fackenheim was working with an understanding of God as omnipotent. Such a notion also conveys a sense of divine goodness and presence, but one that is manifested in domineering and patriarchal ways. It is helpful that Fackenheim's idea of God as commanding presence calls for human response, but it is a response that essentially involves following orders. As Raphael explains, the last thing Jews needed at this point was another voice yelling orders at them.

My analysis of Cone and Jones is parallel to Raphael's response to Fackenheim's theology. All three run into difficulties, from my perspective, when beginning with a classical concept of divine power. Raphael suggests that if one explores women's experiences during the Holocaust, alternative ways of understanding divine power, presence, and goodness are evident. For example, women's relationships of mutual care both depend on divine presence, *Shekhinah*, and elicit further presence when carried out.

On the basis especially of his earlier writings, I surmise that Fackenheim would not have been comfortable with this new interpretation of power. How can a God who persuades, speak to the events of Auschwitz? he might have asked. When God is not "too near," but just near enough, does God still maintain omnipotence, or is divine power abrogated in some way to accommodate divine involvement with the world? In conversation with Elie Wiesel's claim that God was to be found hanging on the gallows as a young boy, Fackenheim explained, "The God that hangs with that boy on the Auschwitz gallows, however, does lack power. He lacks it absolutely, and this because He persists in His intimacy with His people. Is the price paid for that intimacy, then and there, not a *total* loss of the infinity?" For the slightest measure of finitude destroys infinity by definition. Fackenheim asked whether the demand of the Holocaust for absolute intimacy has "fragmented the God of Israel into an intimacy of absolute impotence, and an infinity of absolute indifference?"[49]

I respond to this question with the admission that it is indeed a total loss of power as traditionally understood in theistic traditions. However, if power is reinterpreted to be loving and persuasive instead of dominating, perhaps the divine power is present and displayed in the seemingly impotent intimacy.[50] Given this concept, divine power is present *only* when there is divine intimacy. True power is not the ability to enter into human affairs and forcefully bring about the "good"; it is the patience to allow humanity to strive toward goodness, but also to be present with us when we fail, always persuading us to improve as individuals and as communities. Thus, I understand resistance against dehumanization as human response to divine urging and persuasion, not as obedience to commandment, as did Fackenheim.[51]

One wonders if Fackenheim would have been open to the possibility that God is the sole Power of all history but is present in different ways throughout history. Perhaps God's presence is evident sometimes as a more dominant force, as during the Exodus, and at other times, no less present but in a more subtle way, as in the activities of human free agency. I believe Fackenheim left open the possibility that by responding to God's commanding presence in authentic ways, humans may act as their own fragmentary saving presence. Perhaps it is through these defiant acts of humanity that God may be said to be a saving presence even at Auschwitz and after.[52]

I am intrigued by Fackenheim's implicit suggestion in his later work, particularly in his *To Mend the World*, that divine saving presence may be expressed through human acts of social justice and mending of the ruptures created by the Holocaust. This theological suggestion, taken from Fackenheim's understanding of Lurianic kabbalism, is a profound conception of divine relation to humanity, which is a vital aspect of my own theology. Here, in distinction from Fackenheim's earlier understanding of saving and commanding presence, divine saving presence both requires and is founded on human activity. God remains other to humanity and yet both are most fully and profoundly integrated in the effort to mend the world. This point is not fully developed by Fackenheim perhaps because he felt that too facile an understanding of divine saving presence and human potential for goodness betrays the reality of the divine-human failure to act in such a way during the Holocaust. However, he seemed to want to allow for the possibility that this divine-human activity is possible today because it was in fact actual in some ways even during the Holocaust. This divine saving presence was made manifest in human acts of resistance.

Such a perspective is consistent with the ways that Raphael develops the idea of divine presence as *Shekhinah*, as well as Dwight Hopkins' naming of God as the Spirit of Total Liberation in Us. Similar to my revised humanocentric theism, and in distinction from Jones, Hopkins' notion of the Spirit of Total Liberation in Us unequivocally displays divine goodness. Furthermore, in step with both Jones' and my humanocentric theism, Hopkins' exploration of God and humanity as co-laborers in the struggle for liberation places even greater responsibility on human efforts than does Cone's work. This "third person" of Hopkins' Trinity is good, active, presence that is powerful in a loving, creative, and primarily persuasive sense. This persuasive power calls for human acts of resistance in solidarity with God, in ways that are very much in line with the theological position advanced here. Part of my hesitancy in exactly identifying my revised humanocentric theism with Hopkins' theology is due to the fact that Hopkins still basically asserts the virtual inevitability of liberation because of the divine power in his understanding of God as Way Maker. The designation of the Spirit of Total Liberation in Us is only one person of Hopkins' liberationist "Trinity." Hopkins presents God as Spirit of Total Liberation in Us as part of the larger context that includes God as the Spirit of Total Liberation for Us, which is consistent with God as Way Maker. This notion of God as omnipotent and of liberation as, for all practical purposes, assured acts as an insurance policy or a safety net, should humans fall short of the goal of liberation.

This is precisely where Jones' challenge to black liberation theology is most called for. Jones asserted that humans will resist ethnic suffering and economic, social, and political oppression more vehemently and ferociously in the absence of such a divine insurance policy or safety net. The power of humanocentric theism's bold claim of the functional ultimacy of humanity is to challenge any form of quietism, passivity, or indifference in the face of suffering and moral evil.

Humanocentric theism is a call for people to understand ethnic suffering as evil and an imperative to resist all forms of suffering and moral evil.

In my understanding of the divine-human relationship, humans remain fully human. I am not claiming that we are divine, but that, being created in the image of God, we are most human when we express this image of God in acts of love and social justice, and less human when we carry out oppressive, evil actions. In this way, God remains other to us, yet acts through us in a sense, entering into the most immanent relation with us. God is present to each individual in differing degrees at different times. There exists a mystical union between God and the human in which divine presence may be characterized as an ebb and flow force within us. God inspires and persuades us to act for goodness, liberation, and hope, but it is up to us to actually carry out any form of redemption.

Suffering and evil, according to such a theology, are the fault of humanity directly and God only indirectly. The theodicy problem does not disappear, as one may still question why God was not more present to and within humans who carry out evil actions. Further, such a conception still does not explain natural evils. Rather, it is simply one suggested model of divine-human relation that I believe is more true to human history and our contemporary understandings of the potential for dominant, explicit divine intervention in history. That is, instead of looking to God to step into history to prevent evils from occurring at all, we must become more aware of our own potential to change the course of history. Being created in freedom, we must realize that as a society we will have successes and failures, but this is the human condition. God's immanence within our efforts for the good and God's sustaining persuading power within human history must be the basis for a genuine faith and hope in both God and humanity. Out of love and creativity, God gives humanity free will and persuades us to act toward the good. God gives us space to carry out actions of love, liberation, and hope; God persuades us to do so, and sustains us in such efforts. In this way, divine benevolence and power are manifested.

If we start with conceptions of divine power that differ from classical understandings, then some of the critiques of divine goodness that have been raised in the experience of suffering and oppression are mitigated. The issue becomes whether reinterpretations of divine power as persuasive, such as my revised humanocentric theism, Raphael's formulation of divine presence as *Shekhinah*, and Hopkins' naming of God as the Spirit of Total Liberation in Us, provide meaningful and relevant concepts of God; I believe they do.

Theological Anthropology: Resistance

We now move from our discussion of God to an examination of theological anthropology. After a brief discussion of pertinent aspects of the theological anthropologies of Cone and Fackenheim, I offer my perspective on humanity. Finally, a few examples of resistance are explored in the hope of clarifying this concept as an ethical category, which follows from my theological and anthropological views.

According to Cone, humanity is both sinful and endowed with freedom. Sin is an existential category, rather than a moral one, which is characterized as estrangement from one's true being. For oppressors, sin means standing in the way of another's complete realization of full humanity; for the oppressed, sin is the state of being false to one's true self, or not striving to develop one's full humanity. For Cone, humans are created in the image of God, which means we have the freedom and drive to revolt against forces that oppress us. This human freedom is based on divine freedom. In this sense, God and humanity work with each other to resist oppression. The basis of social justice and resistance movements is the claim that no one is free until we are all free. As free humans, we have a responsibility to strive toward the full liberation and redemption of all humanity, as God acts to liberate the oppressed in history. Thus, we struggle for freedom, but God will carry us forward when and if we fall short of the goal.

According to Fackenheim, humans are created as free beings. Unlike the Christian understanding of original sin, the Jewish concept of sin allows for more flexibility. According to Judaism, humans are created with an inclination toward the good (*yetzer ha-tov*) and toward the bad (*yetzer ha-ra*). We are free to act according to either inclination, though we do tend toward the bad. Like Cone's understanding of the redemption/liberation process, Fackenheim's notion of redemption involves both God and humanity. While we must strive toward redemption, God acts along with us and ultimately is responsible for redemption. Fackenheim's basis for human resistance against despair and oppression in the face of evil is the fact that, during the Holocaust, when there was no divine saving presence apparent, Jews resisted the forces of evil. In his later work, as has been suggested earlier, Fackenheim implies that perhaps these human resistance efforts are in fact aspects of the divine saving presence. At any rate, there is a sense, as in Cone's anthropology, that for Fackenheim, though human efforts are central to redemption, God is the ultimate redeemer of humanity.

For both Cone and Fackenheim, then, we are free, but we tend toward sin; redemption involves both God and humanity, though both thinkers emphasize God's decisive role in this process. Both men reject a naïve optimism concerning humanity, given the horrific and pervasive evils that each man's community has encountered, but both maintain a realistic and hopeful optimism in God and humanity in spite of these evils.

My starting point for theological anthropology is the centrality of our freedom. We are created in the image of God, which for me means that we are created as free individuals and with the purpose of developing and existing in this freedom with one another. I suggest that the biblical pericope of the Fall in the Garden of Eden could be interpreted in a manner consistent with such an understanding of freedom.

Traditionally the Fall of Adam and Eve in Genesis 3 has been interpreted in Christian theology as a fall into sin. By disobeying God's command not to eat from the tree of the knowledge of good and evil, Adam and Eve commit the first sin and are cursed to death. This interpretation leads to an understanding of the divine-human relationship in which God has all the power, humans are sinful, because they are rebellious, and a sense that only God can "fix" us.

This traditional interpretation is rejected as outmoded and oppressive. Instead of as a fall into sin, the story of Adam and Eve should be understood as humanity's metaphorical fall into genuine freedom. Before eating from the tree of the knowledge of good and evil, Adam and Eve have freedom, but it is a naïve freedom. They must have free choice, as they choose to eat from the tree in the first place. However, it is only after eating from the tree that they fully understand, or have knowledge of, their freedom to choose between good and evil. Further, after eating from the tree they begin to realize the nature of both good and evil and their amazing potential for either. In other words, they have become divine-like, in this sense. As in Genesis 3:22: "The man has now become like one of us, knowing good and evil." Rather than a story of sin, this is a story of why we are mortal and why we have freedom.

With our fall into freedom, humanity steps into adulthood as a species. We come to see our potential for great love, community, and progress, as well as our potential for horrific evil, despair, and oppression. We come to see ourselves for what we are: creatures capable of both great good and great evil. The knowledge of this freedom is both our curse and our blessing. We know that it may be within our reach to transform society into a near perfect community, but that we usually fall short of this goal.

Further, it is important to see that the story of Adam and Eve involves more than one individual. It is only after Eve is created from the Adam that their fall into freedom occurs. Our freedom is put to its best use when done in relationship with one another and in partnership with one another.

There is a mixing of the divine and the human in each of us in our encounter with the divine, and yet we remain wholly distinct from God. The entire point of the encounter for both God and humans is that it is an encounter with the Other in which both sides may prosper. We see that we are capable of bettering ourselves morally, spiritually, communally if we try. Despair and oppression are to be resisted. God encourages us to resist forces of despair and oppression both within ourselves and without. It is in this resistance that the full power and manifestation of the proper and best divine-human encounter is exhibited. We are created as beings capable of love, freedom, and creativity. God wants us to be this way, God encourages us to be this way—but God cannot "make" us this way, or else it would not be meaningful. It is in constantly striving toward hope and love, liberation and freedom, that we become what we were created to be. We improve on God's creation, thus improving the God-human relation as a whole, thus, in a way improving God— that is why we are created. Practically speaking, humans must carry out this goal; theologically speaking, it is only because God creates us, God gives us freedom, God gives us love and hope; our efforts are grounded in God's being.

This basically optimistic view of the potential of humanity is founded on the idea of our creation in God's image and the belief that God acts through our freedom. It is claimed that given the above reinterpretation of divine power, as well as contemporary scientific and historical understandings of the limits of dominating divine intervention, God acts through humanity. I agree with Cone and Fackenheim that we are created as free beings who tend toward sin. I also agree that existence in general and the process of redemption in particular involve both God and humanity. However, I emphasize human action over divine. If humanity is to be redeemed it will come through human activities. Granted, these human actions are possible only because of our freedom, which is founded on divine freedom, and on God's goodness and persuasive power, which we work with when we act toward redemption, but when individuals, forces, and institutions impede progress toward redemption, liberation, and hope, we must resist. Our resistance is based on the divine will that we all become fully human. In this way, human resistance efforts carry out and strive for the divine will that we live in freedom. To further clarify the category of resistance suggested here, a few examples are explored. Three compelling types of resistance are care of one another, humor, and social and political liberation movements.

The resistance of care is epitomized in examples such as the parable of the Good Samaritan,[53] in the Holocaust memoirs of the women Melissa Raphael employs as theological sources, as well as in Alice Walker's characters Shug and Celie in *The Color Purple*.[54] In each of these examples, individuals place the needs of others before their own, in an almost entirely altruistic fashion. The individuals in these instances who carry out a resistance of care resist social norms and conventions that dictate that the people they assist are worthless and beyond care. It is by caring for these people thought to be useless and outcast that resistance is carried out with the intent of allowing another's full humanity to flourish in the face of overwhelming oppressive and evil forces. In performing a resistance of care these individuals are depending on their free will, based on divine freedom, and are acting on divine persuasion that encourages such selfless acts of altruism. These are actions taken without concern for reward or gain. They resist evil forces, oppressive social norms, and egoistic selfishness to encourage the full flourishing of another's full humanity, and in this way, their own as well. It is important to add, as much feminist and womanist scholarship has explored, that the type of care expressed here should never involve giving of oneself to the point that one's own humanity is diminished. The resistance of care, as is the case in the next forms of resistance (resistance of humor), need not be limited to great humanitarian efforts, but must be understood as also inclusive of small, simple acts of kindness.

Just as the resistance of care includes ordinary, everyday activities, as well as great acts of humanitarianism, the resistance of humor must be understood as most importantly manifested in private conversations and subtle acts of subversion. There is a generally accepted notion of great traditions of subversive humor among both African Americans and Jews. Humor has been employed by these communities as a psychological coping mechanism as well as a method of coded communication and subversive action. Folktales and jokes serve to overturn oppressive power relations in society either artistically or literally. Poking fun at an oppressor is one way in which oppressed peoples deal with the absurdity of their condition and survive with their full humanity intact. Such humor also serves to encourage the continued struggle for hope and liberation from horrific conditions and to subvert the power of the oppressor. Here are a few examples of such African American and Jewish jokes:

> Pompey, how do I look?
> O, massa mighty.
> What do you mean 'mighty,' Pompey?
> Why, massa, you look noble.
> What do you mean by 'noble'?
> Why, sar you just look like one lion.
> Why, Pompey, where have yo ever seen a lion?
> I see one down in yonder field the other day, massa.
> Pompey, you foolish fellow, that was a jackass.
> Was it, massa? Well you look just like him.[55]

*   *   *

Some years before he became Chancellor, Hitler was making a speech in a Berlin beer hall, and as usual, his voice dripped with anti-Jewish vitriol. To his annoyance, he observed a man in the front row who smiled and chuckled throughout the talk.

When the address was over, Hitler sent word to the stranger that he wished to see him in a nearby coffee house. The man appeared a few minutes later.

"Tell me," said Hitler, noting the stranger's heroic nose, his patriarchal beard and his mannerisms, "aren't you a Jew?"

"Yes, I am."

"Then what were you so pleased about during my lecture? Have you any doubts about my intention to carry out my program against you and your kind?"

"I have no doubts about that at all," answered the old man. "That's why I laughed."

"I don't understand."

"Look at it from my point of view. We Jews have known enemies like you before. Pharaoh thought he could enslave us, and, in honor of our flight to freedom, we celebrate the beautiful festival of Passover. Haman tried to exterminate us and, in commemoration of our survival, we celebrate the joyous occasion of Purim. The destruction of every such despot has brought us another glad holiday. Now you, Hitler, hate us more than did Pharaoh and Haman put together, so I smile and laugh in anticipation of the supremely happy holiday we will observe after we get rid of you, too!"[56]

* * *

During the early part of the Hitler regime, before the infamous "final solution," German Jews taught their children to conform outwardly to Nazi customs, for the sake of survival.

One such Jew was teaching his young son how to conduct himself when eating in a restaurant where he might be observed by others. "When saying the blessing," he reminded the youngster, "the correct form of grace is 'Thank God and the *Fuehrer.*'"

"But suppose the *Fuehrer* dies?" queried the boy.

"In that case, my son," the father explained, "you just thank God."[57]

* * *

In the above examples blacks and Jews resist evil and their oppressive conditions by mocking a slave master or Hitler. In these jokes blacks and Jews resist forces of dehumanization, maintain sanity, overturn false stereotypes, and mitigate the forces of oppression in their lives. In addition, particularly in the folktales and songs of enslaved black Americans, humor could be employed as a means of coded communication, conveying escape plans and news to one another.[58]

In addition to the forms of resistance of care and humor, there also exists the tradition of communal social and political liberation movements. This type of resistance seeks to encourage and even demand the full flourishing of every person's humanity, and especially that of people and groups who are oppressed and marginalized. Though communal in nature, the resistances of social and political movements of this type usually comprise smaller, sometimes individual efforts. This type of movement resists social and political injustices and civil rights violations, environmental degradation, psychological oppression, and any other forces that impede and discourage the full development of humanity. It employs tactics such as political grass roots organization, public protests, and artistic expressions such as graphic arts, music, literature, and sometimes rebellious and revolutionary efforts. Characteristic examples of this type of resistance include the Bar Kochba revolts, Nat Turner's insurrection, Labor Union organization in the early twentieth century in the United States, the Gandhi-led movement for Indian independence, the Warsaw Ghetto Uprising, the civil rights movement in the United States, the Stonewall Rebellion, the protest music of Bob Marley, the antiapartheid efforts in South Africa, the Zapatista movement, and organizations such as Call to Renewal.

As is the case in the other two categories of resistance, it is asserted here also that God is present in such acts of resistance, encouraging our participation and efforts. The claim is that these movements have responded to moments of rare and special opportunity, or *kairos*, that God has presented to us and has persuaded individuals and communities to act on. It is through such movements that God is present to us as liberator (Cone) and as commanding *and* saving presence (Fackenheim). Though God and humanity work together in this type of resistance, as in the other two categories, practically speaking, liberation and salvation are the work and responsibility of humanity.

This category of resistance is admittedly more problematic than the other two in the sense that it is always dangerous and potentially arrogant and misguided to claim that a social or political movement is carried out in response to the will of God and carries the God's full support. This resistance is always based on human interpretation of the social and political scene and therefore fraught with the danger of misinterpretation and political and personal preferences and biases. However, these efforts are nevertheless necessary for us to attain our full humanity and thus fully respond to God's gift of freedom and God's call to liberation from oppression and for hope in the face of terror and despair. The point here is that God carries out acts of liberation through human efforts. If we are to be free from oppression and despair, we must be the ones who carry out the resistance in the struggle for human freedoms and welfare. We must use our God-given freedom and conscience to discern the signs of the times and act out of determination, in love, and for justice.

A corollary to this particular understanding of resistance may seem to be suffering encountered in the process would be interpreted as redemptive. This understanding is rejected here. Suffering is an inevitable and unfortunate aspect of human existence. Suffering is impossible to avoid. Furthermore, suffering is unavoidable in carrying out acts of resistance. Such suffering, however, is not redemptive. The claim that suffering is redemptive is characteristic of Cone's thought, but not Fackenheim's. Fackenheim explicitly rejected interpreting the suffering and death of Jews during the Holocaust as anything but manifestations of human evil. Cone, in contrast, understands suffering to produce some positive effects.

Following the thought of Martin Luther King, Jr. here, Cone asserts that, despite the critiques of William R. Jones, Anthony Pinn, and Delores Williams, among others, suffering encountered in the struggle for the liberation of the oppressed is redemptive. He argues that the life, death, and resurrection of Jesus Christ indicate God's full willingness to suffering with humanity, to suffer as humanity. He continues by asserting that the suffering and resurrection of Jesus give hope and solace to the oppressed of today. The knowledge that Jesus is with them in their suffering encourages them to struggle on through suffering and grow in the faith that God will redeem, that God will liberate. Suffering encountered in the midst of the struggle for liberation is redemptive for Cone.

As stated earlier, I believe suffering is certainly inevitable, but must be understood as a force to be resisted, not embraced. This is not to say that suffering encountered in the struggle for liberation cannot build character or strengthen one's resolve. It certainly may have these effects. However, this need not mean that suffering be interpreted in any positive way, which I feel, it is, if understood as redemptive. Human suffering in the forms of oppression and despair is a result of humans oppressing humans. To understand suffering as redemptive, as having some positive effects, brings into question the goodness of God. We may indeed have to struggle against suffering. The primary positive result that comes from such a struggle is the will to end future suffering and oppression.

The position of humanocentric theism and the category of resistance are based on the work of James Cone and Emil Fackenheim. Though the critiques of their work by various thinkers have been considered and at times accepted as valid, it is still Cone and Fackenheim who provide the primary inspiration for my own theology suggested here. Each theologian has been profoundly influential within his own religious community and I believe each deserves renewed and wider reading. Though differing in important ways from Cone and Fackenheim, I hope that this work will make some small contribution to the conversation.

No matter what theological and ethical perspective one has, the problem of evil and the existence of suffering remain. However, by understanding divine power as persuasive, subtle, and manifested most significantly in human acts of creativity, love, and resistance, we may be led to fight against the oppression and despair to which Cone and Fackenheim responded. In the end such a struggle may also be understood as positively fighting for peace, justice, and redemption in solidarity with God and with each other.

Notes

1 Introducing Black and Jewish Responses to Experiences of Moral Evil and Suffering

1. Some would say that the nature of faith is such that it cannot and should not be analyzed so thoroughly. In other words, it is not supposed to make sense. I am not satisfied by this response. Faith need not always be rational, but surely it need not be irrational.
2. I thank David Tracy for suggesting the need for clarification on this point.
3. Though I am phrasing the issue as one of theodicy, it may in fact be more helpful to understand the positions of many of the thinkers explored in this work (especially Pinn and Rubenstein) as advocating a position of antitheodicy. Antitheodicy may be understood as a position in which there is no compulsion expressed for justifying God as good or powerful. For more on the usefulness or inadequacy of the category of theodicy, see Zachary Braiterman's *(God) After Auschwitz* (Princeton: Princeton University Press, 1998) and Sarah Katherine Pinnock's *Beyond Theodicy* (Albany, NY: State University of New York Press, 2002). I am indebted to Paul Mendes-Flohr for this important insight.
4. I agree with process and feminist theologians who interpret divine power as persuasive and creative, rather than coercive and dominating. However, the concept of God suggested in the present work is much more personal than the God of process theology as I understand it. For further interpretation of process theology in comparison to the theology developed here, see chapter 6.
5. Unlike Jones' humanocentric theism, my revised notion does include God's goodness. See chapter 6 for this distinction.

2 What Does the Christian Gospel Have to Do with the Black Power Movement?: James Cone's God of the Oppressed

1. I thank Nathan Rickard for bringing this to my attention. It was a brief, but very significant moment in my academic life.
2. This assertion is a fundamental aspect of James Cone's theological methodology. Before Cone, and other black theologians, Latin American liberation

theologians, and feminist theologians, it had been assumed, largely by Western, white, male thinkers, that theology should be and was an objective, detached exploration and proclamation of the Word of God, untainted by human concern or ideology. Cone and other progressive thinkers showed that what had been assumed to be objective and universal truth was really nothing more than subjective interpretations based on a white, male worldview and shaped by white, male concerns. Simply put, human experience and human interests shape theology. Consequently, Cone consistently begins theological treatments with a discussion of his history, as well as a more general context of black history in the United States. For Cone's complete spiritual and intellectual autobiography see his *God of the Oppressed*, rev. ed. (Maryknoll, NY: Orbis, 1997), 1–7; *My Soul Looks Back* (Maryknoll, NY: Orbis, 1986); *Risks of Faith: The Emergence of a Black Theology of Liberation, 1968–1998* (Boston: Beacon Press, 1999). See also Cone, "Black Theology: Where We Have Been and a Vision for Where We Are Going," in *Yearning to Breathe Free: Liberation Theologies in the United States*, ed. Mar Peter-Rauol, Linda Rennie Forcey, and Robert Frederick Hunter, Jr. (Maryknoll, NY: Orbis, 1990); Cone, "Looking Back, Going Forward: Black Theology as Public Theology," *Criterion* 38 (Winter 1999): 18–27, 46. Finally, Rufus Burrow, Jr.'s "James H. Cone: Father of Contemporary Black Theology," *Asbury Theological Journal*, (Fall 1993) provides a fairly recent and complete theological biography of Cone.

3. Cone, *God of the Oppressed*, 1.

4. Cone, *My Soul Looks Back*, 29–30.

5. Cone, *God of the Oppressed*, 5.

6. Ibid., 6. Throughout his work, Cone cites Martin Luther King, Jr. and Malcolm X as two of his primary influences. In his early writing Cone turns particularly to Malcolm X and the Black Power movement as theological sources. For discussions of the role of Black Power in his theology see Cone, "Christianity and Black Power," in *Is Anybody Listening to Black America*, ed. C. Eric Lincoln (New York: Seabury Press, 1968); Cone, *Black Theology and Black Power*, 20th anniv. ed. (San Francisco: HarperSanFrancisco, 1989); Cone, "Black Theology and Black Liberation," *Christian Century* 87 (Sept. 16, 1970): 1084–1088; Cone, "Black Theology and the Black Church: Where Do We Go from Here?" *Mid-Stream* 17 (July 1978): 267–277; and Cone, "Looking Back, Going Forward: Black Theology as Public Theology," in *Black Faith and Public Talk: Critical Essays on James H. Cone's* Black Theology and Black Power, ed. Dwight N. Hopkins (Maryknoll, NY: Orbis, 1999).

7. See Cone, *For My People: Black Theology and the Black Church* (Maryknoll, NY: Orbis, 1984), 96–98; and Cone, *A Black Theology of Liberation*, 20th anniv. ed. (Maryknoll, NY: Orbis, 1990), xi–xx.

8. Jacqueline Grant explains that Cone did not address this issue until the mid-1970s. Furthermore, Grant asserts, the first male black theologian who did was William R. Jones in his book, *Is God a White Racist?: A Preamble to Black Theology* (Boston: Beacon Press, 1973). There Jones stated, "[H]ere the issue of divine sexism becomes a live issue. What does Jesus' assumption of a male form imply relative to the coequal status, the cohumanity and

salvation of females?" (126). It would be a few years before the formal beginnings of Womanist Theology came.

9.   Cone, *A Black Theology of Liberation*, xvii.
10. One could say that Cone's work, especially from *God of the Oppressed* (1975) through *Martin & Malcolm & America: A Dream or a Nightmare* (Maryknoll, NY: Orbis, 1991), becomes focused on the links between black oppression in the United States and oppression throughout the world. From an initial analysis of African experience and philosophy as a methodological point, Cone's theology turns next to Latin America and then to Asia in pursuit of a more nuanced and complete treatment of the nature of oppression and the possibility of liberation. On Africa, see Cone and Gayraud S. Wilmore, "Black Theology and African Theology: Consideration for Dialogue, Critique and Integration," in *Black Faith and Black Solidarity: Pan-Africanism and Faith in Christ*, ed. Priscilla Massie (New York: Friendship Press, 1973). On Latin America, see Cone, "From Geneva to Sao Paulo: A Dialogue between Black Theology and Latin American Liberation Theology," in *The Challenge of Basic Christian Communities: Papers from the International Ecumenical Congress of Theology, February 20–March 2, 1980, Sao Paulo, Brazil*, ed. Sergi Torres and John Eagleson (Maryknoll, NY: Orbis, 1981). On Asia, see Cone, "Asian Theology Today: Searching for Definitions," *Christian Century* (May 23, 1979): 589–591. On the relationship between black theology and third world theology in more general terms, see Cone, "Reflections from the Perspective of U.S. Blacks: Black Theology and Third World Theology," in *Irruption of the Third World: Challenge to Theology: Papers from the Fifth International Conference of the Ecumenical Association of Third World Theologians, August 17–29, 1981, New Delhi, India*, ed. Virginia Fabella and Sergios Torres (Maryknoll, NY: Orbis, 1983); Cone, "Black Theology and Third World Theologies," *Chicago Theological Seminary Register* 73:1 (1983): 3–12; Cone, "Black Theology: Its Origin, Methodology, and Relationship to Third World Theologies," in both *Doing Theology in a Divided World: Papers from the Sixth International Conference of the Ecumenical Association of Third World Theologians, January 5–13, 1983, Geneva, Switzerland*, ed. Virginia Fabella and Sergio Torres (Maryknoll, NY: Orbis, 1985), and in *Church in Struggle: Liberation Theologies and Social Change in North America*, ed. William K. Tabb (New York: Monthly Review Press, 1986). Ironically enough, Cone's attention to third world oppression preceded his recognition of the connections between black oppression in the United States and oppression of other minorities *within* his own country. On these relationships, see his *For My People*, 157–174.
11. Cone, *A Black Theology of Liberation*, xviii; Cone, *For My People*, 88–96.
12. Cone, *A Black Theology of Liberation*, xviii.
13. Cone often turned to Karl Barth, Paul Tillich, Albert Camus, and Jean-Paul Sartre, among other white thinkers, throughout *Black Theology and Black Power* and *Black Theology of Liberation*. By his *Spirituals and the Blues: An Interpretation* (Maryknoll, NY: Orbis, 1992) and *God of the Oppressed* (1975, 1997) Cone had fully and consciously made the transition to building

his constructive theology on black experience and black history, at the exclusion of, or at least suspicion of, white sources. For a curiously intense and superficial white critique of Cone's reliance on "white" sources at the neglect of "the black religious experience," see Frederick Sontag's "Coconut Theology: Is James Cone the 'Uncle Tom' of Black Theology?" *Journal of Religious Thought* 36 (Fall–Winter 1979): 5–12; see also Archie Smith, Jr.'s "A Black Response to Sontag's 'Coconut Theology' " *Journal of Religious Thought* 36 (Fall–Winter 1979): 13–25. Smith retorts that Cone's methodological danger is not his portrayal of the black religious experience, but rather his "uncritical acceptance and seemingly idolatrous allegiance to black power." Clearly, Cone has been criticized for everything from "being too black" to not being the right type of black to not "being black enough." To an extent, these wide-ranging criticisms from all sides indicate not that Cone is misguided but, on the contrary, that he was quite insightful in his theology, in my opinion.

14. Cone acknowledges that several of the early representatives of black theology, including Gayraud Wilmore, Cecil Cone, Charles Long, and Henry Mitchell, emphasized this point (*For My People*, 86–88). These thinkers maintained that, for black theology to be truly black, one had to turn to the black experience in the United States, and eventually and fundamentally to African sources. On this point, see Gayraud Wilmore, *Black Religion and Black Radicalism: An Examination of the Black Experience in Religion* (Garden City, NY: Anchor Press, 1973); Cecil Cone, *The Identity Crisis in Black Theology* (Nashville: AMEC, 1975); and Charles Long, "Perspectives for a Study of Afro-American Religion in the United States," *History of Religions* 11(Aug. 1971); and Long, "Structural Similarities and Dissimilarities in Black and African Theologies," *Journal of Religious Thought* 32 (Fall–Winter 1975).

15. Gustavo Gutierrez, *A Theology of Liberation: History, Politics, and Salvation*, rev. ed. (Maryknoll, NY: Orbis, 1988), 11.

16. In his early work, Cone meant African Americans in particular when he used the word oppressed. As previously indicated, he later came to nuance his understanding of oppression to include the complexities of sexism, classism, and imperialism (see his preface to the 1986 edition of *A Black Theology of Liberation*, his preface to the 1997 edition of *God of the Oppressed*, chapter 5 of *For My People*), and chapters 4 and 5 of *My Soul Looks Back*. I would agree with Cone's later conception of oppression as being complex, multifaceted, and interrelated. Oppression occurs whenever an individual or community is not able to strive toward their full humanity as intended by God because of the sins of another individual or community standing in their way. Thus, though oppression is a broad, holistic category, including both socioeconomic realities as well as psychological phenomena, it usually is systemic and involves those with power, specifically economic, social, cultural, and/or sexual power, standing over and against those without power.

17. Cone, *A Black Theology of Liberation*, 5.

18. Paul Tillich, *Systematic Theology*, vol. 1 (Chicago: University of Chicago Press, 1951), 66.

19. For Cone's critique of white theology and the white church see chapter three of his *Black Theology & Black Power* (1989) and chapter 2 of *For My People* (1984). According to Cone, the failure of white theologians to see that the liberation of the oppressed is the will of God is compounded by the claim that their theologies are objective and universal interpretations of the Gospel, whereas Cone's was based on ideology. If a Christian theology refuses to consider the experiences of the oppressed of society, then that theology is not Christian in content or in form. In Cone's words, it is impossible "to do Christian theology apart from the biblical claim that God came in Christ to set the captives free." In a footnote to this comment, Cone explains, "Everything I have written has been an explication of this central thesis" ("What is Christian Theology?" *Encounter* 43 no. 2 [Spring 1982]: 122).

20. Cone, *My Soul Looks Back*, 38–39.

21. See Steven W. Stall, "Sociology of Knowledge, Relativism, and Theology," in *Religion and the Sociology of Knowledge: Modernization and Pluralism in Christian Thought and Structure*, ed. Barbara Hargrove (New York: Edwin Mellon Press, 1984). Stall critiques Cone and other liberation theologians, not for claiming the social contextualization of all theology, but for not recognizing their own ideological turn in claiming their stance to be correct and all others false. In other words, according to Stall the sociology of knowledge approach states that all statements are related to context, not that some are false and others are true. Therefore, in making the claim that white theology is heretical and that black theology is the true interpretation of the message of the Bible, Cone is guilty of the same offense for which he indicts white Christians. Of course, Cone might argue that liberation is revealed as the Word of God, not the word of humanity, in the Bible as he does in "Black Theology and Ideology: A Response to My Respondents," *Union Seminary Quarterly Review* 31:1 (Fall 1975). Stall argues that Cone's claim of divine revelation as source of his liberation stance is still not valid, but he does not further explain this denial in his essay.

22. Cone, *A Black Theology of Liberation*, 18–20.

23. Ibid., 38.

24. In other places, Cone seems to say that the Bible and his Christian identity come before the primacy of black experience in his theology: see his "What is Christian Theology?" 118. The reason for the apparent discrepancy is that Cone does not see the issue as an either/or methodological consideration. In other words, the choice between being black and being Christian is no choice at all because to be Christian is to be black, and vice versa, as Cone interprets both terms.

25. Cone, "The Dialectic of Theology and Life or Speaking the Truth," *Union Seminary Quarterly Review* 24 no. 2 (Winter 1974): 75.

26. Cone, *Black Theology and Black Power*, 8–9.

27. Ibid., 11.

28. Cone, *A Black Theology of Liberation*, 24.

29. Ibid., 25.

30. Ibid., 23–25. On the importance of the black experience as a theological source and its relationship to the Bible, see also "The Dialectic of Theology

and Life or Speaking the Truth." In this essay Cone discusses the black experience through specifically religious manifestations of the sermon, prayer, and song.

31. Cone, *A Black Theology of Liberation*, 26.
32. Ibid., 25–27.
33. Ibid., 27–29.
34. Ibid., 29–33.
35. In addition to his fuller treatments of the Bible as a source for black theology present in his books, Cone's "Biblical Revelation and Social Existence," *Interpretation* 28:4 (Oct. 1974): 422–440, provides a very thorough treatment of his biblical hermeneutics. There Cone states, *"The hermeneutical principle for an exegesis of the scriptures is the revelation of God in Christ as the liberator of the oppressed from social oppression and to political struggle, wherein the poor recognize that their fight against poverty and injustice is not only consistent with the gospel but is the gospel of Jesus Christ"* (439). One would be hard pressed to find a more complete and succinct statement of not only Cone's biblical hermeneutic, but also his entire theological enterprise. For more on Cone's use of the Bible, see Robert A. Bennett, "Biblical Theology and Black Theology," *Journal of the Interdenominational Theological Center* 3 (Spring 1976): 1–16.
36. Cone, *A Black Theology of Liberation*, 31.
37. Cone, *Black Theology and Black Power*, 120.
38. Cone, *A Black Theology of Liberation*, 1–2.
39. Ibid., 31.
40. Ibid.
41. Ibid., 46.
42. Ibid., 60.
43. Albert Cleage, *The Black Messiah* (Trenton, NJ: Africa World Press, 1989 ed.), 41, 45.
44. Ibid., 73.
45. Ibid., 115, 138.
46. Cone, *A Black Theology of Liberation*, 100.
47. Cone, "Biblical Revelation and Social Existence," 424.
48. Cleage, *The Black Messiah*, 73, 92, 244.
49. Cone, *A Black Theology of Liberation*, 104.
50. Cone, "Biblical Revelation and Social Existence," 426.
51. Cone, *Black Theology and Black Power*, 64.
52. Cone, "Biblical Revelation and Social Existence," 430.
53. Cleage, *The Black Messiah*, 45.
54. Ibid., 71.
55. Cone, *A Black Theology of Liberation*, 123.
56. Ibid., 121.
57. Ibid., 63.
58. On the issue of literal and symbolic blackness, as well as the more general topic of universals and particulars, William Hordern's interview with Cone is enlightening: "Dialogue on Black Theology," *Christian Century* 88 no. 37 (Sept. 15, 1971): 1079–1085. In this brief interview, the dialectical character

of Cone's theology is evident. Never straying from the commitment to blackness and particularity, Cone also discusses the role of symbolic blackness that is universally accessible and necessary. According to Cone, theology of liberation must begin with the particular experience of oppression and then, only after time and struggle, move toward a more universal notion of liberation. The assertion that the universal notion of liberation cannot fully encompass the particularity of oppression marks Cone's theology as dialectical. In other words, a give-and-take relationship must always characterize the interplay of the particular and the universal. For an insightful analysis of what Cone's category of "blackness" means for a theological category of "whiteness," see Glenn R. Bucher, "Liberation in the Church: Black and White," *Union Seminary Quarterly Review* 29 (Winter 1974): 91–105. Bucher examines how white liberation from the role of the oppressor is dependent on black liberation from oppression.

59. Cleage, *The Black Messiah*, 45, 91.
60. Cone, *Black Theology and Black Power*, 33.
61. Ibid., 74. On the white corruption of Christianity during slavery, see Dwight Hopkins, *Shoes That Fit Our Feet: Sources for a Constructive Black Theology* (Maryknoll, NY: Orbis, 1993), 20–22.
62. Some of Cone's work may be seen as a Christian apologetic written to black Americans, especially to younger, more militant blacks of the late 1960s and early 1970s who claimed that Christianity is incurably the white man's religion. For his defense of the liberating power of Christianity, properly interpreted, see "Black Theology and the Black College Student," *The Journal of Afro-American Issues* 4 nos. 3–4 (Summer/Fall 1976): 420–431. On Cone's rejection of black nationalist and black Marxist groups that misunderstood and too strongly criticized the black church, see *My Soul Looks Back*, 54–57. There he claims that some black nationalist groups unknowingly offered the same critique of the black church as "otherworldly and compensatory" as white racist groups had.
63. Cone, *Black Theology and Black Power*, ix.
64. Cone cites this passage throughout his work and, generally, relies more on Luke's gospel account than any other. For example, see *A Black Theology of Liberation*, 3; *Black Theology and Black Power*, 35; and "Biblical Revelation and Social Existence," 434.
65. Cone, *A Black Theology of Liberation*, 6.
66. Ibid., 128.
67. Cone, *Black Theology and Black Power*, 36.
68. Cone, *A Black Theology of Liberation*, 114.
69. Ibid., 115.
70. Ibid., 118.
71. Cone, *Black Theology and Black Power*, 35.
72. Cone, *A Black Theology of Liberation*, 32.
73. Cone, *Black Theology and Black Power*, xii.
74. Ibid., 38.
75. Cone, *A Black Theology of Liberation*, 121.
76. Ibid., 119–124.

77. See Kelly Brown Douglas, *The Black Christ* (Maryknoll, NY: Orbis, 1994), 68. According to Cone, the universal message of liberation through Christ may be accessed only through the particularity of Christ as he identifies with the oppressed and downtrodden, taking on their experiences and struggling to overcome oppression in their lives.

78. Cone, *Black Theology and Black Power*, 1.

79. Ibid., 32.

80. Ibid., 31.

81. The dialectical relationship between the black experience and the interpretation of the Bible characterizes Cone's work. His early writings sought to bring the Black Power movement into relation with the Bible and the Christian tradition. Particularly from his *Spirituals and the Blues* (1972, 1992) onward, Cone traces the belief in God as liberator through black experience and history. Before the early 1970s he had believed that experience must shape how one encounters the Bible. After 1972, Cone began to demonstrate that this claim was not a new one, but rather had characterized black Christian thought all along. That is, for Cone, the black experience, though inseparable from the encounter with the Bible, in and of itself points to God as liberator. For example, in the black spirituals one already finds a faith in God as liberator that paradoxically seems to both precede and be based on the black encounter with the Bible. In addition to *Spirituals and the Blues*, see also Cone, "The Meaning of God in the Black Spirituals," in *God as Father?* ed. Johannes-Baptist Metz and Edward Schillebeeckx (Edinburgh: T & T Clark, 1981).

82. Cone, *A Black Theology of Liberation*, 45.

83. Ibid., 70–71.

84. Ibid., 45.

85. Ibid., 46.

86. Ibid.

87. For a fascinating discussion of the differences between ideology and theology, specifically on how to differentiate between the Word of God and the words of humanity, see Cone, "Black Theology and Ideology."

88. Cone, *God of the Oppressed*, 90.

89. Cone, *A Black Theology of Liberation*, 46.

90. Cone, *God of the Oppressed*, 57.

91. Cone, "Biblical Revelation and Social Existence."

92. Cone, *A Black Theology of Liberation*, 75.

93. Cone, *Black Theology and Black Power*, 29.

94. Cone, *God of the Oppressed*, 134.

95. Cone, *Black Theology and Black Power*, 39.

96. Cone, *God of the Oppressed*, 64.

97. Ibid., 58.

98. Cone, *A Black Theology of Liberation*, 2.

99. See Delores S. Williams, *Sisters in the Wilderness: The Challenge of Womanist God-Talk* (Maryknoll, NY: Orbis, 1993).

100. The dilemma occurs when black liberation theologians identify with the Israelites who, after having been oppressed in Egypt, become oppressors in Canaan. Furthermore, this change in status is apparently carried out at

the behest of God. If God sides with the oppressed of the land, would God side with the conquering Israelites or the conquered Canaanites? This problem indicates a serious ambiguity and potential danger inherent in liberation theology. For a Palestinian liberation interpretation, see Naim Ateek, *Justice and Only Justice: A Palestinian Theology of Liberation* (Maryknoll, NY: Orbis, 1989); for a Native American view, see Robert Allen Warrior, "Canaanites and Conquerors," *Christianity and Crisis* 49 no. 12 (Sept. 11, 1989).

101. Cone, *A Black Theology of Liberation*, 110.
102. Ibid., 38. In quoted passages throughout the book the original italicized emphasis has been maintained.
103. Ibid., 114. In quoted passages throughout the book the original italicized emphasis has been maintained.
104. Cone, *God of the Oppressed*, 74.
105. Cone, *A Black Theology of Liberation*, 3.
106. In "The Liberator as Exorcist: James Cone and the Classic Doctrine of Atonement," *Religion in Life* 49 (Winter 1980): 477–487, David L. Weddle places Cone's Christology within the context of traditional Christian theologians, including Anselm. Oddly, Weddle understands Cone's Christ as a triumphalistic exorciser of the demon of racism. Further, he misinterprets Cone as advocating violence as the *only* means to black liberation.
107. Cone, *A Black Theology of Liberation*, 118.
108. Ibid., 121.
109. Cone, *God of the Oppressed*, 125–126.
110. Cone, *A Black Theology of Liberation*, 121.
111. Ibid., 60.
112. Cone, *God of the Oppressed*, 57.
113. Cone, *A Black Theology of Liberation*, 81.
114. Ibid.
115. Cone, *The Spirituals and the Blues*, 65.
116. Cone, *A Black Theology of Liberation*, 63.
117. Cone, *Black Theology and Black Power*, 152.
118. Ibid., 151.
119. Cone, *A Black Theology of Liberation*, 63.
120. Ibid., 64.
121. Cone, *God of the Oppressed*, 126.
122. Cone, *A Black Theology of Liberation*, 76.
123. Cone, "The Meaning of God in the Black Spirituals."
124. Cone, *A Black Theology of Liberation*, 76–77.
125. Cone, "Biblical Revelation and Social Existence," 425.
126. Cone, *A Black Theology of Liberation*, 77.
127. Cone's thinking on love and justice is deeply influenced by Martin Luther King. Cone explains that King in turn had been influenced primarily by the black church tradition, but also by white liberal Protestantism and the writings of Henry David Thoreau and Mohandas Gandhi. King's fundamental assertion was that love and justice could not be separated without falsely altering the meaning of both concepts. See Cone, "The Theology of Martin Luther King, Jr.," *Union Seminary Quarterly Review* 40 no. 4 (1986): 21–39.

128. Cone, *A Black Theology of Liberation*, 68.
129. Ibid., 67.
130. Ibid., 2.
131. Ibid., 70.
132. Ibid., 71.
133. Ibid., 73–74.
134. Ibid., 70.
135. Ibid.
136. Ibid., 72–73.
137. Reinhold Niebuhr, *The Nature and Destiny of Man: a Christian Interpretation*, vol. 1, *Human Nature* (New York: Scribner's, 1941), 222–223.
138. Cone, *A Black Theology of Liberation*, 82.
139. See Edward K. Braxton, "Bernard Lonergan and Black Theology," in *Civilisation noire et Eglise catholique*, ed. L. P. Ngongo et al. (Paris: Presence Africaine, 1978). Braxton argues that Cone's designation of theoretical issues, such as God's existence, theodicy, Christology, as white and practical issues, such as survival and liberation, as black is too general and simplistic. Braxton claims that though perhaps most blacks are not concerned with these theoretical and philosophical questions, certainly some are. Likewise, many poor whites worry more about their next meal than they do about the persons of the Trinity. I believe Braxton's response is a common, and to an extent valid, response to Cone's statements. However, Braxton misunderstands Cone's notions of blackness and whiteness. Those who are black, literally and symbolically, *are* concerned more with survival than with philosophy. Here, blackness means those who are oppressed, poor, and powerless in society. Cone's immediate concern is certainly those who are literally black, but his theology extends to a greater group than this.
140. Cone, *A Black Theology of Liberation*, 83.
141. Ibid., 83.
142. I agree with Cone that theology must not ignore the human situation, in concrete, real terms. Theology should not simply be abstract philosophical reflection done in a social and historical vacuum. I also agree that to make claims about humanity and about God and not to take human suffering and oppression into account is to invalidate the latter, or at least to make them questionable. However, I do not believe that many of the white theologians Cone lumps together consciously chose to ignore racism and oppression. Rather, they differed from Cone methodologically and, as a result, believed theology to be concerned first with God, and with all else after. This explains, but does not excuse, their overwhelming ignorance of or apathy toward social affairs in general, though there certainly were white theologians concerned with social justice. I am thinking in particular of Reinhold Niebuhr and Walter Rauschenbusch.
143. Cone, *A Black Theology of Liberation*, 84.
144. Ibid., 108.
145. Cone writes, "Sin, then, is the failure of Israel to recognize the liberating work of God. It is believing that liberation is not the definition of being in the world" (Ibid., 105).

146. Sin, then, is both epistemological and ethical. Epistemologically, we sin when we lack knowledge of our true selves and our history. This is the importance of Black Power and Black Consciousness. Thinkers such as Malcolm X and Steve Biko taught that black history reveals the value and beauty of black history and culture. As Malcolm X asserted, "[t]he worst crime the white man has committed has been to teach us to hate ourselves" (cited by Cone in *Black Theology and Black Power*, 18). Ethically, we sin when we fail to act on such epistemological revelations. To know that we should act morally and justly, striving for the liberation of the oppressed is only the first step. We sin also unless we act for the liberation of the oppressed.

147. Cone, "Freedom, History, and Hope," in *Liberation, Revolution, and Freedom: Theological Perspectives*, ed. Thomas M. McFadden (New York: Seabury, 1975), 60.

148. Ibid., 59.

149. Cone, *A Black Theology of Liberation*, 94.

150. Ibid., 93.

151. Ibid., 89.

152. Ibid., 88.

153. Cone, "Freedom, History, and Hope," 64.

154. Cone, *God of the Oppressed*, 127.

155. Cone, *A Black Theology of Liberation*, 87–88.

156. Cone, *Black Theology and Black Power*, 125.

157. Cone, "Freedom, History, and Hope," 63.

158. Cone, *Black Theology and Black Power*, 137.

159. Cone, *A Black Theology of Liberation*, 85.

160. Ibid., 128.

161. Cone, *God of the Oppressed*, 130.

162. Cone, *A Black Theology of Liberation*, 97.

163. Ibid., 80.

164. Cone, *God of the Oppressed*, 159.

165. Ibid., 159.

166. Ibid., 161.

167. Ibid., 163.

168. Ibid., xviii.

169. Ibid., xvii.

170. Ibid., xvii.

171. Cone reiterates his perspective on suffering and theodicy in "Calling the Oppressors to Account: Justice, Love, and Hope in Black Religion," in *The Courage to Hope: From Black Suffering to Human Redemption*, ed. Quinton Hosford Dixie and Cornel West (Boston: Beacon Press, 1999); this essay is reprinted as "God is the Color of Suffering," in *The Changing Face of God*, ed. Frederick Schmidt (Atlanta: Morehouse Publishing, 2000). See also Warren McWilliams, "Theodicy according to James Cone," *Journal of Religious Thought* 36 (Fall–Winter 1979): 45–54 and McWilliams, "Divine Suffering in Contemporary Theology," *Scottish Journal of Theology* 33 no. 1 (1980): 39–43.

172. Cone, *Black Theology and Black Power*, 12.

173. Cone, *The Spirituals and the Blues*, 23.

174. Cone, *Black Theology and Black Power*, 137.

175. Cone, "Black Theology and Ideology," 78.

176. On the biblically based imperative to resist dehumanization and social injustice see Cone, "Christian Faith and Political Praxis," *Encounter* 43 no. 2 (Spring 1982): 12, 17–19; and Cone, "What is Christian Theology?" 118–119.

177. Cone cites inspiration from these black resistance leaders in many places, including his "Black Theology: Its Origin, Methodology, and Relationship to Third World Theologies"; "Black Theology on Revolution, Violence, and Reconciliation," in *Modern American Protestantism and Its World: Historical Articles on Protestantism in American Religious Life, Vol. 9: Native American Religion and Black Protestantism*, ed. Martin Marty (Munich: Saur, 1993), 293; and "Black Spirituals: A Theological Interpretation," *Theology Today* 29 no. 1 (1972): 57–58. Also notice that a religious basis for resistance may be claimed for all of these historical figures.

178. This option is explored in depth in chapter 3 of this work.

179. On these differences between Cone's theistic basis for resistance and Jones' humanistic foundation, see Cone, "What is Christian Theology?" 125–128, and Cone, "Christian Faith and Political Praxis," 135–142. On the importance of hope in the freedom struggle see Cone, "Martin Luther King: The Source for His Courage to Face Death," in *Martyrdom Today*, ed. Johannes-Baptist Metz and Edward Schillebeeckx (Edinburgh: T & T Clark, 1983).

180. I venture to claim that Cone would approve of any religious or philosophical basis that both encourages acts of social justice for the oppressed of society as well as instills hope that liberation will be actualized. For example, in the preface to the 1989 edition of *Black Theology and Black Power* he explains, "As in 1969, I still regard Jesus Christ today as the chief focus of my perspective on God but not to the exclusion of other religious perspectives. God's reality is not bound by one manifestation of the divine in Jesus but can be found wherever people are being empowered to fight for freedom" (xii).

181. Cone, *The Spirituals and the Blues*, 33.

182. Karl Marx, "Criticism of Religion Is the Presupposition of All Criticism," in *The Karl Marx Library*, vol. 5, *On Religion*, ed. Saul K. Padover (New York: McGraw Hill, 1974), 35–36.

183. Cone, "The Meaning of God in the Black Spirituals," 59. Cone discusses this aspect of the spiritual in "Black Spirituals," 60–63.

184. Cone, *The Spirituals and the Blues*, 80.

185. Ibid., 87–88.

186. Cone, "Demystifying Martin and Malcolm," *Theology Today* 51 (Apr. 1994): 30.

187. Cone, *Martin & Malcolm & America*, 2. Cone's book is the best book-length comparative study of Malcolm X and Martin Luther King, Jr. For a chapter-length examination of the importance of Malcolm X and King for contemporary black theology of liberation, see Hopkins' *Shoes That Fit Our Feet*.

188. Cone, *Martin & Malcolm & America*, 50–51.

189. In Ibid., 89.

190. Ibid., 104.

191. Ibid., 108.
192. Malcolm X, *Malcolm X Speaks*, ed. George Breitman (New York: Grove Weidenfeld, 1965), 38–40.
193. Cone, "Martin and Malcolm on Nonviolence and Violence," *The Princeton Seminary Bulletin* 20 no. 3 (1999): 259–261.
194. Malcolm X, *The Autobiography of Malcolm X* (New York: Ballantine, 1964), 383.
195. Malcolm X, *Malcolm X Speaks*, 10.
196. Malcolm X, *The Autobiography of Malcolm X*, 427.
197. Cone, *Martin & Malcolm & America*, 131.
198. Ibid., 78.
199. In Cone, *Martin & Malcolm & America*, 78.
200. Ibid.
201. Martin Luther King, Jr., *Where Do We Go from Here? Chaos or Community?* (Boston: Beacon, 1967), 105.
202. King, *Why We Can't Wait* (New York: New American Library, 1963), 82.
203. Noel Leo Erskine, *King among the Theologians* (Cleveland: Pilgrim, 1994), 152.
204. In Cone, *Martin & Malcolm & America*, 222.
205. Ibid., 233.
206. King, *Where Do We Go from Here?* 21.
207. King, *Strength to Love* (Philadelphia: Fortress), 1981 ed., 97.
208. Cone, *Martin & Malcolm & America*, 223.
209. Ibid., 224–225.
210. Ibid., 237.
211. Ibid., 240.
212. Ibid., 236.
213. Ibid., 84.
214. Ibid., 129–130.
215. For critical discussions of the role of violence in Cone's theological ethics, see Herbert O. Edwards, "Black Theology and the Black Revolution" and Paul L. Lehmann's "Black Theology and 'Christian' Theology," both in *Union Seminary Quarterly Review* 31 no. 1 (Fall 1975): 23–30, 31–37. This issue includes an essay by Cone on violence and reconciliation, responses by several thinkers, and Cone's rejoinder in which he distinguishes his theology from ideology.

3   Why Divine Goodness or Power? Why God? Why Liberation?: Critiques and Affirmations of James Cone

1. William R. Jones, "Theodicy and Methodology in Black Theology: A Critique of Washington, Cone, and Cleage," *Harvard Theological Review* 64 (Oct. 1971): 543.
2. Ibid., 551.

3. Ibid., 550.
4. Henry James Young argued that Jones' humanistic perspective misunderstands tenets fundamental to black theism. Young asserts that God promises that black liberation will come in the future. Maintaining eschatological hope in the future activity of God overcomes the contradiction between divine benevolence and black suffering, he claims. Further, Jones' presupposition that God is the sum of God's acts is anthropomorphic, according to Young. Finally, the exaltation-liberation event that Jones demands for eschatological hope to be warranted is existentially evident in the black community's struggle for freedom, Young suggests. Whether or not Young is correct in his assertions concerning the nature of black theism, it is apparent that Jones relies on an internal criticism of Cone's thought. That is, Cone himself demands that hope be based on evidence, that we know God from God's activity, and that liberation be an already, but not yet, achieved reality. For Young's assessment of Jones' thought, see "Black Theology and the Work of William R. Jones," *Religion in Life* 44 no. 1 (Spring 1975): 14–28.
5. Cone, *A Black Theology of Liberation*, 27.
6. Jones, *Is God a White Racist?: A Preamble to Black Theology*, rev. ed. (Boston: Beacon Press, 1998). Jones claims that any Black theodicy must meet the following dozen points: (1) suffering must not be ultimately blamed on God; (2) divine racism cannot be assumed as false; (3) no perpetuation of black suffering; (4) no divine sexism or black racism; (5) must be monotheistic; (6) no theodicy of deserved punishment; (7) no theodicy of "beyond human comprehension"; (8) must include possibility of "present and/or subsequent amelioration of black oppression" in this life; (9) suffering is negative or oppressive; (10) human efforts are necessary; (11) extermination of oppressive suffering is possible; and (12) must be internally consistent and systematically coherent (174–175).
7. Jones, *Is God a White Racist?* 172.
8. Ibid., 186.
9. Ibid., 187.
10. Ibid.
11. Ibid., 194.
12. Ibid., 191.
13. In ibid., 192.
14. Ibid., 201.
15. Anthony Pinn makes this point in his *Varieties of African American Religious Experience* (Minneapolis: Fortress, 1998) and his *Terror and Triumph: the Nature of Black Religion* (Minneapolis: Fortress, 2003).
16. Jones, "The Case for Black Humanism," in *Black Theology II: Essays on the Formation and Outreach of Contemporary Black Theology*, ed. Calvin E. Bruce and William R. Jones (Lewisburg: Bucknell University Press, 1978), 217–218.
17. On this point, see especially Pinn, ed., *By These Hands: A Documentary History of African American Humanism* (New York: New York University Press, 2001).

18. Jones, "Religious Humanism: Its Problems and Prospects in Black Religion and Culture," *Journal of the Interdenominational Theological Center* 7 (Spring 1980): 179.

19. Jones, "Process Theology: Guardian of the Oppressor or Goad to the Oppressed: An Interim Assessment," *Process Studies* 18 no. 4 (Winter 1989): 277.

20. Cone, "Epilogue," in *Black Theology: A Documentary History, 1966–1979*, ed. Gayraud S. Wilmore, Jr. and James H. Cone (Maryknoll, NY: Orbis, 1979), 437–438.

21. Cone, *God of the Oppressed*, 188.

22. Ibid., 177.

23. Rufus Burrow, Jr. also points out this flaw in Cone's response and the necessity of an adequate consideration of this point for the future of black liberation theology. See especially Burrow, *James H. Cone and Black Liberation Theology* (Jefferson, NC: McFarland & Company, 1994), 196–202.

24. Pinn, *Why Lord?: Suffering and Evil in Black Theology* (New York: Continuum, 1995), 19.

25. Ibid., 99.

26. Ibid., 97–100.

27. Ibid., 87.

28. Ibid., 89.

29. Pinn, *Why Lord?* 141.

30. Ibid., 158.

31. Pinn, *Varieties of African American Religious Experience*, chapter four.

32. Pinn, *By These Hands*, 10.

33. Ibid., 8.

34. Pinn, *Why Lord?* 157.

35. Ibid., 158.

36. Hopkins, in *Moral Evil and Redemptive Suffering: A History of Theodicy in African-American Religious Thought*, ed. Anthony Pinn (Gainesville: University Press of Florida, 2002), 17.

37. Jones, "Theodicy: The Controlling Category for Black Theology," *Journal of Religious Thought* 30 no. 1 (1973): 32.

38. Alice Walker, *In Search of Our Mothers' Gardens: Womanist Prose* (San Diego: Harcourt Brace Jovanovich, 1983), xi–xii. "Womanist 1. From womanish (Opp. Of 'girlish,' i.e., frivolous, irresponsible, not serious) A black feminist or feminist of color. From the black folk expression of mothers to female children, 'You acting womanish,' i.e., like a woman. Usually referring to outrageous, audacious, courageous, or willful behavior. Wanting to know more and in greater depth than is considered 'good' for one. Interested in grown-up doings. Acting grown up. Being grown up. Interchangeable with another black folk expression: 'You trying to be grown.' Responsible. In charge. Serious. 2. Also: A woman who loves other women, sexually and/or nonsexually. Appreciates and prefers women's culture, women's emotional flexibility (values tears as natural counterbalance of laughter), and women's strength. Sometimes loves individual men, sexually and/or nonsexually. Committed to the survival and wholeness of entire

people, male and female. Not a separatist, except periodically, for health. Traditionally universalist, as in 'Mama, why are we brown, pink, and yellow, and our cousins are white, beige, and black?' Ans.: 'Well, you know the colored race is just like a flower garden, with every color flower represented.' Traditionally capable, as in 'Mama, I'm walking to Canada and I'm taking you and a bunch of other slaves with me.' Reply: 'It wouldn't be the first time.' 3. Loves music. Loves the moon. Loves the Spirit. Loves love and food and roundness. Loves struggle. Loves the Folk. Loves herself. Regardless. 4. Womanist is to feminist as purple is to lavender."

39. Delores Williams, "The Color of Feminism," *Christianity and Crisis* 45 (Apr. 29, 1985): 164–165. Williams, *Sisters in the Wilderness*; Williams, "Womanist/Feminist Dialogue: Problems and Possibilities," *Journal of Feminist Studies in Religion* 9 (Spring–Fall 1993): 67–73.

40. For Williams' initial articulation of "womanist theology," see her "Womanist Theology: Black Women's Voices," in *Weaving the Visions: New Patterns in Feminist Spirituality*, ed. Judith Plaskow and Carol P. Christ (San Francisco: HarperSanFrancisco, 1989).

41. Included among these early womanist works are Katie G. Cannon, *Black Womanist Ethics* (Atlanta: Scholar's Press, 1988); Jacquelyn Grant, *White Women's Christ and Black Women's Jesus: Feminist Christology and Womanist Response* (Atlanta: Scholar's Press, 1989); and Williams, *Sisters in the Wilderness* (1993).

42. Autobiography and literature are two of these sources. For a brief autobiographical essay, see Williams, " 'Keep on Climbing Up': Spiritual Mentors," *Christian Century* 110 (Oct. 6, 1993): 927–928. The literature of African American women as an expression of this experience is frequently used as a source for womanist theology, including and especially that of Delores Williams. Williams draws especially from Margaret Walker, Zora Neale Hurston, and Alice Walker. See Williams, "Women as Makers of Literature," in *Women's Spirit Bonding*, ed. Janet Kalven and Mary I. Buckley (New York: Pilgrim Press, 1984); Williams, "Women's Oppression and Lifeline Politics in Black Women's Religious Narratives," *Journal of Feminist Studies in Religion* 1 no. 2 (Fall 1985): 59–71; Williams, "Black Women's Literature and the Task of Feminist Theology," in *Immaculate and Powerful: The Female in Sacred Image and Social Reality*, ed. Clarissa W. Atkinson, Constance H. Buchanan, and Margaret R. Miles (Boston: Beacon Press, 1985); Williams, " 'The Color Purple': What Was Missed," *Christianity and Crisis* 46 (July 14, 1986): 230–232. For an example of the use of black women's literature, Toni Morrison in particular, used as a source by a male black theologian of liberation, see Dwight Hopkins, "Black Women's Spirituality of Funk," in *Shoes That Fit Our Feet*.

43. For Williams' treatment of the depth and breadth of forms of oppression, see Williams, "Christmas Families," *Christianity and Crisis* 49 (Dec. 11, 1989): 371–372; Williams, "Liberation: Summing Up the Negatives," *Christianity and Crisis* 49 (June 12, 1989): 183–184; Williams, "Exposing False Distinctions," *Sojourners* 19 (Aug.–Sept. 1990): 19–21; Williams, "The 'Sense' of Advent," *Christian Century* 107 (Nov. 21–28, 1990): 1092;

Williams, "A Time of Decision for the Black Community," *Sojourners* 20 (Oct. 1991): 22–23; and Williams, "Kairos Time: Challenge of the Centrisms," *Christianity and Crisis* 52 (Feb. 3, 1992): 16–18.

44. See Mark Chapman, *Christianity on Trial: African-American Religious Thought Before and After Black Power* (Maryknoll, NY: Orbis, 1996), 156.

45. Williams, *Sisters in the Wilderness*, 144.

46. Ibid., 146–147.

47. Ibid., 108.

48. See Elsa Tamez, "The Woman Who Complicated the History of Salvation," in *New Eyes for Reading: Biblical and Theological Reflections by Women from the Third World*, ed. John S. Pobee and Barbel von Wartenberg-Potter (Geneva: WCC, 1986). The demand to encounter the Bible from a non-Jewish perspective has also been made by Palestinian Christians, such as Ateek in *Justice and Only Justice* and Native Americans, such as Warrior in "Canaanites and Conquerors."

49. Williams, *Sisters in the Wilderness*, 60–62.

50. Ibid., 70–71.

51. Ibid., 81.

52. Williams, "Women's Oppression and Lifeline Politics." On the "doctrine of resistance" based on black women's "resistance rituals," see also Williams, "Womanist/Feminist Dialogue."

53. For a critique of traditional Christology and discussion of womanist Christology, see Williams' "Rituals of Resistance in Womanist Worship," in *Women at Worship: Interpretations of North American Diversity*, ed. Marjorie Procter-Smith and Janet R. Walton (Louisville: Westminster/John Knox Press, 1993).

54. Williams, *Sisters in the Wilderness*, 161–162.

55. Ibid., 167.

56. Williams, "A Crucifixion Double Cross? The Violence of Our Images May Do More Harm than Good," *Other Side* 29 (Sept.–Oct. 1993): 25–27. For a critique of Williams' perspective on the crucifixion, see Joanne Terrell, *Power in the Blood?: The Cross in the African-American Experience* (Eugene, OR: Wipf and Stock, 2005).

57. Williams, *Sisters in the Wilderness*, 164.

58. Ibid., 164–165.

59. Ibid., 198.

60. See Cone's 1997 edition of *God of the Oppressed* (Maryknoll, NY: Orbis), 162, 170, for specific allusion to Anthony Pinn. Pinn's *Why Lord?* was published after the first edition of Cone's work, but before the revised edition.

61. Cone, *Black Theology & Black Power*, 124–125.

62. Ibid., 117.

63. Hopkins, *Shoes That Fit Our Feet*; Hopkins, *Down, Up, and Over: Slave Religion and Black Theology* (Minneapolis: Fortress, 2000); Hopkins, *Being Human: Race, Culture, and Religion* (Minneapolis: Fortress, 2005). In *Shoes* Hopkins outlines five sources for a black theology of liberation: slave religion, black women's experience, folk culture, politics, and social analysis. In *Down, Up, and Over* Hopkins fully develops slave religion as a theological source. *Being Human* is an exploration of contemporary theological anthropology.

64. For his conception of God, see Hopkins, "Black Theology on God: The Divine in Black Popular Religion," in *The Ties That Bind: African American and Hispanic American/Latino a Theologies in Dialogue*, ed. Anthony B. Pinn and Benjamin Valentin (New York: Continuum, 2001).

65. Thus, for the purposes of the present work, Hopkins serves not so much as a thinker who is critical of Cone's work as much as one who incorporates the work of Cone's critics into his thinking, especially that of Womanists, and builds on Cone's theology by developing a detailed methodology and branching into new directions such as black folk culture, political economy, and gender. On folk culture, see Hopkins, " 'Now, You Gointer Hear Lies above Suspicion," in *Shoes That Fit Our Feet*; and Hopkins, "Culture: Labor, Aesthetic, and Spirit" and "Conclusion as Introduction" in *Being Human* (2005). On political economy, see Hopkins, "W. E. B. DuBois: Theological Reflections on Democratized Political Power," in *Shoes That Fit Our Feet*; Hopkins, "Social Justice Struggle," in *Spirituality and the Secular Quest*, ed. Peter H. Van Ness (New York: Crossroad, 1996); and Hopkins, "The Religion of Globalization," in *Religions/Globalizations: Theories and Cases*, ed. Hopkins, Lois Ann Lorentzen, Eduardo Mendieta, and David Batstone (Durham, NC: Duke University Press, 2001). On his work with womanist thought, see his "Black Women's Spirituality of Funk."; Hopkins and Linda Thomas, "Womanist Theology and Black Theology: Conversational Envisioning of an Unfinished Dream," in *A Dream Unfinished*, ed. Eleazar S. Fernandez and Fernando F. Segovia (Maryknoll, NY: Orbis, 2001); and Hopkins, "Black Theology of Liberation and the Impact of Womanist Theology," *Heart and Head: Black Theology—Past, Present and Future* (New York: Palgrave, 2002). On gender, see Hopkins, "A New Black Heterosexual Male," *Heart and Head* (2002).

66. For example, see Hopkins, "Theological Method and Cultural Studies: Slave Religious Culture as a Heuristic," in *Changing Conversations: Religious Reflection and Cultural Analysis*, ed. Hopkins and Sheila Greeve Davaney (New York: Routledge, 1996).

67. Hopkins, *Shoes That Fit Our Feet*, 84.

68. Ibid., 24. I believe Hopkins would point to this event as refutation of William R. Jones' claim that God does not act decisively in history as liberator of African Americans.

69. Ibid., 85–93.

70. Hopkins, *Down, Up, and Over*, 159.

71. Hopkins, *Shoes That Fit Our Feet*, 88.

72. Hopkins, *Down, Up, and Over*, 160.

73. Ibid., 163.

74. Ibid., 210.

75. Ibid., 228.

76. Ibid., 234.

77. Ibid., 239.

78. Ibid., 128.

79. Ibid., 129–135, 254–273; and Hopkins, *Shoes That Fit Our Feet* (1993).

80. I believe Hopkins' interest in humor, as well as folk culture and literature, show the influence of postmodernism on his work. That is, these expressions of everyday people, though fragmentary and quotidian, may be understood as more honest and accurate articulations of black experiences because they do not claim the authority of metanarrative. For one of his brief considerations of postmodernism, see Hopkins, "Postmodernity, Black Theology of Liberation and the U.S.A.: Michel Foucault and James H. Cone," in *Liberation Theologies, Postmodernity, and the Americas*, ed. David Batstone, Eduardo Mendieta, Lois Ann Lorentzen, and Dwight N. Hopkins (New York: Routledge, 1997).
81. Hopkins, *Down, Up, and Over*, 255.
82. Ibid., 256.
83. Ibid., 257.

4   A New Sinai? A New Exodus? Divine Presence During and After the Holocaust in the Theology of Emil Fackenheim

1. Emil Fackenheim, *God's Presence in History: Jewish Affirmations and Philosophical Reflections* (New York: New York University, 1970), 84.
2. Fackenheim, *The Jewish Return into History: Reflections in the Age of Auschwitz and a New Jerusalem* (New York: Schocken, 1978), xi; Fackenheim, *Encounters between Judaism and Modern Philosophy: A Preface to Future Jewish Thought* (New York: Basic Books, 1973), 213–229. Fackenheim asserted, "For unlike matters of science, theological matters are of intimate personal concern to us. Our personal experience here inevitably enters into our conclusions, and this experience is necessarily partial and limited." Fackenheim, "Judaism and the Idea of Progress," *Quest for Past and Future: Essays in Jewish Theology* (Bloomington: Indiana University Press, 1968), 83.
3. For a brief account of Fackenheim's intellectual biography, see Fackenheim, "The Development of My Thought," *Religious Studies Review* 13 no. 3 (July 1987): 204–206. See also Fackenheim, *An Epitaph for German Judaism: From Halle to Jerusalem* (Madison: University of Wisconsin Press, 2002).
4. Fackenheim, *To Mend the World*, rev. ed. (Bloomington: Indiana University, 1994), xxxiii–xxxvi.
5. Fackenheim, "Sachsenhausen 1938: Groundwork for Auschwitz," in *The Jewish Return into History* (New York: Schocken Books, 1978), 60.
6. Fackenheim's philosophical work from this period includes *Metaphysics and Historicity* (Milwaukee: Marquette University Press, 1961) and *The Religious Dimension in Hegel's Thought* (Bloomington: Indiana University Press, 1967).
7. Fackenheim, "The Development of My Thought," 204.
8. Ibid., 204.
9. Ibid.

10. For his biblical hermeneutics, see Fackenheim, *What Is Judaism?: An Interpretation for the Present Age*, rev. ed. (Syracuse, NY: Syracuse University Press, 1999) and Fackenheim, *The Jewish Bible after the Holocaust: A Re-Reading* (Bloomington: Indiana University Press, 1991). Fackenheim reads the Bible seriously, but not literally. My treatment of Fackenheim's method does not follow the above investigation of Cone's method in an exact manner. Though Fackenheim wrote with great theological and philosophical depth and breadth, he was not a systematic writer. Most of his published books are collections of essays, articles, and lectures, with *To Mend the World* and *What Is Judaism?* being the exceptions. While it would be possible to explore Fackenheim's method traditionally, that is to identify the sources and norm of his theology, I do not believe it is fruitful. He himself does not consciously carry out such an exercise, and I believe by doing so I would be unnecessarily imposing external categories and expectations on his theological enterprise. However, my exploration of Fackenheim's method does, as was the case in the analysis of Cone, precede the examination of his theology. I believe a statement of Fackenheim's theological impetus, the questions and issues that drove his work, help to set the stage for the analysis to follow.
11. Tillich, *Systematic Theology*, Vol 1 (Chicago: University of Chicago Press, 1951), 64.
12. Fackenheim does not specify which thinkers he has in mind as "classical" theologians.
13. Fackenheim, "An Outline of Modern Jewish Theology," in *Quest for Past and Future*, 101.
14. Ibid.
15. Fackenheim, "The Development of My Thought," 204.
16. Ibid.
17. Fackenheim, "These Twenty Years: A Reappraisal," *Quest for Past and Future*, 9.
18. Fackenheim, *The Jewish Return into History*, xii.
19. Fackenheim, "Can There Be Judaism without Revelation," *Quest for Past and Future*, 75. For more of Fackenheim's early conception of faith, see his "Self-realization and the Search for God," *Judaism* 1 no. 4 (Oct. 1952): 302–303.
20. Fackenheim, "These Twenty Years: A Reappraisal," 9.
21. Ibid., 9–10.
22. Fackenheim, "An Outline of Modern Jewish Theology," 105–106.
23. Fackenheim, *God's Presence in History*, 9.
24. Ibid., 32.
25. Ibid., 11–14.
26. Ibid., 16.
27. Ibid., 16–18.
28. In "Many Genocides, One Holocaust?: The Limits of the Rights of States and the Obligations of Individuals," *Modern Judaism* 1 no. 1 (May 1981): 74–89, Irving Louis Horowitz denies Fackenheim's claim that the Jewish Holocaust is unique. I believe Horowitz ignores the theological ramifications of interpreting the Holocaust as unique in a commendable effort to link resistance

movements against the genocide of any people. It seems to me that any event of genocide is historically, sociologically, culturally, politically, ethically, and theologically unique; and yet, there are certainly points of comparison that are worthwhile to explore. The import of Fackenheim's claim that the Holocaust is unique is that the response to it must be unique also. Fackenheim validly asserted that Jews were singled out as Jews and that their crime was existence as Jews; thus, Jewish response to the Nazi logic of destruction, with absolutely theological aspects, must be survival *as Jews*. Along with Fackenheim, I cannot imagine that this is the exact proposed response to any other act of genocide. Horowitz's challenge, then, really raises the issue of whether respondents to genocidal acts may find solidarity with one another if, in fact, what they are responding to are "unique" events. Must the responses to unique events be themselves unique? I hope to show that, though important distinctions, especially theological ones remain, there may be points of similarity found in the responses to dehumanization, oppression, and despair. For a pertinent discussion of how theological methodology encounters history, see Fackenheim, "Judaism, Christianity and Reinhold Niebuhr—A Reply to Levi Olan," *Judaism* 5 no. 4 (Fall 1956): 316–324.

29. Fackenheim, *To Mend the World*, 12.
30. Ibid., 12–13.
31. Ibid., 183.
32. Ibid., 235.
33. Ibid., 237.
34. Ibid., 238.
35. Fackenheim, "On Life, Death, and Transfiguration of Martyrdom: The Jewish Testimony to the Divine Image in Our Time," in *The Jewish Return into History*, 246.
36. Ibid., 246–247.
37. Fackenheim, *God's Presence in History*, 26.
38. Ibid., 73.
39. Ibid., 72.
40. Ibid., 69.
41. Ibid., 73.
42. Ibid., 27.
43. Ibid.
44. Ibid., 29.
45. Ibid.
46. Ibid., 29–30.
47. Fackenheim, *To Mend the World*, xlvi.
48. Fackenheim *God's Presence in History*, 74.
49. Ibid., 74–75.
50. Fackenheim, "These Twenty Years: A Reappraisal," 18.
51. Fackenheim's category of resistance is further explored below.
52. On Fackenheim's assessment of modern philosophy, see his *The Religious Dimension in Hegel's Thought* and his *Encounters between Judaism and Modern Philosophy*. See also Louis Greenspan and Graeme Nicholson, eds., *Fackenheim: German Philosophy and Jewish Thought* (Toronto: University

of Toronto Press, 1992). Fackenheim always considered himself to be both a philosopher and a theologian. He often posed philosophical questions and responded with religious answers.

53. Throughout his work, particularly his early work, Fackenheim challenges the modern dependence on naturalism and rationalism. See especially Fackenheim, "In Praise of Abraham, Our Father," *Quest for Past and Future;* Fackenheim, "Self-realization and the Search for God"; Fackenheim, "On the Self-exposure of Faith to the Modern-Secular World: Philosophical Reflections in the Light of Jewish Experience" *Quest for Past and Future;* and Fackenheim, "Man and His World in the Perspective of Judaism: Reflections on Expo '67," *The Jewish Return into History.*

54. Fackenheim, *God's Presence in History*, 17.

55. See Fackenheim, "Jewish Existence and the Living God," *Quest for Past and Future.*

56. Fackenheim, "Self-realization and the Search for God," 298 and "An Outline of a Modern Jewish Theology," *Judaism* 3 no. 3 (Summer 1954): 246.

57. Fackenheim, *What Is Judaism?* 283.

58. Fackenheim, *God's Presence in History*, 5.

59. Ibid., 6.

60. Ibid., 43.

61. Fackenheim, *To Mend the World*, 138.

62. Ibid., 139.

63. Ibid.

64. Fackenheim, *God's Presence in History*, 52–53.

65. Fackenheim, *What Is Judaism?* 283.

66. For more on the issue of the covenant in the context of universalism and particularism, see Fackenheim, "The Commandment to Hope: A Response to Contemporary Jewish Experience" in *The Future of Hope*, ed. Walter H. Capps (Philadelphia: Fortress Press, 1970).

67. Fackenheim, *What Is Judaism?* 284.

68. Ibid., 110–112.

69. Ibid., 112–113.

70. Fackenheim, *God's Presence in History*, 25.

71. Fackenheim, *What Is Judaism?* 115.

72. For Fackenheim's early discussion of the covenant, see his "Judaism and the Meaning of Life," *Quest for Past and Future.* For a more recent and fuller treatment of this topic see chapter 5 of his *What Is Judaism?*

73. As we will see in the work of Marc Ellis in chapter 5 of this work, the idea of chosenness has been challenged and reinterpreted by Jewish theologians as well as thinkers from outside the tradition.

74. Fackenheim, *What Is Judaism?* 112. This topic also has obvious ramifications in terms of one's understanding of religious pluralism, which is discussed in chapter 6 of this work.

75. Exodus 19:4–6.

76. God enters into the covenant with Jews, "not for the sake of Israel only, but for the world." The universal mission of the particular community of people is explored below in the section on Fackenheim's understanding of *tikkun.*

For a brief, but lucid, response to the charge of elitism or even racism, see Fackenheim, "A Response to Five Questions," *Quest for Past and Future*.

77. Fackenheim, *What Is Judaism?* 117.

78. Ibid., 113.

79. Fackenheim, *God's Presence in History*, 15.

80. Ibid., 23.

81. Ibid., 15.

82. Ibid., 17.

83. For Fackenheim's discussions of this issue, see Fackenheim, "The Dilemma of Liberal Judaism" and "The Revealed Morality of Judaism and Modern Thought," *Quest for Past and Future*; Fackenheim, "Human Freedom and Divine Power," *Judaism* 12 no. 3 (Summer 1963) and; Fackenheim, "Responsibility and Freedom" *Judaism* 14 no. 2 (Spring 1965). In his ruminations on the relationship between human freedom and divine power in regard to commanding presence, Fackenheim used Kant as an interlocutor. According to Kant, morality cannot be revealed. If it is revealed, then it is heteronomous and it is followed for the sake of another and is therefore not truly moral. If one could arrive at this revealed morality independently of the revelation, if it is autonomously derived, then it is not truly revealed. Kant's own resolution of the dilemma was to claim that a person should not accept a law as moral because it is from God, but rather assert that a law is divine *because* it is moral. Furthermore, one can use reason, apart from revelation, to decide the morality of a given law. Fackenheim, on the contrary, claimed that Judaism has resolved the dilemma by understanding the "essential togetherness" of autonomy and heteronomy in revealed morality. He explained that in Judaism "the Divine manifests Itself as *commanding*, and in order to do so it requires real human freedom . . . . The freedom required in the pristine moment of divine commanding Presence, then, is nothing less than *the freedom to accept or reject the divine commanding Presence as a whole, and for its own sake—that is, for no other reason than that it is that Presence*." When autonomously accepted in its entirety, the divine will is accepted as one's own.

84. Fackenheim, "Human Freedom and Divine Power," 342. It is this understanding of the relationship between religion and philosophy, life and thought, that will provide space for Fackenheim's turn to acts of resistance carried out during the Holocaust when reason will not allow an "explanation" for the event.

85. Fackenheim turned to *midrash* and personal testimonies throughout his work for this reason. In the light of his claim that the Holocaust denies rationalization, Fackenheim depended on the fragmentary yet profound insights of *midrash* and the work of Holocaust survivors such as Elie Wiesel and Primo Levi. See especially Fackenheim, "Demythologizing and Remythologizing in Jewish Experience: Reflections Inspired by Hegel's Philosophy" and "Midrashic Existence after the Holocaust: Reflections Occasioned by the Work of Elie Wiesel," in *The Jewish Return into History*. This literature *expresses*, but does not explain, the realities of the Holocaust world and the Jewish responses to it. As an aside, it is interesting to me that, given his view of the ability of literature to convey the Holocaust world,

Fackenheim did not turn to music or art for similar reasons. For one exception to this, see Fackenheim, "Philosophical Reflections on Claude Lanzmann's *Shoah*," in *Faith and Freedom: A Tribute to Franklin H. Littell*, ed. Richard Libowitz (Oxford: Pergamon Press, 1987).

86. Fackenheim, *Quest for Past and Future*, 39.

87. Ibid.

88. On process theology, see especially the works of Charles Hartshorne and David Ray Griffin.

89. Fackenheim, "Two Types of Reform," *Quest for Past and Future*.

90. Ibid., 175.

91. Fackenheim, "Human Freedom and Divine Power."

92. As is explained in chapter 6 of this work, though certainly sharing similarities with process thought, my own interpretation of divine power owes a primary debt to feminist and womanist theology. The only explicit Jewish feminist encounter with Holocaust theology of which I know is Melissa Raphael's "Is Patriarchal Theology Still Patriarchal? Reading Theologies of the Holocaust from a Feminist Perspective," *Journal of Feminist Studies in Religion* 18 no. 2 (Fall 2002). Raphael takes Holocaust theologians, including Fackenheim, to task for first imposing masculine understandings of power on God and then attempting to formulate theology in light of the failure of this dominating and controlling type of divine power during the Holocaust. In other words, if divine power is reinterpreted along feminist lines (God as relational, empathetic, and present in human communities) some of the traditional theodicy problems *begin* to fall away. See also Raphael, "When God Beheld God: Notes towards a Jewish Feminist Theology of the Holocaust," *Feminist Theology* 21 (1999): 53–78; and Raphael, *The Female Face of God in Auschwitz: A Jewish Feminist Theology of the Holocaust* (London and New York: Routledge, 2003).

93. For a challenging critique of Fackenheim's denial of a saving divine presence after the Holocaust, see Sandra Lubarsky, "Ethics and Theodicy: Tensions in Emil Fackenheim's Thought," *Encounter* 44 (Winter 1983): 59–72. I believe that Fackenheim's focus on human acts of resistance and the possibility of a fragmentary *tikkun olam*, or mending of the world, leave open the hope for redemption. For a useful and clear contextualization of Jewish responses to the Holocaust, including Fackenheim's understanding of divine presence after the Holocaust, see Alan L. Berger, "Holocaust and History: A Theological Reflection," *Journal of Ecumenical Studies* 25 no. 2 (Spring 1988).

94. For his initial articulation of his well-known assertion of the Commanding Voice, see Fackenheim, "Jewish Values in the Post-Holocaust Future: A Symposium," *Judaism* 16 no. 3 (Summer 1967): 266–299; and Fackenheim, *God's Presence in History*.

95. On authenticity, see Fackenheim, "Concerning Authentic and Unauthentic Responses to the Holocaust," *Holocaust and Genocide Studies* 1 no. 1 (1986): 101–120.

96. Fackenheim's articulations of the Commanding Voice of Auschwitz and of the human response to it are explored in the next section on humanity. I believe it makes the most sense to address this aspect of Fackenheim's

theology in the section on humanity rather than in the section on God because, as Fackenheim maintained, the commanding presence of God both overwhelms *and requires* free human response. In other words, as divine commanding presence is fulfilled through human response, this aspect of Fackenheim's theology, existentially speaking, is best understood through an exploration of his theological anthropology.

97. "Man" is used here to indicate Fackenheim's language choice, particularly in his early writings. In his more recent works, Fackenheim uses gender-inclusive language.

98. Fackenheim, "Judaism, Christianity and Reinhold Niebuhr."

99. Compare especially Niebuhr's *The Nature and Destiny of Man* with Fackenheim's early writings such as "Self-realization and the Search for God" (1952) and "An Outline of a Modern Jewish Theology."

100. For more on the divine-human relationship along these lines, see Fackenheim, "An Outline of a Modern Jewish Theology"; Fackenheim, "Judaism, Christianity and Reinhold Niebuhr"; Fackenheim, "Human Freedom and Divine Power, 342–343; Fackenheim, "The Commandment to Hope," 74–77; and "Concerning Authentic and Unauthentic Responses to the Holocaust," 117.

101. Fackenheim, *Quest for Past and Future*, 261–262.

102. Ibid., 78.

103. Ibid., 261.

104. Genesis 9:8–17.

105. Fackenheim, *Quest for Past and Future*, 208.

106. Ibid., 209.

107. Ibid.

108. Ibid., 211–212.

109. Fackenheim, *The Jewish Return into History*, 60.

110. Fackenheim, *The Jewish Return into History*, 109. Sandra Lubarsky compellingly critiques Fackenheim for separating God's saving presence from God's commanding presence in the face of Auschwitz ("Ethics and Theodicy: Tensions in Emil Fackenheim's Thought," *Encounter* 44 no. 1 (Winter 1983)). If the two aspects of divine nature were completely separated, the resulting God would be inadequate, as she argues. However, as will become evident, Fackenheim leaves space for fragmentary divine saving presence in human activity. As this point is mostly clearly developed in Fackenheim's *To Mend the World* (1982), perhaps Lubarsky did not have access to the argument for her own article. This suggestion is supported by the fact that she does not cite Fackenheim's 1982 work.

111. Fackenheim, *God's Presence in History*, 83.

112. See Michael Morgan, "Historicism, Evil, and Post-Holocaust Moral Thought," in *Remembering for the Future: Working Papers and Addenda: Vol. 1: Jews and Christians During and After the Holocaust*, ed. Yehuda Bauer et al. (Oxford: Pergamon Press, 1989). Morgan develops an ethics of resistance based on Fackenheim's categories. In this essay Morgan questions the basis of the imperative to survive as Jews and to resist dehumanization and despair.

113. Fackenheim, "The Commandment to Hope," 89. Ellen T. Charry argues that Fackenheim's articulation of the Commanding Voice of Auschwitz is the same thing as "Jews demanding justice for themselves," thus ignoring Fackenheim's emphasis that the Voice be other than human. See Charry, "Jewish Holocaust Theology: An Assessment," *Journal of Ecumenical Studies* 18 no. 1 (Winter 1981): 132.

114. Fackenheim, *To Mend the World*, 217.

115. Ibid., 218.

116. Fackenheim stopped tantalizingly short of explicitly identifying this voice as divine, although I believe it is strongly implied. Perhaps Fackenheim's formulation of this voice remains inclusive of religious and secular responses if he does not specify the identity of the speaker. On this point see Howard R. Burkle, *God, Suffering, & Belief* (Nashville: Abingdon, 1977), especially 47–49. Furthermore, Laurie McRobert has suggested that Fackenheim's development of the Commanding Voice of Auschwitz in his *To Mend the World* is intended to address Christian as well as Jewish responses (McRobert, "Emil L. Fackenheim: Encounters with Christianity," *Toronto Journal of Theology* 5 no. 2 [Fall 1989]). While I believe Christians did respond during the Holocaust, and must still today, in ways consistent with the Commanding Voice of Auschwitz, I believe Fackenheim's notion of divine commanding presence speaks directly to Jews in their particularity as Jews. While the Holocaust challenges, if not destroy, faith in God and humanity for both Jews and Christians, it does so in different ways for each group and requires unique responses along these lines. In chapter 6 of this work, more is said on Jewish-Christian relations and present-day responses to the Holocaust world.

117. Fackenheim, *God's Presence in History*, 84.

118. Ibid., 92.

119. Fackenheim, *To Mend the World*, 24–25.

120. For more on Fackenheim's development on this point between 1970 and 1982, see Morgan, "Historicism, Evil, and post-Holocaust Moral Thought," 1045–1049.

121. In this section I am addressing Fackenheim's account of Jewish resistance during the Holocaust. This sets the stage for the next section's exploration of forms of resistance after the Holocaust.

122. Fackenheim, *To Mend the World*, 25.

123. Ibid., 223–224.

124. Fackenheim, *The Jewish Return into History*, 60.

125. Ibid., 63–64.

126. Fackenheim, *To Mend the World*, 220.

127. Ibid., 239.

128. Ibid.

129. For a development of the ethics of resistance that remains loyal to Fackenheim's category, see Morgan, "Jewish Ethics after the Holocaust," *Journal of Religious Ethics* 12 no. 2 (1984): 256–277. In the article Morgan also includes more examples of Jewish resistance during the Holocaust.

130. Fackenheim, "The Commandment to Hope."

131. Fackenheim, *God's Presence in History*, 95.

132.   In choosing these three categories, I intend to make an implicit comparison between the theologies of Cone and Fackenheim. Though different in important ways, both in form and content, there are points of similarity between Cone's development of the spirituals and blues and Fackenheim's understanding of *midrash*. Both are creative artistic expressions of theological paradoxes and claims that are best conveyed through story and song. The compelling critiques of racism and anti-Semitism and the resulting emphasis on group solidarity, identity, and strength in the life of Malcolm X and implicitly in the assertion of the importance of the state of Israel provide interesting parallels as well. Finally, the assertion that hope and redemption remain possible and that a divine-human activity must bring it to fruition despite opposing forces of evil, is voiced by both Martin Luther King, Jr. and in Fackenheim's notion of *tikkun olam*. In the end, these three categories were selected because Fackenheim himself develops them as examples of resistance.

133.   McRobert comes to this conclusion in "Emil L. Fackenheim: Encounters with Christianity": 214. Though I agree with this conclusion, I disagree with her that the imperative for Christian activity in bringing about *tikkun* is based on the Commanding Voice of Auschwitz. Though Christians certainly must respond to the Holocaust, I believe Fackenheim interprets the divine commanding presence of the Holocaust to speak specifically to Jews.

134.   Fackenheim, "Midrashic Existence," 264.

135.   Fackenheim, *God's Presence in History*, 20.

136.   Fackenheim, "Midrashic Existence," 263–264.

137.   Ibid., 266.

138.   Ibid., 266–269.

139.   Ibid., 269.

140.   Fackenheim relies heavily of the works of Elie Wiesel, which poetically express life lived in the madness of *midrashic* existence.

141.   Fackenheim, "Demythologizing and Remythologizing in Jewish Experience," 124–126.

142.   Fackenheim, *To Mend the World*, 14, 255.

143.   Fackenheim, "The People Israel Lives: How My Mind Has Changed," *The Jewish Return into History*, 54.

144.   Fackenheim, *To Mend the World*, 284–285.

145.   For more on the role of Israel in Fackenheim's thought, see the essays in part three of his *The Jewish Return into History*, and Fackenheim, "The Zionist Imperative," *First Things* 50 (Feb. 1995): 18–23.

146.   Fackenheim, *God's Presence in History*, 86.

147.   Fackenheim, "The Holocaust and the State of Israel: Their Relation," *The Jewish Return into History*, 279.

148.   Ibid., 282.

149.   The issue of the politics of Israel is central to the discussion in my presentation and critique of the work of Marc Ellis in chapter 5 of this work. Ellis' critique of the type of support for Israel he finds in Fackenheim's writings has been controversial, to say the least.

150.   Fackenheim based his account of this kabbalistic concept on the work of Gershom Scholem. See especially Scholem, *Major Trends in Jewish*

Mysticism, 3rd rev. ed. (New York: Schocken, 1995), 265–278. For an interesting discussion of how the idea of *tikkun* has been incorporated in recent thought, including Fackenheim's use, see Lawrence Fine's "*Tikkun:* A Lurianic Motif in Contemporary Jewish Thought," in *From Ancient Israel to Modern Judaism: Intellect in Quest of Understanding: Essays in Honor of Marvin Fox, Vol 4: The Modern Age: Theology, Literature, History*, ed. Jacob Neusner, Ernest S. Frerichs, and Nahum M. Sarna (Atlanta: Scholars Press, 1989). Fine points out that Isaac Luria had intended *tikkun* to be a cosmic process brought about by contemplative action, such as prayer, performance of commandments, and rituals.

151. Fackenheim, *To Mend the World*, 253.
152. Fackenheim, "Can There Be Judaism without Revelation," 78.
153. Fackenheim, *To Mend the World*, 141.
154. Fackenheim, "Can There Be Judaism without Revelation," 79.
155. Fackenheim, *To Mend the World*, 254.
156. On this point, see especially Morgan, "Historicism, Evil, and Post-Holocaust Moral Thought."
157. Fackenheim, *To Mend the World*, 300.
158. Ibid., 309–310.
159. Ibid., 256.
160. Ibid., 310.
161. Fackenheim, "Religious Responsibility for the Social Order," *Quest for Past and Future*, 193–194.

5   After the Holocaust: The Destruction of the God of History, of Chosenness, and of Patriarchy; Critiques and Affirmations of Emil Fackenheim

1. Ignaz Maybaum, *The Face of God after Auschwitz* (Amsterdam: Polak and Van Gennep, 1965); Richard Rubenstein, *After Auschwitz: Radical Theology and Contemporary Judaism* (New York: Macmillan, 1966) and; Fackenheim, *God's Presence in History*, (1970).
2. For Rubenstein's intellectual autobiography, see *Power Struggle: An Autobiographical Confession* (New York: Scribner's Son, 1974); and Rubenstein, "A Twentieth-Century Journey" in *From the Unthinkable to the Unavoidable: American Christian and Jewish Scholars Encounter the Holocaust*, ed. Carol Rittner and John K. Roth (Westport: Praeger, 1997).
3. For Rubenstein's early response to his critics, see Rubenstein, "Auschwitz and Covenant Theology" *Christian Century* 86 (May 21, 1969): 716–718. For a recent, kinder assessment of Rubenstein's status in contemporary Jewish thought, see Zachary Braiterman, *(God) after Auschwitz: Tradition and Change in Post-Holocaust Jewish Thought* (Princeton: Princeton University Press, 1998). For Rubenstein's own account of early understandings

of his work, see Rubenstein, "Reason's Deadly Dreams," in *The Bent World: Essays on Religion and Culture*, ed. John R. May (Ann Arbor: Edwards Brothers, 1981) and; Rubenstein, "A Twentieth-Century Journey." In these essays and in the second, enlarged edition of *After Auschwitz: History, Theology, and Contemporary Judaism*, 2nd ed. (Baltimore: Johns Hopkins, 1992), Rubenstein explains that his early theological writings were wrongly interpreted as Jewish "Death-of-God" theology. In truth, Rubenstein's work asserts that we live in the time of the death of the God of history, who acts benevolently and powerfully for Israel. He discussed God after the death of this God and focused his interpretation of Judaism on its communal and ritualistic elements. This point is explored in greater detail below.

4. I have in mind here especially Rubenstein, *The Cunning of History: The Holocaust and the American Future* (New York: Harper, 1978); Rubenstein, *The Age of Triage: Fear and Hope in an Over-crowded World* (Boston: Beacon Press, 1983) and; Rubenstein, ed., *Modernization: The Humanist Response to Its Promise and Problems* (Washington: Paragon House, 1982).

5. Rubenstein, *After Auschwitz* (1st ed.), 50–58.

6. Ibid., 152.

7. For Rubenstein's interpretation of divine power in traditional Jewish thought, see Rubenstein, "God's Omnipotence in Rabbinic Judaism" *Judaism* 9 (Spring 1960): 120–128. For a clear explanation of Rubenstein's developing reflections on the Holocaust, see Rubenstein, "Reason's Deadly Dreams" and; Rubenstein, "Radical Theology and the Holocaust," in *The Death of God Movement and the Holocaust: Radical Theology Encounters the Shoah*, ed. Stephen R. Haynes and John K. Roth (Westport: Greenwood Press, 1999).

8. Rubenstein, *After Auschwitz* (1st ed.), 153.

9. Ibid., 136.

10. Ibid., 140.

11. Ibid.

12. Rubenstein, *After Auschwitz* (2nd ed.), xiii. Rubenstein's understanding of the state of Israel is explored further below.

13. Ibid., 298.

14. Ibid.

15. Ibid., 302.

16. Rubenstein, "Reason's Deadly Dreams," 7.

17. See above, chapter 3, for a detailed discussion of Fackenheim's understanding of divine commanding presence.

18. Rubenstein, "Emil Fackenheim's Radical Monotheism," *Soundings* 57 no. 2 (Summer 1974), 238.

19. Ibid., 245–246.

20. For Marc H. Ellis' discussion of the works of Emil Fackenheim, Richard Rubenstein, Irving Greenberg, and Elie Wiesel, see Ellis, *Toward a Jewish Theology of Liberation* (Maryknoll, NY: Orbis, 1987), 7–46; Ellis, *Beyond Innocence and Redemption: Confronting the Holocaust and Israeli Power: Creating a Moral Failure for the Jewish People* (San Francisco: Harper & Row, 1990), 1–31 and; Ellis, "Holocaust Theology and Latin American Liberation Theology: Suffering and Solidarity," in *Remembering for the*

Future: Working Papers and Addenda, Vol. 1: Jews and Christians During and After the Holocaust, ed. Yehuda Bauer et al. (Oxford: Pergamon Press, 1989), 584–587. Ellis tends to group these thinkers together as a homogenized school of thought, "Holocaust theology," and sometimes ignores very genuine differences among their work. Some of these differences are expressed in the above treatments of Fackenheim and Rubenstein.

21.   Ellis, "Holocaust Theology," 585.

22.   Ibid., 586.

23.   Ibid.

24.   Ellis, *Toward a Jewish Theology of Liberation*, 114.

25.   Ibid., 116. Acts of aggression and injustice perpetrated by both Israelis and Palestinians against one another have been copiously rehearsed by many writers and activists in many places. Ellis' accounts of Israeli oppression of Palestinians are present in almost all of his works, but particularly so in *Beyond Innocence and Redemption*, 79–133; Ellis, *Unholy Alliance: Religion and Atrocity in Our Time* (Minneapolis: Fortress, 1997), chapters 1 and 3; Rosemary Radford Ruether and Marc H. Ellis, eds. *Beyond Occupation: American Jewish, Christian, and Palestinian Voices for Peace* (Boston: Beacon Press, 1990), introduction and; Ellis, *Revolutionary Forgiveness: Essays on Judaism, Christianity, and the Future of Religious Life* (Waco, TX: Baylor University Press, 2000), chapters 14 and 15. These realities are excluded here not to mitigate or deny their seriousness but rather because few would deny them.

26.   Ellis has been strongly influenced by his time spent at the Maryknoll School of Theology, as well as his readings of and relationships with such thinkers and activists as Dorothy Day, Daniel Berrigan, and Gustavo Gutierrez. For his autobiographical essays discussing these experiences, see part I of his *Revolutionary Forgiveness*. See also Ellis, "The Legacy of Peter Maurin," *CrossCurrents* 34 no. 3 (Fall 1984): 294–304.

27.   For an illustration of how Ellis incorporates his advocacy of the Palestinian people into his theology, see Ellis, 54–64 in "After Auschwitz and the Palestinian Uprising," in *Contemporary Jewish Religious Responses to the Shoah*, ed. Steven L. Jacobs (Lanham: University Press of America, 1993), 54–64.

28.   Ellis, *Toward a Jewish Theology of Liberation*, 75.

29.   Ibid., 74.

30.   Of course, for Fackenheim, the Holocaust, though sharing some characteristics with other forms of oppression and events of genocide, is a wholly unique event in human history.

31.   Ellis, "Holocaust Theology," 593–594.

32.   Ibid., 595. For Ellis' further reflections on Jewish-Christian relations, see Ellis, *Beyond Innocence and Redemption*, 134–155; Ellis, "Jews, Christians, and Liberation Theology: A Response," in *Judaism, Christianity, and Liberation: An Agenda for Dialogue*, ed. Otto Maduro (Maryknoll, NY: Orbis, 1991) and; Ellis, *Ending Auschwitz: the Future of Jewish and Christian Life* (Louisville: John Knox Press, 1994), 56–130.

33.   Ellis, *Toward a Jewish Theology of Liberation*, 111–112. Though remaining consistent with these characteristics, Ellis does not fully develop this

theology. He claims only to outline features of a theology to be developed by another theologian.

34. For Ellis' interpretation and reworking of Fackenheim's categories of the 614th commandment and *tikkun*, see Ellis, "Restoring the Ordinary: An Inquiry into the Jewish Covenant at the End of Auschwitz," *Asia Journal of Theology* 10 no. 2 (Oct. 1996): 402–406.

35. See Monique McClellan's interview with Ellis, "Power and Empowerment," *One World* no. 145 (May 1989): 17–19.

36. Raphael cites Judith Plaskow, *Standing Again at Sinai: Judaism from a Feminist Perspective* (San Francisco: HarperCollins, 1990) and Rachel Adler, *Engendering Judaism: An Inclusive Theology and Ethics* (Philadelphia: Jewish Publication Society, 1998) as the only two book-length Jewish feminist theologies. There is only a passing reference to the Holocaust in each. Raphael's position says as much about the lack of published Jewish feminist theology as Plaskow and Adler's works. Raphael's early work in feminist thought, theology, and goddess religion includes " 'Cover Not Our Blood with Thy Silence': Sadism, Eschatological Justice and Female Images of the Divine," *Feminist Theology* no. 8 (Jan. 1995): 85–105; *Thealogy and Embodiment: The Post-patriarchal Reconstruction of Female Sacrality* (Sheffield: Sheffield Academic Press, 1996); "Truth in Flux: Goddess Feminism as a Late Modern Religion," *Religion* 26 (July 1996): 199–213; "Real-izing the Material: Spiritual Feminism and the Resacralization of the Earth," in *The Ideal in the World's Religions: Essays on the Person, Family Society and Environment*, ed. Robert Carter and Sheldon Isenberg (St. Paul: Paragon House, 1997); "Thealogy and the Parthenogenetic Reproduction of Femaleness," in *Religion and Sexuality*, ed. Michael A. Hayes, Wendy Porter, and David Tombs (Sheffield: Sheffield Academic Press, 1998); " 'I Will Be Who I Will Be': The Representation of God in Postmodern Jewish Feminist Theology and Contemporary Education," *British Journal of Religious Education* 21 (Spring 1999): 69–79; "Monotheism in Contemporary Feminist Goddess Religion: A Betrayal of Early Thealogical Non-realism?" in *Is There a Future for Feminist Theology?* ed. Deborah F. Sawyer and Diane M. Collier (Sheffield: Sheffield Academic Press, 1999) and; *Introducing Thealogy: Discourse on the Goddess* (Cleveland: The Pilgrim Press, 2000).

37. For a concise statement of this critique, see Raphael, "Is Patriarchal Theology Still Patriarchal? Reading Theologies of the Holocaust from a Feminist Perspective," *Journal of Feminist Studies in Religion* 18 no. 2 (Fall 2002): 105–113.

38. Raphael, *The Female Face of God*, 28.

39. Ibid., 30.

40. Ibid., 30–31.

41. Ibid., 31–32.

42. Two points are important here. First, Raphael defends her use of a, by no means complete or random, selection of memoirs as the basis of her theology of redemption through mutually caring relationships. Responding to Lawrence Langer's claim that Holocaust accounts "nurture not ethical insight but

confusion, doubt, and moral uncertainty," Raphael insists that "theology is not a purely evidential project" and that "the accounts of camp sisterhood need not, then, only be weighed historiographically against their counter-evidential opposite, but can be read theologically as *midrashim* or narrative commentaries on the presence or face of God in Auschwitz." See Langer, *Holocaust Testimonies: The Ruins of Memory* (New Haven: Yale University Press, 1991), 26 and; Raphael, *The Female Face of God in Auschwitz*, 8–9. Langer's argument, applicable to Fackenheim as well as Raphael, echoes Anthony Pinn's claim that James Cone and Dwight Hopkins were reading God and religion *into* slave narratives. I agree with Raphael's response, implied by Fackenheim, Cone, and Hopkins, that theology shares more in common with the arts than the sciences in that theology does not purport to be objective, disinterested, or concerned primarily with the face value of history or reality. The second point is that Raphael claims and adequately demonstrates that her focus on and discussion of women's experiences does not restrict men's experiences or the potential for similar understandings of divine presence and human relationship from a male perspective. On this issue, see Raphael, *The Female Face of God in Auschwitz*, 10, 123.

43. Raphael, *The Female Face of God in Auschwitz*, 54.
44. For more on Raphael's use and critique of Jewish mysticism, see "When God Beheld God," 53–78.
45. Raphael, *The Female Face of God in Auschwitz*, 55.
46. Ibid.
47. Ibid., 61.
48. Ibid., 90.
49. Ibid.
50. Ibid., 95.
51. The category of resistance developed in chapter 6 includes the claim that a variety of individuals with genuine differences may align in support of one another for the common goal of resistance to oppression. I have in mind particularly Jewish-Black and Jewish-Christian efforts.
52. Raphael, *The Female Face of God in Auschwitz*, 98.
53. Ibid., 100.
54. Ibid., 101.
55. Ibid., 74.
56. Ibid., 79.
57. Ibid., 134.
58. Although she does not fully develop her critique of the reliance of Eliezer Berkovits and Arthur A. Cohen on a patriarchal understanding of humans as autonomous and free (see Raphael, "When God Beheld God," 65–66), as I understand it, she would also have objections to the centrality of human freedom in the theology that is developed in the present work.
59. Morgan, "Mendelssohn's Defense of Reason in *Jerusalem*," *Judaism* 38 no. 4 (Fall 1989): 449–459; Morgan, "Martin Buber, Cooperation, and Evil," *Journal of the American Academy of Religion* 58 (Spring 1990): 99–109 and; Morgan, *Dilemmas in Modern Jewish Thought: The Dialectics of Revelation and History* (Bloomington: Indiana University Press, 1992).

60. See Morgan, ed., *Emil Fackenheim: Jewish Philosophers and Jewish Philosophy* (Bloomington: Indiana University Press, 1996); Morgan, ed., *A Holocaust Reader: Responses to the Nazi Extermination* (Oxford: Oxford University Press, 2000) and; Morgan, *Beyond Auschwitz: Post-Holocaust Jewish Thought in America* (Oxford: Oxford University Press, 2001).

61. Morgan, "Jewish Philosophy and Historical Self-consciousness," *Journal of Religion* 71 no. 1 (Jan. 1991): 45.

62. Morgan, "Historicism, Evil, and Post–Holocaust Moral Thought," 1044.

63. Ibid., 1045.

64. Ibid.

65. Morgan, *Beyond Auschwitz*, 182.

66. Ibid.

67. Ibid., 189–190.

68. Morgan, *Interim Judaism: Jewish Thought in a Century of Crisis* (Bloomington: Indiana University Press, 2001), 119.

69. Though Morgan treats the search for transcendence separately from the problem of objectivity, focusing on the relationship between human language and divine-human relation in Buber and Rosenzweig in regard to the former, I understand these aspects as overlapping and almost identical. In addition, where Fackenheim is a central figure in Morgan's articulation of the problem of objectivity, he is peripheral to Morgan's exploration of the search for transcendence in *Interim Judaism*. For these reasons, the present work addresses Morgan's writings on the first two aspects of interim Judaism at the same time. Following this, Morgan's third aspect of messianism and politics is dealt with on its own.

70. Morgan, *Interim Judaism*, 3.

71. Ibid., 27–28.

72. Ibid., 42.

73. Ibid., 113.

74. Ibid., 115.

6   A Consideration of Humanocentric Theism, Resistance, and Redemption

1. Eric Sundquist, *Strangers in the Land: Blacks, Jews, Post-Holocaust America* (Cambridge, MA: The Belknap Press of Harvard University Press, 2005), 18.

2. Ibid., 4.

3. Ibid., 2–3.

4. Ibid., 96, 110.

5. Cheryl Lynn Greenberg, *Troubling the Waters: Black-Jewish Relations in the American Century* (Princeton: Princeton University Press, 2006), 75.

6. Sundquist, *Strangers in the Land*, 66.

7. C.L. Greenberg, *Troubling the Waters*, 74–75.

8. Ibid., 92, 121.

9. Ibid., 117.

10. See C. L. Greenberg, *Troubling the Waters*, chapter 4 for a full discussion of each of these realms.
11. Sundquist, *Strangers in the Land*, 37–38.
12. C. L. Greenberg, *Troubling the Waters*, 59.
13. Sundquist, *Strangers in the Land*, 17–23, 23–30. Though neither James Cone nor Emil Fackenheim wrote very directly about the other contemporary community, it is interesting that both men were most famously active during this very time when black-Jewish relations began to become most strained.
14. C. L. Greenberg, *Troubling the Waters*, 225–227.
15. Sundquist, *Strangers in the Land*, 75.
16. Ibid., 152.
17. Ibid., 110.
18. Ibid., 160.
19. C. L. Greenberg, *Troubling the Waters*, 159.
20. Ibid., 166.
21. Ibid., 206.
22. Ibid., 237.
23. Sundquist, *Strangers in the Land*, 1.
24. Ibid., 15.
25. C. L. Greenberg, *Troubling the Waters*, 207.
26. Ibid., 234–235.
27. Ibid., 208.
28. Krister Stendahl, "Response to *For the Sake of Heaven and Earth*," in Irving Greenberg, *For the Sake of Heaven and Earth: The New Encounter between Judaism and Christianity* (Philadelphia: Jewish Publication Society, 2004), 263.
29. Irving Greenberg. *For the Sake of Heaven and Earth: The New Encounter between Judaism and Christianity* (Philadelphia: Jewish Publication Society, 2004), 44.
30. There are many detailed accounts of Jewish-Christian relations. The primary one consulted here is Tikva Frymer-Kensky et al., eds., *Christianity in Jewish Terms* (Boulder, CO: Westview Press, 2000). Robert Chazan's "Christian-Jewish Interactions over the Ages" in this text speaks most directly to these issues. See also Byron L. Sherwin and Harold Kasimow, eds., *John Paul II and Interreligious Dialogue* (Maryknoll, NY: Orbis Books, 1999), and James Aitken and Edward Kessler, eds., *Challenges in Jewish-Christian Relations* (New York: Paulist Press, 2006).
31. Irving Greenberg, "The Shoah and the Legacy of Anti-Semitism: Judaism, Christianity, and Partnership after the Twentieth Century," in *Christianity in Jewish Terms*, ed. Tikva Frymer-Kensky et al., 33.
32. Austin Flannery, O. P., ed. *Vatican Council II: The Conciliar and Post Conciliar Documents* (Collegeville, MN: Liturgical Press, 1975), 738–749.
33. Diana Eck, *Encountering God: A Spiritual Journey from Bozeman to Banaras* (Boston: Beacon Press, 1993), 191.
34. Ibid., 192.
35. Ibid., 193–196.
36. Ibid., 197–199.

37. Thomas Merton, *Faith and Violence: Christian Teaching and Christian Practice* (Notre Dame, IN: University of Notre Dame Press, 1968), 152.
38. Eck, *Encountering God*, 229.
39. This link between interreligious dialogue and liberation theology must be further developed for the sake of both fields. For important efforts to examine and nuance this connection, see especially the work of Paul Knitter. A particular text that I have in mind in this regard is Knitter, *One Earth Many Religions: Multifaith Dialogue and Global Responsibility* (Maryknoll, NY: Orbis, 1995).
40. Jones, "Process Theology," 278.
41. Howard R. Burkle, *The Non-Existence of God* (New York: Herder & Herder, 1977).
42. Jones, "Process Theology," 278.
43. Ibid., 277.
44. One question then still raised is whether one may claim that *all* people in fact are free in a meaningful and effective way. I thank Anthony Pinn for this question in his response to my paper, "Toward a Revised Humanocentric Theism: A Consideration of William R. Jones on Divine Power and Human Freedom and Suffering," American Academy of Religion Annual Meeting, Washington, DC (2006). My answer is an appeal to an existential freedom, which I believe all people do in fact have access to, rather than to economic, social, and political forms of freedom, to which all certainly do not have access. Such a response may admittedly be a product of my white, male, middle-class, and academic identity. Interestingly, Melissa Raphael critiques some male Holocaust theologians, especially Arthur A. Cohen, for making human freedom a norm in his work.
45. Jones, "Process Theology," 278.
46. Jones, *Is God a White Racist?* 174–175.
47. Jones, "Process Theology," 277.
48. This notion is in part inspired by one of Abraham Joshua Heschel's essays. In speaking about the situation during the Vietnam War and his reading of the Hebrew prophets, Heschel wrote, "Morally speaking there is no limit to the concern one must feel fro the suffering of human beings. It also became clear to me that in regard to cruelties committed in the name of a free society, some are guilty, while all are responsible. I did not feel guilty as an individual American for the bloodshed in Vietnam, but I felt deeply responsible." See Heschel, *Moral Grandeur and Spiritual Audacity*, ed. Susannah Heschel (New York: Farrar, Straus and Giroux, 1996), 225.
49. Fackenheim, *What Is Judaism?* 289–290.
50. For a process-influenced critique of Fackenheim's theology along these lines, see Howard Burkle, *God, Suffering, & Belief* (Nashville: Abingdon, 1977). Burkle, my former professor at Grinnell College, provides one of the only simultaneous analyses of black theology (William R. Jones) and post-Holocaust Jewish theology (Fackenheim) of which I am aware. Burkle also treats existentialism and feminism, examining each school of thought in turn.
51. The question explored later is whether divine commandment is a possible, or is necessary impetus for human ethical action after the Holocaust. For,

the Holocaust calls into question not only whether God is present, but also whether the actions of humanity depend in any way on this presence. Does humanity have the ethical resources to respond to a God who persuades, but does not coerce, who acts as immanent guiding force, not dominant overwhelming power, in the world?

52. See Michael Oppenheim, "Theology and Community: The Work of Emil Fackenheim," *Religious Studies Review* 13 no. 3 (July 1987): 206–210. Oppenheim also states that Fackenheim made this very move in his *To Mend the World.*

53. Luke 10:25–37.

54. Alice Walker, *The Color Purple: A Novel* (New York: Harcourt, Brace, and Jovanovich, 1982).

55. Gilbert Osofsky, ed., *Puttin' on Ole Massa: The Slave Narratives of Henry Bibb, William Wells Brown, and Solomon Northup* (San Francisco: Harper and Row, 1969), 22. This joke is cited in Dwight Hopkins, *Down, Up, and Over*, 255.

56. Henry D. Spalding, ed., *Encyclopedia of Jewish Humor: From Biblical Times to the Modern Age* (New York: Jonathan David Publishers, 1969), 187–188.

57. Ibid., 199.

58. For further examples of black humor, see Daryl Cumber Dance, *Shuckin' and Jivin': Folklore from Contemporary Black Americans* (Bloomington: Indiana University Press, 1978); for a theological interpretation of the role of humor as resistance, see Hopkins, *Down, Up, and Over*, 254–261.

Bibliography

Adams, Maurianne and John Bracey, eds., *Strangers and Neighbors: Relations between Blacks and Jews in the United States.* Amherst: University of Massachusetts Press, 1999.

Adler, Rachel. *Engendering Judaism: An Inclusive Theology and Ethics.* Philadelphia: Jewish Publication Society, 1998.

Aitken, James and Edward Kessler, eds. *Challenges in Jewish-Christian Relations.* New York: Paulist Press, 2006.

Anderson, Victor. *Beyond Ontological Blackness: An Essay on African American Religious and Cultural Criticism.* New York: Continuum, 1995.

———. Review of *Why Lord? Suffering and Evil in Black Theology,* by Anthony B. Pinn. *Cross Currents* 47 (Fall 1997): 410–413.

Ateek, Naim S. *Justice, and Only Justice: A Palestinian Theology of Liberation.* Maryknoll, NY: Orbis, 1989.

Ateek, Naim S., Marc H. Ellis, and Rosemary Radford Ruether, eds., *Faith and the Intifada: Palestinian Christian Voices.* Maryknoll, NY: Orbis, 1992.

Baker-Fletcher, Garth Kasimu. *Xodus: An African American Male Journey.* Minneapolis: Fortress, 1996.

Baker-Fletcher, Karen and Garth Kasimu Baker-Fletcher. *My Sister, My Brother: Womanist and Xodus God-Talk.* Maryknoll, NY: Orbis, 1997.

Berenbaum, Michael. "Women, Blacks, and Jews: Theologians of Survival." *Religion in Life* 45, no. 1 (Spring 1976): 106–118.

Berger, Alan L. "Holocaust and History: A Theological Reflection." *Journal of Ecumenical Studies* 25, no. 2 (Spring 1988): 194–211.

Bosch, David J. "Currents and Crosscurrents in South African Black Theology." *Journal of Religion in Africa* 6 (1974): 1–22.

Boshoff, Carel. "Christ in Black Theology." *Missionalia* 9 (N 1981): 107–125.

Braiterman, Zachary. *(God) After Auschwitz: Tradition and Change in Post-Holocaust Jewish Thought.* Princeton: Princeton University Press, 1998.

Braxton, Edward K. "Bernard Lonergan and Black Theology." In *Black Civilization and the Catholic Church*, edited by Societe africaine de culture. Paris: Presence Africaine, 1978.

Brown, Charles S. "Present Trends in Black Theology." *Journal of Religious Thought* 32 (Fall–Winter 1975): 60–68.

Buber, Martin. *Eclipse of God.* New York: Harper & Row, 1952.

———. *Good and Evil.* New York: Scribner's, 1953.

Buber, Martin. *I and Thou*. Translated by Walter Kaufmann. New York: Scribner's, 1970.

Bucher, Glenn R. "Liberation in the Church: Black and White." *Union Seminary Quarterly Review* 29 no. 2 (Winter 1974): 91–105.

Buhring, Kurt. "Toward a Revised Humanocentric Theism: A Consideration of William R. Jones on Divine Power and Human Freedom and Suffering." Paper presented at the Annual Meeting of the American Academy of Religion, Washington, DC, Nov. 2006.

Burkle, Howard R. *God, Suffering, & Belief*. Nashville: Abingdon Press, 1977. 47–49.

Burrow, Rufus, Jr. *James H. Cone and Black Liberation Theology*. Jefferson, NC: McFarland, 1994. 196–202.

———. "Toward Womanist Theology and Ethics." *Journal of Feminist Studies in Religion* 15 (Spring 1999): 77–95.

Cannon, Katie G. *Black Womanist Ethics*. Atlanta: Scholar's Press, 1988.

Chapman, G. Clarke, Jr. "Black Theology and Theology of Hope? What Have They to Say to Each Other?" *Union Seminary Quarterly Review* 29 no. 2 (Winter 1974): 107–129.

Chapman, Mark L. *Christianity on Trial: African-American Religious Thought Before and After Black Power*. Maryknoll, NY: Orbis, 1996. 156.

Charry, Ellen T. "Jewish Holocaust Theology: An Assessment." *Journal of Ecumenical Studies* 18 no. 1 (Winter 1981): 128–139. 132.

Cleage, Albert B, Jr. *The Black Messiah*. Trenton, NJ: Africa World Press, 1968. 41, 45, 71, 73, 91–92, 115, 138, 244.

Cohen, Arthur A. *The Tremendum: A Theological Interpretation of the Holocaust*. New York: Continuum, 1981.

Cohen, Rich. *The Avengers: A Jewish War Story*. New York: Knopf, 2000.

Cohn-Sherbok, Dan. "Jewish Faith and the Holocaust." *Religious Studies* 26 (1990): 277–293.

Coleman, Will. Review of *Why Lord? Suffering and Evil in Black Theology* by Anthony B. Pinn. *Journal of the American Academy of Religion* 66 (Summer 1998): 461–464.

Cone, Cecil. *The Identity Crisis in Black Theology*. Nashville: AMEC, 1975.

Cone, James H. "An African-American Perspective on the Cross and Suffering." In *The Scandal of a Crucified World: Perspectives on the Cross and Suffering*, edited by Yacob Tesfai. Maryknoll, NY: Orbis, 1994.

———. "America: A Dream of a Nightmare?" *Journal of the Interdenominational Theological Center* 13 (Spring 1986): 263–278.

———. "Asian Theology Today: Searching for Definitions." *Christian Century* (May 23, 1979): 589–591.

———. "Biblical Revelation and Social Existence." *Interpretation* 28 no. 4 (Oct. 1974): 422–440. 424–426, 430, 434, 439.

———. "A Black American Looks at African Theology." *Worldview* 22 (Dec. 1979): 26, 36–38.

———. "Black Consciousness and the Black Church: An Historical-Theological Interpretation." In *Black Renaissance*, edited by Thoahlane Thoahlane. Johannesburg: Ravan Press, 1975.

———. "Black Liberation Theology and Black Catholics: A Critical Conversation." *Theological Studies* 61 no. 4 (Dec. 2000): 731–747.

———. "Black Power, Black Theology, and the Study of Theology and Ethics." *Theological Education* 6 (Spring 1970): 202–215.

———. "Black Spirituals: A Theological Interpretation." *Theology Today* 29 no. 1 (Apr. 1972): 54–69. 57–58, 60–63.

———. "Black Theology and Black Liberation." *Christian Century* 87 no. 37 (Sept. 16, 1970): 1084–1088.

———. *Black Theology and Black Power*. 20th anniv. ed. San Francisco: Harper & Row, 1989. ix, xii, 1, 8–9, 11–12, 18, 29, 31–33, 35–36, 38–39, 64, 74, 117, 120, 124–125, 137, 151–152.

———. "Black Theology and Ideology: A Response to My Respondents." *Union Seminary Quarterly Review* 31 no. 1 (Fall 1975): 71–86, 78.

———. "Black Theology and the Black Church: Where Do We Go from Here?" *Mid-Stream* 17 no. 3 (July 1978): 267–277.

———. "Black Theology and the Black College Student." *The Journal of Afro-American Issues* 4 nos. 3–4 (Summer/Fall 1976): 420–431.

———. "Black Theology and the Imperative and Dilemma of Solidarity." In *Struggles for Solidarity: Liberation Theologies in Tension*, edited by Lorine M. Getz and Ruy Costa. Minneapolis: Fortress Press, 1992.

———. "Black Theology and Third World Theologies." *Chicago Theological Seminary Register* 73 no. 1 (1983): 3–12.

———. "Black Theology from a Historical Perspective." *Bangalore Theological Forum* 22 (June 1990): 1–25.

———. "Black Theology in American Religion." *Introduction to Christian Theology: Contemporary North American Perspectives*, edited by Roger A. Badham. Louisville: Westminster John Knox Press, 1998.

———. "Black Theology in the United States." *Journal of the Interdenominational Theological Center* 16 (1988–1989): 279–283.

———. "Black Theology: Its Origin, Methodology, and Relationship to Third World Theologies." In *Doing Theology in a Divided World: Papers from the Sixth International Conference of the Ecumenical Association of Third World Theologians, January 5–13, 1983, Geneva, Switzerland*, edited by Virginia Fabella and Sergio Torres. Maryknoll, NY: Orbis, 1985.

———. "Black Theology: Its Origins, Method, and Relation to Third World Theologies." In *Churches in Struggle: Liberation Theologies and Social Change in North America*, edited by William K. Tabb. New York: Monthly Review Press, 1986.

———. *A Black Theology of Liberation*. 20th anniv. ed. Maryknoll, NY: 1990. Xi–xx, 1–3, 5, 6, 18–20, 23–33, 38, 45, 46, 60, 63–64, 67–68, 70–77, 80–85, 87, 89, 93–94, 97, 100, 104–105, 108, 110, 114–115, 118–124, 128.

———. "Black Theology on Revolution, Violence, and Reconciliation." In *Modern American Protestantism and Its World: Historical Articles on Protestantism in American Religious Life, Vol. 9: Native American Religion and Black Protestantism*, edited by Martin E. Marty. Munich: Saur, 1993. 293.

———. "Black Theology: Where We Have Been and a Vision for Where We Are Going." In *Yearning to Breathe Free: Liberation Theologies in the United States*, edited by Mar Peter-Raoul, Linda Rennie Forcey, and Robert Frederick Hunter, Jr. Maryknoll, NY: Orbis, 1990.

Cone, James H. "Black Theology on Revolution, Violence, and Reconciliation." *Union Seminary Quarterly Review* 31 no. 1 (Fall 1975): 5–14.

———. "Calling the Oppressors to Account: Justice, Love, and Hope in Black Religion." In *The Courage to Hope: From Black Suffering to Human Redemption*, edited by Quinton Hosford Dixie and Cornel West. Boston: Beacon Press, 1999.

———. "Christian Faith and Political Praxis." *Encounter* 43 no. 2 (Spring 1982): 129–142. 135–142.

———. "Christian Faith and Political Praxis." In *Confronting Life: Theology out of Context*, edited by M. P. Joseph. ISPCK, 1995. 12, 17–19.

———. "Christianity and Black Power." In *Is Anybody Listening to Black America?* edited by C. Eric Lincoln. New York: Seabury Press, 1968.

———. "Christian Theology and Scripture as the Expression of God's Liberating Activity." *Bangalore Theological Forum* 22 (June 1990): 26–39.

———. "A Critical Response to Schubert Ogden's *Faith and Freedom: Toward a Theology of Liberation.*" *The Perkins School of Theology Journal* 33 (Fall 1979): 51–55.

———. "Demystifying Martin and Malcolm." *Theology Today* 51 no. 1 (Apr. 1994): 27–37. 30.

———. "The Dialectic of Theology and Life or Speaking the Truth." *Union Seminary Quarterly Review* 29 no. 2 (Winter 1974): 75–89. 75.

———. "A Dream or a Nightmare? Martin Luther King, Jr. and Malcolm X: Speaking the Truth about America." *Sojourners* 15 no. 1 (Jan. 1986): 26–30.

———. "Ecumenical Association of Third World Theologians." *Ecumenical Trends* 14 no. 8 (Sept, 1985): 119–122.

———. "Epilogue." In *Black Theology: A Documentary History, 1966–1979*, edited by Gayraud S. Wilmore and James H. Cone. Maryknoll, NY: Orbis, 1979. 437–438.

———. "Evangelization and Politics: A Black Perspective." *Bulletin of African Theology* 4 no. 7 (1982): 5–15.

———. "First EATWOT Inter-Continental Dialogue." *Voices* 22 no. 2 (Dec. 1999): 179–188.

———. *For My People.* Maryknoll, NY: Orbis, 1984. 86–98, 157–174.

———. "Freedom, History, and Hope." In *Liberation, Revolution, and Freedom: Theological Perspectives*, edited by Thomas M. Mcfadden. New York: Seabury, 1975. 59–60, 63–64.

———. "From Geneva to Sao Paulo: A Dialogue between Black Theology and Latin American Liberation Theology." In *The Challenge of Basic Christian Communities: Papers from the International Ecumenical Congress of Theology, February 20–March 2, 1980, Sao Paolo, Brazil*, edited by Sergio Torres and John Eagleson. Maryknoll, NY: Orbis, 1981.

———. "God is the Color of Suffering." In *The Changing Face of God*, edited by Frederick W. Schmidt. Atlanta: Morehouse Publishing, 2000.

———. *God of the Oppressed.* Rev. ed. Maryknoll, NY: Orbis, 1997. Xvii–xviii, 1–7, 57–58, 64, 74, 90, 125–127, 130, 134, 159, 161–163, 170, 177, 188.

———. " 'God Our Father, Christ Our Redeemer, Man Our Brother': A Theological Interpretation of the A.M.E. Church." *Journal of the Interdenominational Theological Center* 4 (Fall 1976): 25–33.

———. "In Search of a Definition of Violence." *Church and Society* 85 (Jan.–Feb. 1995): 5–7.

———. "Looking Back, Going Forward: Black Theology as Public Theology." *Criterion* 38 (Winter 1999): 18–27, 46.

———. "Malcolm X: The Impact of a Cultural Revolutionary." *Christian Century* 109 no. 38 (Dec. 23–30 1992): 1189–1195.

———. *Martin & Malcolm & America: A Dream or a Nightmare.* Maryknoll, NY: Orbis, 1992. 2, 50–51, 78, 84, 89, 104, 108, 129–131, 222–225, 233, 236–237, 240.

———. "Martin and Malcolm on Nonviolence and Violence." *The Princeton Seminary Bulletin* 20 no. 3 (1999): 251–263. 259–261.

———. "Martin Luther King, Jr., and the Third World." In *The Future of Liberation Theology: Essays in Honor of Gustavo Gutierrez*, edited by Marc Ellis and Otto Maduro. Maryknoll, NY: Orbis, 1989.

———. "Martin Luther King, Jr., and the Third World." In *World Order and Religion*, edited by Wade Clark Roof. New York: SUNY Press, 1991.

———. "Martin Luther King, Jr., Black Theology—Black Church." *Theology Today* 40 No. 4 (Jan. 1984): 409–420.

———. "Martin Luther King, Jr.: Sixty-Fifth Anniversary Overview and Assessment." *Journal of the Interdenominational Theological Center* 21 (1993–1994): 1–9.

———. "Martin Luther King: The Source for His Courage to Face Death." In *Martyrdom Today*, edited by Johannes-Baptist Metz and Edward Schillebeeckx. Edinburgh: T&T Clark, 1983.

———. "Martin, Malcolm, and Black Theology." In *The Future of Theology: Essays in Honor of Jurgen Moltmann*, edited by Miroslav Volf, Carmen Krieg, and Thomas Kucharz. Grand Rapids: Eerdmans, 1996.

———. "The Meaning of God in the Black Spirituals." In *God as Father?* edited by Johannes-Baptist Metz and Edward Schillebeeckx. Edinburgh: T&T Clark, 1981. 59.

———. *My Soul Looks Back.* Maryknoll, NY: Orbis, 1986. 29–30, 38–39, 54–57.

———. "One Lord: 'Who is Our Lord?' " In *Proceedings of the Fourteenth World Methodist Conference*, edited by Joe Hale. World Methodist Council, 1982.

———. "Reflections from the Perspective of U.S. Blacks: Black Theology and Third World Theology." In *Irruption of the Third World: Challenge to Theology: Papers from the Fifth International Conference of the Ecumenical Association of Third World Theologians, August 17–29, 1981, New Delhi, India*, edited by Virginia Fabella and Sergio Torres. Maryknoll, NY: Orbis, 1983.

———. *Risks of Faith: The Emergence of a Black Theology of Liberation, 1968–1998.* Boston: Beacon Press, 1999. xxii.

———. "Sanctification, Liberation and Black Worship." *Nexus* 24 nos. 1–2 (1981–1982): 2–12.

———. "The Servant Church." In *The Pastor as Servant*, edited by Earl E. Shelp and Ronald H. Sunderland. New York: Pilgrim Press, 1986.

Cone, James H. *Speaking the Truth*. Grand Rapids: Eerdmans, 1986.

———. *The Spirituals and the Blues: An Interpretation*. Maryknoll, NY: Orbis, 1992. 23, 33, 65, 80, 87–88.

———. "The Struggle, the Song: An Interview of James Cone." Interviewed by John Alexander. *The Other Side* 31 (Nov.–Dec. 1995): 30–32.

———. "Theological Reflection on Black Theology." In *We Are One Voice*, edited by Simon S. Maimela and Dwight N. Hopkins. Johannesburg: Skotaville Publishers, 1989.

———. "Theology as the Expression of God's Liberating Activity for the Poor." In *The Vocation of the Theologian*, edited by Theodore W. Jennings, Jr. Philadelphia: Fortress Press, 1985.

———. "The Theology of Martin Luther King, Jr." *Union Seminary Quarterly Review* 40 no. 4 (1986): 21–39.

———. "Theology, the Bible, and the Poor." In *Standing with the Poor: Theological Reflections on Economic Reality*, edited by Paul Plenge Parker. Cleveland: Pilgrim Press, 1992.

———. "Toward the Morning." *Sojourners* 13 no. 9 (Oct. 1984): 13–16.

———. "Two Roads to Freedom: Martin Luther King, Jr., and Malcolm X." *Bangalore Theological Forum* 22 (June 1990): 40–61.

———. "The Vocation of a Theologian." In *Theology & Corporate Conscience: Essays in Honor of Frederick Herzog*, edited by M. Douglas Meeks, Jurgen Moltmann, and Frederick R. Trost. Minneapolis: Kirk House, 1999.

———. "What is Christian Theology?" *Encounter* 43 no. 2 (Spring 1982): 117–128. 118–119, 122, 125–128.

———. "What is the Church?" In *Hammering Swords into Ploughshares: Essays in Honor of Archbishop Mpilo Desmond Tutu*, edited by B. Tlhagale and Itumenleng Mosala. Johannesburg: Skotaville Publishers, 1987.

———. "Whose Earth Is It Anyway?" *CrossCurrents* 50 nos. 1–2 (Spring/Summer 2000): 36–46.

———. "Women's Experience of the Sacred: An African American Male Theological Response." *Voices* 19 (June 1996): 162–169.

———. " 'Women's Experience of the Sacred': An Interpretation of EATWOT's 3rd International Dialogue." *Voices* 19 (June 1996): 195–213.

Cone, James H. and Gayraud S. Wilmore, Jr. "Black Theology and African Theology: Consideration for DialogueCritique and Integration." In *Black Faith and Black Solidarity: Pan-Africanism and Faith in Christ*, edited by Priscilla Massie. New York: Friendship Press, 1973.

Cone, James H. and William Hordern. "Dialogue on Black Theology." *Christian Century* 88 no. 37 (Sept. 15 1971): 1079–1085.

Dance, Daryl Cumber. *Shuckin' and Jivin': Folklore from Contemporary Black Americans*. Bloomington: Indiana University Press, 1978.

Douglas, Kelly Brown. *The Black Christ*. Maryknoll, NY: Orbis, 1994. 68.

Eck, Diana. *Encountering God: A Spiritual Journey from Bozeman to Banaras*. Boston: Beacon Press, 1993. 191–199, 229.

Edwards, Herbert O. "Black Theology and the Black Revolution." *Union Seminary Quarterly Review* 31 no. 1 (Fall 1975): 23–30.

———. "Black Theology: Retrospect and Prospect." *Journal of Religious Thought* 32 (Fall/Winter 1975): 46–59.

Ellis, Marc H. "After Auschwitz and the Palestinian Uprising." In *Contemporary Jewish Religious Responses to the Shoah*, edited by Steven L. Jacobs. Lanham: University Press of America, 1993. 54–64.

———. *Beyond Innocence and Redemption: Confronting the Holocaust and Israeli Power: Creating a Moral Future for the Jewish People*. San Francisco: Harper & Row, 1990. 1–31, 79–133, 134–155.

———. *Ending Auschwitz: The Future of Jewish and Christian Life*. Louisville: John Knox Press, 1994. 56–130.

———. "Ending the Era of Auschwitz." *Christian Century* 116 (Oct. 6 1999): 938–941.

———. *Faithfulness in the Age of Auschwitz*. Amity, NY: Amity House, 1986.

———. "Holocaust Theology and Latin American Liberation Theology: Suffering and Solidarity." In *Remembering for the Future: Working Papers and Addenda, Vol. 1: Jews and Christians During and After the Holocaust*, edited by Yehuda Bauer, Alice Eckardt, Franklin H. Littell, David Patterson, Elisabeth Maxwell, and Robert Maxwell. Oxford: Pergamon Press, 1989. 584–587, 593–595.

———. "Imagining Judaism and Jewish Life on the Threshold of the Twenty-First Century: A Commentary on the Wye Memorandum." *Journal of Church and State* 41 (Winter 1999): 5–12.

———. *Israel and Palestine out of the Ashes: The Search for Jewish Identity in the Twenty-First Century*. London: Pluto Press, 2002.

———. "Jews, Christians, and Liberation Theology: A Response." In *Judaism, Christianity, and Liberation: An Agenda for Dialogue*, edited by Otto Maduro. Maryknoll, NY: Orbis, 1991.

———. "The Legacy of Peter Maurin." *CrossCurrents* 34 no. 3 (Fall 1984): 294–304.

———. *O Jerusalem! The Contested Future of the Jewish Covenant*. Minneapolis: Fortress, 1999.

———. *Peter Maurin: Prophet in the Twentieth Century*. New York: Paulist Press, 1981.

———. "Power and Empowerment." *One World* 145 (May 1989): 17–19.

———. *Practicing Exile: The Religious Odyssey of an American Jew*. Minneapolis: Fortress Press, 2002.

———. "Restoring the Ordinary: An Inquiry into the Jewish Covenant at the End of Auschwitz." *The Asia Journal of Theology* 10 no. 2 (Oct. 1996): 377–413. 402–406.

———. *Revolutionary Forgiveness: Essays on Judaism, Christianity, and the Future of Religious Life*. Waco, Texas: Baylor University Press, 2000.

———. "Theology, Politics, and Peace: A Jewish Perspective." In *Theology, Politics, and Peace*, edited by Theodore Runyon. Maryknoll, NY: Orbis, 1989.

———. *Toward a Jewish Theology of Liberation*. Maryknoll, NY: Orbis, 1987. 7–46, 74–75, 111–112, 114, 116.

———. *Unholy Alliance: Religion and Atrocity in Our Time*. Minneapolis: Fortress, 1997.

———. *A Year at the Catholic Worker*. New York: Paulist Press, 1978.

Ellis, Marc H. and Otto Maduro, eds., *Expanding the View: Gustavo Gutierrez and the Future of Liberation Theology*. Maryknoll, NY: Orbis, 1990.

———. *The Future of Liberation Theology: Essays in Honor of Gustavo Gutierrez*. Maryknoll, NY: Orbis, 1989.

Erskine, Noel Leo. *King among the Theologians*. Cleveland: Pilgrim Press, 1994. 152.

Fackenheim, Emil L. "The Commandment to Hope: A Response to Contemporary Jewish Experience." In *The Future of Hope*, edited by Walter H. Capps. Philadelphia: Fortress Press, 1970. 74–77, 89.

———. "Concerning Authentic and Unauthentic Responses to the Holocaust." *Holocaust and Genocide Studies* 1 no. 1 (1986): 101–120. 117

———. "The Development of My Thought." *Religious Studies Review* 13 no. 3 (July 1987): 204–206.

———. *Encounters between Judaism and Modern Philosophy: A Preface to Future Jewish Thought*. New York: Basic Books, 1973. 213–229.

———. *An Epitaph for German Judaism: from Halle to Jerusalem*. Madison: University of Wisconsin Press, 2002.

———. "Germany's Worst Enemy." *Commentary* 90 no. 4 (Oct. 1990): 31–34.

———. *God's Presence in History: Jewish Affirmations and Philosophical Reflections*. New York: NYU Press, 1970. 5–6, 9, 11–18, 20, 23, 25–26, 27, 29–30, 32, 43, 52–53, 69, 72–75, 83–84, 86, 92, 95.

———. "Holocaust and Weltanschung: Philosophical Reflections on Why They Did It." In *Remembering for the Future: Working Papers and Addenda, Vol. 1: Jews and Christians During and After the Holocaust*, edited by Yehuda Bauer Alice Eckardt, Franklin H. Littell, David Patterson, Elisabeth Maxwell, and Robert Maxwell. Oxford: Pergamon Press, 1989.

———. "Human Freedom and Divine Power." *Judaism* 12 no. 3 (Summer 1963). 342–343.

———. "Jerusalem 'Above' and Jerusalem 'Below': The Mystery of the Togetherness." In *Jerusalem: City of Ages*, edited by Alice L. Eckardt. Lanham: University Press of America, 1987.

———. *The Jewish Bible after the Holocaust: A Re-Reading*. Bloomington: Indiana University Press, 1991.

———. "Jewish Philosophy in the Academy." In *Teaching Jewish Civilization: A Global Approach to Higher Education*, edited by Moshe Davis. New York: NYU Press, 1995.

———. *The Jewish Return into History: Reflections in the Age of Auschwitz and a New Jerusalem*. New York: Schocken Books, 1978. xi–xii, 54, 60, 63–64, 109, 124–126, 246–247, 263–264, 266–269, 279, 282.

———. *The Jewish Thought of Emil Fackenheim: A Reader*, edited by Michael L. Morgan. Detroit: Wayne State University Press, 1987.

———. "Jewish Values in the Post-Holocaust Future: A Symposium." *Judaism* 16 no. 3 (Summer 1967): 266–299.

———. "Judaism, Christianity and Reinhold Niebuhr—A Reply to Levi Olan." *Judaism* 5 no. 4 (Fall 1956): 316–324.

———. *Metaphysics and Historicity*. Milwaukee, WI: Marquette University Press, 1961.

———. "New Hearts and the Old Covenant: On Some Possibilities of a Fraternal Jewish-Christian Reading of the Jewish Bible Today." In *The Divine Helmsman: Studies on God's Control of Human Events, Presented to Lou H. Silberman*, edited by James L. Crenshaw and Samuel Sandmel. New York: KTAV Publishing House, 1980.

———. "An Outline of a Modern Jewish Theology." *Judaism* 3 no. 3 (Summer 1954): 246.

———. *Paths to Jewish Belief: A Systematic Introduction*. New York: Behrman House, 1960.

———. "Pesach after Saddam Hussein." In *What Kind of God? Essays in Honor of Richard L. Rubenstein*, edited by Betty Rogers Rubenstein and Michael Berenbaum. Lanham: University Press of America, 1995.

———. "Philosophical Reflections on Claude Lanzmann's *Shoah*." In *Faith and Freedom: A Tribute to Franklin H. Littell*, edited by Richard Libowitz. Oxford: Pergamon Press, 1987.

———. "The Possibility of the Universe in al-Farabi, Ibn Sina, and Maimonides." *Proceedings of the American Academy for Jewish Research* 16 (1947): 39–70.

———. *Quest for Past and Future: Essays in Jewish Theology*. Bloomington: Indiana University Press, 1968. 9–10, 18, 39, 75, 78–79, 83, 101, 105–106, 175, 193–194, 208–209, 211–212, 261–262.

———. "Raul Hillberg and the Uniqueness of the Holocaust." *Holocaust and Genocide Studies* 3 no. 4 (1988): 491–494.

———. "The Rebirth of the Holy Remnant." In *Major Changes within the Jewish People in the Wake of the Holocaust*, edited by Yisrael Gutman. Jerusalem: Yad Vashem, 1996.

———. *The Religious Dimension in Hegel's Thought*. Bloomington: Indiana University Press, 1967.

———. "Responsibility and Freedom." *Judaism* 14 no. 2 (Spring 1965): 237–238.

———. Review of *Man Is Not Alone: A Philosophy of Religion* by Abraham Joshua Heschel. *Judaism* 1 no. 1 (Jan. 1952): 85–89.

———. "Self-realization and the Search for God." *Judaism* 1 no. 4 (Oct. 1952): 298–303. 298.

———. "The Systematic Role of the Matrix (Existence) and Apex (Yom Kippur) of Jewish Religious Life in Rosenzweig's 'Star of Redemption.' " In *Der Philosoph Franz Rosenzweig (1886–1929), Internationaler Kongress-Kassel 1986, Bd 2: Das neue Denken und seine Dimensionen*, edited by Wolfdietrich Schmied-Kowarzik. Freiburg/Munchen: Verlag Karl Alber, 1988.

———. *To Mend the World: Foundations of Post-Holocaust Jewish Thought*. Rev.ed. Bloomington: Indiana University Press, 1994. xxxiii–xxxvi, xlvi, 12–14, 24–25, 138–139, 141, 183, 217–218, 220, 223–224, 235, 237–239, 253–256, 284–285, 300, 309–310.

———. *What Is Judaism? An Interpretation for the Present Age*. Syracuse, NY: Syracuse University Press, 1999. 110–113, 115, 117, 283–284, 289–290.

———. "The Zionist Imperative." *First Things* 50 (Feb. 1995): 18–23.

Felder, Cain Hope. *Troubling Biblical Waters: Race, Class, and Family*. Maryknoll, NY: Orbis, 1989.

Fine, Lawrence. "*Tikkun*: A Lurianic Motif in Contemporary Jewish Thought." In *From Ancient Israel to Modern Judaism: Intellect in Quest of Understanding: Essays in Honor of Marvin Fox, Vol. 4: The Modern Age: Theology, Literature, History*, edited by Jacob Neusner, Ernest S. Frerichs, and Nahum M. Sarna. Atlanta: Scholars Press, 1989.

Flannery, Austin, O. P., ed., *Vatican Council II: The Conciliar and Post Conciliar Documents*. Collegeville, MN: Liturgical Press, 1975. 738–749.

Frymer-Kensky, Tikva David Novak, Peter Ochs, David Fox Sandmel, Michael A. Signer, eds., *Christianity in Jewish Terms*. Boulder, CO: Westview Press, 2000.

Goatley, David Emmanuel. *Were You There? Godforsakenness in Slave Religion*. Maryknoll, NY: Orbis, 1996.

Gollwitzer, Helmut. "Why Black Theology?" *Union Seminary Quarterly Review* 31 no. 1 (Fall 1975): 38–58.

Grant, Jacqueline. "Black Christology: Interpreting Aspects of the Apostolic Faith." *Mid-Stream* 24 no. 4 (Oct. 1985): 366–375.

———. *White Women's Christ and Black Women's Jesus: Feminist Christology and Womanist Response*. Atlanta: Scholar's Press, 1989.

Greenberg, Cheryl Lynn. *Troubling the Waters: Black-Jewish Relations in the American Century*. Princeton: Princeton University Press, 2006. 59, 74–75, 92, 117, 121, 159, 166, 206–208, 225–227, 234–235, 237.

Greenberg, Irving. *For the Sake of Heaven and Earth: The New Encounter between Judaism and Christianity*. Philadelphia: The Jewish Publication Society, 2004. 44.

———. "The Shoah and the Legacy of Anti-Semitism: Judaism, Christianity, and Partnership after the Twentieth Century." In *Christianity in Jewish Terms*, edited by Tikva Frymer-Kensky David Novak, Peter Ochs, David Fox Sandmel, Michael A. Signer. Boulder, CO: Westview Press, 2000. 33.

Greenspan, Louis and Graeme Nicholson, eds., *Fackenheim: German Philosophy and Jewish Thought*. Toronto: University of Toronto Press, 1992.

Gutierrez, Gustavo. *On Job: God-Talk and the Suffering of the Innocent*. Translated by Matthew J. O'Connell. Maryknoll, NY: Orbis, 1987.

———. *A Theology of Liberation: History, Politics, and Salvation*. Rev. ed. Translated and edited by Sister Caridad Inda and John Eaglson. Maryknoll, NY: Orbis, 1988. 11.

Gutman, Israel. *Resistance: The Warsaw Ghetto Uprising*. Boston: Houghton Mifflin, 1994.

Hanson, Geddes W. Review of *Is God a White Racist?* by William R. Jones. *Theology Today* 31, no. 1 (Apr. 1974): 76–81.

Herzog, Frederick. "Theology at the Crossroads." *Union Seminary Quarterly Review* 31 no. 1 (Fall 1975): 59–68.

Heschel, Abraham Joshua. *Moral Grandeur and Spiritual Audacity*. Edited by Susannah Heschel. New York: Farrar, Straus and Giroux, 1996. 225.

Hopkins, Dwight N. *Being Human: Race, Culture, and Religion*. Minneapolis: Fortress, 1995.

———, ed., *Black Faith and Public Talk: Critical Essays on James H. Cone's Black Theology & Black Power*. Maryknoll, NY: Orbis, 1999.

———. "Black Theology and a Second Generation: New Scholarship and New Challenges." In *Black Theology: A Documentary History, Volume Two: 1980–1992*, edited by James H. Cone and Gayraud S. Wilmore. Maryknoll, NY: Orbis, 1993.

———. "Black Theology on God: The Divine in Black Popular Religion." In *The Ties That Bind: African American and Hispanic American/Latino/a Theologies In Dialogue*, edited by Anthony B. Pinn and Benjamin Valentin. New York: Continuum, 2001.

———. *Black Theology USA and South Africa: Politics, Culture, and Liberation.* Maryknoll, NY: Orbis, 1989.

———. *Down, Up, and Over: Slave Religion and Black Theology.* Minneapolis: Fortress, 2000. 128–135, 159–160, 163, 210, 228, 234, 239, 254–273.

———. *Heart and Head: Black Theology—Past, Present, and Future.* New York: Palgrave, 2002.

———. *Introducing Black Theology of Liberation.* Maryknoll, NY: Orbis, 1999.

———. "Postmodernity, Black Theology of Liberation and the U.S.A.: Michel Foucault and James H. Cone." In *Liberation Theologies, Postmodernity, and the Americas*, edited by David Batston, Eduardo Mendieta, Lois Ann Lorentzen, and Dwight N. Hopkins. London: Routledge, 1997.

———. "The Religion of Globalization." In *Religions/Globalizations: Theories and Cases*, edited by Dwight N. Hopkins, Lois Ann Lorentzen, Eduardo Mendieta, and David Batstone. Durham, NC: Duke University Press, 2001.

———. *Shoes That Fit Our Feet: Sources for a Constructive Black Theology.* Maryknoll, NY: Orbis, 1993. 20–22, 24, 84–93.

———. "Social Justice Struggle." In *Spirituality and the Secular Quest*, edited by Peter H. Van Ness. New York: Crossroad, 1996.

———. "Spirituality and Transformation in Black Theology." In *Spirituality of the Third World: A Cry for Life*, edited by K. C. Abraham and Bernadette Mbuy-Beya. Maryknoll, NY: Orbis, 1994.

———. "Theological Method and Cultural Studies: Slave Religious Culture as a Heuristic." In *Changing Conversations: Religious Reflection and Cultural Analysis*, edited by Dwight N. Hopkins and Sheila Greeve Davaney. New York: Routledge, 1996

Hopkins, Dwight N. and Linda E. Thomas. "Voices from the Margins in the United States." In *The Twentieth Century: A Theological Overview*, edited by Gregory Baum. Maryknoll, NY: Orbis, 1999.

———. "Womanist Theology and Black Theology: Conversational Envisioning of an Unfinished Dream," in *A Dream Unfinished*, edited by Eleazar S. Fernandez and Fernando F. Segovia. Maryknoll, NY: Orbis, 2001.

Horowitz, Irving Louis. "Many Genocides, One Holocaust? The Limits of the Rights of States and the Obligations of Individuals." *Modern Judaism* 1 no. 1 (May 1981): 74–89.

Jones, William R. "The Case for Black Humanism." In *Black Theology II: Essays on the Formation and Outreach of Contemporary Black Theology*, edited by Calvin E. Bruce and William R. Jones. Lewisburg: Bucknell University Press, 1978. 217–218.

Jones, William R. "Functional Ultimacy as Authority in Religious Humanism." *Religious Humanism* 12, no. 1 (Winter 1978): 28–32.

———. *Is God a White Racist? A Preamble to Black Theology.* Boston: Beacon Press, 1998. 126, 172, 174–175, 186–187, 191–192, 194, 201.

———. "Liberation Strategies in Black Theology: Mao, Martin, or Malcolm?" *Chicago Theological Seminary Register* 73, no. 1 (Winter 1983): 38–48.

———. "Process Theology: Guardian of the Oppressor or Goad to the Oppressed: An Interim Assessment." *Process Studies* 18 no. 4 (Winter 1989): 268–281. 277–278.

———. "Purpose and Method in Liberation Theology: Implications for an Interim Assessment." In *Liberation Theology: North American Style*, edited by Deane William Ferm. New York: International Religious Foundation, 1987.

———. "Reconciliation and Liberation in Black Theology: Some Implications for Religious Education." *Religious Education* 67 (Sept.–Oct. 1972): 383–389.

———. "Religion as Legitimator and Liberator: A Worm's Eye View of Religion and Contemporary Politics." In *Spirit Matters: The Worldwide Impact of Religion on Politics*, edited by Richard L. Rubenstein. New York: Paragon, 1987.

———. "Religious Humanism: Its Problems and Prospects in Black Religion and Culture." *Journal of the Interdenominational Theological Center* 7 (Spring 1980): 169–186. 179.

———. "The Religious Legitimation of Counterviolence; Insights from Latin American Liberation Theology." In *The Terrible Meek: Religion and Revolution in Cross-Cultural Perspective*, edited by Lonnie D. Kliever. New York: Paragon, 1987.

———. "Theism and Religious Humanism: The Chasm Narrows." *Christian Century* 92 (May 21 1975): 520–525.

———. "Theodicy and Methodology in Black Theology: A Critique of Washington, Cone and Cleage." *Harvard Theological Review* 64 (Oct. 1971): 541–557. 543, 550–551.

———. "Theodicy: The Controlling Category for Black Theology." *Journal of Religious Thought* 30, no. 1 (1973): 28–38. 32.

———. "Toward a Black Theology." *Mid-Stream* 13 (Fall–Winter 1973–1974): 2–9.

———. "Toward an Interim Assessment of Black Theology." *Christian Century* 89 (May 3 1972): 513–517.

King, Martin Luther, Jr. *Strength to Love.* Cleveland: Collins Publishing Co., 1963. 97.

———. *Stride toward Freedom.* New York: Harper, 1958.

———. *A Testament to Hope: The Essential Writings of Martin Luther King, Jr.*, edited by James M. Washington. San Francisco: Harper & Row, 1986.

———. *Trumpet of Conscience.* New York: Harper & Row, 1967.

———. *Where Do We Go from Here? Chaos or Community?* Boston: Beacon Press, 1967. 21, 105.

———. *Why We Can't Wait.* New York: New American Library, 1963. 82.

Knitter, Paul. *One Earth Many Religions: Multifaith Dialogue and Global Responsibility.* Maryknoll, NY: Orbis Books, 1995.

Langbein, Hermann. *Against All Hope: Resistance in the Nazi Concentration Camps 1938–1945.* Translated by Harry Zohn. New York: Continuum, 1996.

Langer, Lawrence. *Holocaust Testimonies: The Ruins of Memory*. New Haven: Yale University Press, 1991. 26.

Leaman, Oliver. *Evil and Suffering in Jewish Philosophy*. Cambridge: Cambridge University Press, 1995.

Lehmann, Paul L. "Black Theology and 'Christian' Theology." *Union Seminary Quarterly Review* 31 no. 1 (Fall 1975): 31–37.

Levi, Primo. *Survival in Auschwitz: The Nazi Assault on Humanity*. New York: Simon & Schuster, 1996.

Lincoln, C. Eric. "A Perspective on James H. Cone's Black Theology." *Union Seminary Quarterly Review* 31 no. 1 (Fall 1975): 15–22.

Long, Charles. "Perspectives for a Study of Afro-American Religion in the United States." *History of Religions* 11 (Aug. 1971).

———. "Structural Similarities and Dissimilarities in Black and African Theologies." *Journal of Religious Thought* 32 (Fall–Winter 1975).

Lubarsky, Sandra. "Ethics and Theodicy: Tensions in Emil Fackenheim's Thought." *Encounter* 44 no. 1 (Winter 1983): 59–72.

Malcolm X. *The Autobiography of Malcolm X: As Told to Alex Haley*. New York: Ballantine, 1964. 383, 427.

———. *Malcolm X Speaks: Selected Speeches and Statements*, edited by George Breitman. New York: Grove Press, 1966. 10, 38–40.

Marx, Karl. "Criticism of Religion is the Presupposition of All Criticism." In *The Karl Marx Library*. Vol. 5, *On Religion*, edited by Saul K. Padover. New York: McGraw Hill, 1974. 35–36.

Maybaum, Ignaz. *The Face of God after Auschwitz*. Amsterdam: Polak and Van Gennep, 1965.

McDaniel, Jay. "The God of the Oppressed and the God Who is Empty." *Journal of Ecumenical Studies* 22 no. 4 (Fall 1985): 687–702.

McGowan, Daniel A. and Marc H. Ellis, eds., *Remembering Deir Yassin: The Future of Israel and Palestine*. New York: Olive Branch Press, 1998.

McRobert, Laurie. "Emil L. Fackenheim and Radical Evil." *Journal of the American Academy of Religion* 57 no. 2 (1989): 325–340.

———. "Emil L. Fackenheim: Encounters with Christianity." *Toronto Journal of Theology* 5 no. 2 (Fall 1989): 206–222. 214.

McWilliams, Warren. "Divine Suffering in Contemporary Theology." *Scottish Journal of Theology* 33 (1980): 35–53.

———. "Theodicy According to James Cone." *Journal of Religious Thought* 36 (Fall–Winter 1979): 45–54.

Merton, Thomas. *Faith and Violence: Christian Teaching and Christian Practice*. Notre Dame, IN: University of Notre Dame Press, 1968. 152.

Morgan, Michael L. *Beyond Auschwitz: Post-Holocaust Jewish Thought in America*. Oxford: Oxford University Press, 2001. 182, 189–190.

———. "The Curse of Historicity: The Role of History in Leo Strauss's Jewish Thought." *The Journal of Religion* 61 no. 4 (O 1981): 345–363.

———. *Dilemmas in Modern Jewish Thought: The Dialectics of Revelation and History*. Bloomington: Indiana University Press, 1992.

———. "Historicism, Evil, and Post-Holocaust Moral Thought." In *Remembering for the Future: Working Papers and Addenda, Vol. 1: Jews and Christians*

During and After the Holocaust, edited by Yehuda Bauer Alice Eckardt, Franklin H. Littell, David Patterson, Elisabeth Maxwell, and Robert Maxwell. Oxford: Pergamon Press, 1989. 1044–1049.

Morgan, Michael L. "History and Modern Jewish Thought: Spinoza and Mendelssohn on the Ritual Law." *Judaism* 30 no. 4 (Fall 1981): 467–478.

———. *Interim Judaism: Jewish Thought in a Century of Crisis*. Bloomington: Indiana University Press, 2001. 3, 27–28, 42, 113, 115, 119.

———. "Jewish Ethics after the Holocaust." *Journal of Religious Ethics* 12 no. 2 (Fall 1984): 256–277.

———. "Jewish Philosophy and Historical Self-Consciousness." *The Journal of Religion* 71 no. 1 (Jan. 1991): 36–49. 45.

———. "Jewish Thought Today." *The Journal of Religion* 68 no. 4 (Oct. 1988): 575–580.

———. "Martin Buber, Cooperation, and Evil." *Journal of the American Academy of Religion* 58 (Spring 1990): 99–109.

———. "Mendelssohn's Defense of Reason in *Jerusalem*." *Judaism* 38 no. 4 (Fall 1989): 449–459.

———. "Overcoming the Remoteness of the Past: Memory and Historiography in Modern Jewish Thought." *Judaism* 38 no. 4 (Spring 1989): 160–173.

———, ed., *Emil Fackenheim: Jewish Philosophers and Jewish Philosophy*. Bloomington: Indiana University Press, 1996.

———. *A Holocaust Reader: Responses to the Nazi Extermination*. New York: Oxford University Press, 2001.

Motlhabi, Mokgethi. "The Historic Origins of Black Theology." *Bulletin de Theologie Africaine* 6 no. 12 (June–Dec. 1984): 211–226.

Muehl, William. Review of *Is God a White Racist?* by William R. Jones. *Christian Century* 91 (Fall 1974): 208–209.

Niebuhr, Reinhold. *The Nature and Destiny of Man: A Christian Interpretation*, Vol. 1, *Human Nature*. New York: Scribner's, 1941. 222–223.

Olds, Mason. "Humanism and Liberation Theology." *Religious Humanism* 21 no. 3 (Summer 1987): 98–109.

Oppenheim, Michael. "Theology and Community: The Work of Emil Fackenheim." *Religious Studies Review* 18 no. 3 (July 1987): 206–210.

Osofsky, Gilbert, ed., *Puttin' on Ole Massa: The Slave Narratives of Henry Bibb, William Wells Brown, and Solomon Northup*. Reprint, San Francisco: Harper and Row, 1969. 22.

Pinn, Anthony B. "Black Theology, Black Bodies, and Pedagogy." *CrossCurrents* 50, nos. 1–2 (Spring–Summer 2000): 196–202.

———, ed., *By These Hands: A Documentary History of African American Humanism*. New York: New York University Press, 2001. 4, 8, 10.

———. " 'Double Consciousness' in Nineteenth-Century Black Nationalism: Reflections on the Teachings of Bishop Henry McNeal Turner." *Journal of Religious Thought* 52 (Summer–Fall 1995): 15–26.

———, ed., *Moral Evil and Redemptive Suffering: A History of Theodicy in African-American Religious Thought*. Gainesville: University Press of Florida, 2002. 17.

———. "Religion and 'America's Problem Child': Notes on Pauli Murray's Theological Development." *Journal of Feminist Studies in Religion* 15 (Spring 1999): 21–39.

———. "Rethinking the Nature and Tasks of African American Theology: A Pragmatic Perspective." *American Journal of Theology & Philosophy* 19, no. 2 (May 1998): 191–208.

———. *Terror and Triumph: The Nature of Black Religion.* Minneapolis: Fortress, 2003.

———. *Varieties of African American Religious Experience.* Minneapolis: Fortress, 1998.

———. *Why Lord? Suffering and Evil in Black Theology.* New York: Continuum, 1995. 19, 87, 89, 97–100, 141, 157–158.

Pinn, Anthony B., and Benjamin Valentin, eds., *The Ties That Bind: African American and Hispanic American/Latino/a Theologies in Dialogue.* New York: Continuum, 2001.

Pinnock, Sarah Katherine. *Beyond Theodicy: Jewish and Christian Continental Thinkers Respond to the Holocaust.* Albany, NY: State University of New York Press, 2002.

Plaskow, Judith. *Standing again at Sinai: Judaism from a Feminist Perspective.* San Francisco: HarperCollins, 1990.

Premnath, D. N. "Comparative and Historical Sociology in Old Testament Research: A Study of Isaiah 3:12–15." *Bangalore Theological Forum* 17 no. 4 (Oct.–Dec. 1985): 19–36.

Raphael, Melissa. "At the East End of Eden: A Feminist Spirituality of Gardening: Our Way Past the Flaming Sword." *Feminist Theology* no. 4 (Sept. 1993): 101–110.

———. " 'Cover Not Our Blood with Thy Silence': Sadism, Eschatological Justice and Female Images of the Divine." *Feminist Theology* no. 8 (Jan. 1995): 85–105.

———. "The Face of God in Every Generation: Jewish Feminist Spirituality and the Legend of the Thirty-Six Hidden Saints." In *Spirituality and Society in the New Millennium,* edited by Ursula King, with Tina Beattie. Brighton: Sussex Academic Press, 2001.

———. *The Female Face of God in Auschwitz: A Jewish Feminist Theology of the Holocaust.* London: Routledge, 2003. 8–10, 28, 30–32, 54–55, 61, 74, 79, 90, 95, 98, 100–101, 123, 134.

———. "Goddess Religion, Postmodern Jewish Feminism, and the Complexity of Alternative Religious Identities." *Nova Religio* 1 no. 2 (Apr. 1998): 198–215.

———. *Introducing Thealogy: Discourse on the Goddess.* Cleveland: Pilgrim Press, 2000.

———. "Is Patriarchal Theology Still Patriarchal? Reading Theologies of the Holocaust from a Feminist Perspective." *Journal of Feminist Studies in Religion* 18 no. 2 (Fall 2002): 105–113.

———. " 'I Will Be Who I Will Be': The Representation of God in Postmodern Jewish Feminist Theology and Contemporary Education." *British Journal of Religious Education* 21 (Spring 1999): 69–79.

Raphael, Melissa. "Monotheism in Contemporary Feminist Goddess Religion: A Betrayal of Early Thealogical Non-Realism?" In *Is There a Future for Feminist Theology?* edited by Deborah F. Sawyer and Diane M. Collier. Sheffield: Sheffield Academic Press, 1999.

———. "Real-izing the Material: Spiritual Feminism and the Resacralization of the Earth." In *The Ideal in the World's Religions: Essays on the Person, Family, Society and Environment*, edited by Robert Carter and Sheldon Isenberg. St. Paul, MN: Paragon, 1997.

———. *Rudolf Otto and the Concept of Holiness.* Oxford: Clarendon Press, 1997.

———. *Thealogy and Embodiment: The Post-Patriarchal Reconstruction of Female Sacrality.* Sheffield: Sheffield Academic Press, 1996.

———. "Thealogy and the Parthenogenetic Reproduction of Femaleness." In *Religion and Sexuality*, edited by Michael A. Hayes, Wendy Porter, and David Tombs. Sheffield: Sheffield Academic Press, 1998.

———. "Thealogy, Redemption and the Call of the Wild." *Feminist Theology* no. 15: (May 1997): 55–72.

———. "Truth in Flux: Goddess Feminism as a Late Modern Religion." *Religion* 26 no. 3 (July 1996): 199–213.

———. "When God Beheld God: Notes towards a Jewish Feminist Theology of the Holocaust." *Feminist Theology* no. 21 (May 1999): 53–78. 65–66.

Roberson, Rachel. "Seeking 'A Way out of No Way.' " *The Witness* 83 no. 4 (Apr. 2000): 30–31.

Roberts, J. Deotis. *Liberation and Reconciliation: A Black Theology.* Rev. ed. Maryknoll, NY: Orbis, 1994.

Roseman, Mark. *A Past in Hiding: Memory and Survival in Nazi Germany.* New York: Metropolitan Books, 2000.

Rosenzweig, Franz. *The Star of Redemption.* Translated by William H. Hallo. New York: Holt, Rinehart, and Winston, 1970.

Rubenstein, Betty Rogers and Michael Berenbaum, eds., *What Kind of God? Essays in Honor of Richard L. Rubenstein.* Lanham: University Press of America, 1995.

Rubenstein, Richard L. "1881: Watershed Year of Modern Jewish History." In *Events and Movements in Modern Judaism*, edited by Raphael Patai and Emanuel S. Goldsmith. Washington: Paragon House, 1995.

———. *After Auschwitz: History, Theology, and Contemporary Judaism.* 2nd ed. Baltimore: Johns Hopkins University Press, 1992. xiii, 298, 302.

———. *After Auschwitz: Radical Theology and Contemporary Judaism.* New York: Macmillan Publishing, 1966. 50–58, 136, 140, 152–153.

———. *The Age of Triage: Fear and Hope in an Over-crowded World.* Boston: Beacon Press, 1983.

———. "Auschwitz and Covenant Theology." *Christian Century* (May 21, 1969). 716–718.

———. "The Cave, the Rock, and the Tent: the Meaning of Place." *Continuum* 6 no. 2 (Summer 1968): 143–155.

———. "Covenant and Holocaust (1)." In *Remembering for the Future: Working Papers and Addenda, Vol. 1: Jews and Christians During and After the Holocaust*, edited by Yehuda Bauer. Oxford: Pergamon Press, 1989.

———. "The Convent at Auschwitz and the Imperatives of Pluralism in the Global Electronic Village." In *Memory Offended: The Auschwitz Convent Controversy*, edited by Carol Rittner and John K. Roth. New York: Praeger, 1991.

———. *The Cunning of History: The Holocaust and the American Future.* New York: Harper, 1978.

———. "Did Christians Fail Israel?" *The Lutheran Quarterly* 20 (Aug. 1968): 251–254.

———. "Discussion: Jewish Self-Understanding and the Land and State of Israel." With Uriel Tal, Jakob J. Petuchowski and Arthur Hertzberg. *Union Seminary Quarterly Review* 26 (Summer 1971): 368–371.

———. "Emil Fackenheim's Radical Monotheism: A Review Essay." *Soundings* 57 no. 2 (Summer 1974): 236–251. 238, 245–246.

———. "Freud and Judaism: A Review Article." *The Journal of Religion* 47 no 1 (Jan. 1967): 39–44.

———. "Freud, God, and Jewish Mysticism." In *Problems in Contemporary Jewish Theology,* edited by Dan Cohn-Sherbok. Lewiston: Edwin Mellen Press, 1992.

———. "God as Cosmic Sadist: In Reply to Emil Fackenheim." *Christian Century* (July 29, 1970).

———. "God's Omnipotence in Rabbinic Judaism." *Judaism* 9 (Spring 1960): 120–128.

———. "Holocaust, Sunyata, and Holy Nothingness: An Essay in Interreligious Dialogue." In *Divine Emptiness and Historical Fullness: A Buddhist-Jewish-Christian Conversation with Masao Abe*, edited by Christopher Ives. Valley Forge: Trinity Press International, 1995.

———. "The Human Condition in Jewish Thought and Experience." In *The Human Condition in the Jewish and Christian Traditions*, edited by Frederick E. Greenspahn. Hoboken: KTAV Publishing, 1986.

———. "Japan and the Jews: The Roots of a Modern Myth." In *Aus zweier Zeugen Mund*, edited by Julius H. Schoeps. Gerlingen: Bleicher, 1992.

———. "Jews, Israel, and Liberation Theology." In *Judaism, Christianity, and Liberation: An Agenda for Dialogue*, edited by Otto Maduro. Maryknoll, NY: Orbis, 1991.

———. "Job and Auschwitz." *Union Seminary Quarterly Review* 25 no 4 (Summer 1970): 421–437.

———. "Journey to Poland." *Judaism* 15 (Fall 1966): 474–482.

———. "Liberalism and the Jewish Interests." *Judaism* 21 (Winter 1972): 16–19.

———. "The Meaning of Anxiety in Rabbinic Judaism." In *Judaism and Psychoanalysis*, edited by Mortimer Ostow. New York: KTAV Publishing, 1982.

———. "The Meaning of Sin in Rabbinic Theology." *Judaism* 10 (Summer 1961): 227–236.

———. *Morality and Eros.* New York: McGraw-Hill, 1970.

———. *My Brother Paul.* New York: Harper & Row, 1972.

———. "On Death in Life: Reflections on Franz Rosenzweig." *Soundings* 55 no. 2 (Summer 1972): 216–235.

———. "The Philosopher and the Jews: The Case of Martin Heidegger." *Modern Judaism* 9 no. 2 (May 1989): 179–196.

Rubenstein, Richard L. "Radical Theology and the Holocaust." In *The Death of God Movement and the Holocaust: Radical Theology Encounters the Shoah*, edited by Stephen R. Haynes and John K. Roth. Westport, CT: Greenwood Press, 1999.

———. "Reason's Deadly Dreams." In *The Bent World: Essays on Religion and Culture*, edited by John R May. Ann Arbor: Edwards Brothers, 1981. 7.

———. "Religion and History: Power, History, and the Covenant at Sinai." In *Take Judaism, for Example: Studies toward the Comparison of Religions*, edited by Jacob Neusner. Chicago: University of Chicago Press, 1983.

———. "Religion and the Academic Community: The Creative Tensions of Faith and Learning." *Judaism* 8 (Spring 1959): 142–151.

———. *The Religious Imagination: A Study in Psychoanalysis and Jewish Theology*. New York: Bobbs-Merrill, 1968.

———. "Science and Spirit in Contemporary Jewish Mysticism." *CrossCurrents* (Winter 1983–1984): 400–405.

———. "Scribes, Pharisees, and Hypocrites: A Study in Rabbinic Psychology." *Judaism* 12 (Aug. 1963): 456–468.

———. "The South Encounters the Holocaust: William Styron's *Sophie's Choice*." In *Varieties of Southern Religious Experience*, edited by Samuel S. Hill. Baton Rouge: Louisiana State University Press, 1988.

———. "A Twentieth-Century Journey." In *From the Unthinkable to the Unavoidable: American Christian and Jewish Scholars Encounter the Holocaust*, edited by Carol Rittner and John K. Roth. Westport, CT: Praeger, 1997

———. "The Wannsee Conference and the Rationalization of Genocide." In *Remembrance and Recollection: Essays on the Centennial Year of Martin Niemoller and Reinhold Niebuhr and the Fiftieth Year of the Wannsee Conference*, edited by Hubert G. Locke and Marcia Sachs Littell. Lanham: University Press of America, 1995.

Rubenstein, Richard L., ed., *Modernization: The Humanist Response to Its Promise and Problems*. Washington: Paragon House, 1982.

Rubenstein, Richard L. and John K. Roth, eds., *Approaches to Auschwitz: The Holocaust and Its Legacy*. Atlanta: John Knox Press, 1987.

Ruether, Rosemary Radford. "The Black Theology of James Cone." *Catholic World* (Oct. 1971): 18–20.

———. "Re-Contextualizing Theology." *Theology Today* 43 no. 1 (Apr. 1986): 22–27.

Ruether, Rosemary Radford and Marc H. Ellis, eds., *Beyond Occupation: American Jewish, Christian, and Palestinian Voices for Peace*. Boston: Beacon Press, 1990.

Scholem, Gershom. *Major Trends in Jewish Mysticism*. 3rd Rev. ed. New York: Schocken, 1995. 265–278.

Seaton, Derry. Review of *Is God a White Racist?* by William R. Jones. *Review and Expositor* 71 (Summer 1974): 417–418.

Shapiro, Susan E. "For Thy Breach is Great like the Sea; Who Can Heal Thee?" *Religious Studies Review* 13 no. 3 (July 1987): 210–213.

Sherwin, Byron L. and Harold Kasimow, eds., *John Paul II and Interreligious Dialogue*. Maryknoll, NY: Orbis, 1999.

Shulman, Harvey. "The Theo-Political Thought of Emil Fackenheim." *Judaism* 39 no. 2 (Spring 1990): 221–231.

Smith, Archie, Jr. "A Black Response to Sontag's 'Coconut Theology.' " *Journal of Religious Thought* 36 (Fall–Winter 1979): 13–25.

Sontag, Frederick. "Coconut Theology: Is James Cone the 'Uncle Tom' of Black Theology?" *Journal of Religious Thought* 36 (Fall–Winter 1979): 5–12.

———. "Liberation Theology and the Interpretation of Political Violence." In *The Politics of Latin American Liberation Theology: The Challenge to U.S. Public Policy*, edited by Richard L. Rubenstein and John K. Roth. Washington, DC: Washington Institute Press, 1988.

Spalding, Henry D., ed., *Encyclopedia of Jewish Humor: From Biblical Times to the Modern Age*. New York: Jonathan David Publishers, 1969. 187–188, 199.

Stall, Steven W. "Sociology of Knowledge, Relativism, and Theology." In *Religion and the Sociology of Knowledge: Modernization and Pluralism in Christian Thought and Structure*, edited by Barbara Hargrove. New York: Edwin Mellen Press, 1984.

Stendahl, Krister. "Response to *For the Sake of Heaven and Earth*." In *For the Sake of Heaven and Earth: The New Encounter between Judaism and Christianity*, by Irving Greenberg. Philadelphia: Jewish Publication Society, 2004. 263.

Stern, David and Paul Mendes-Flohr, eds., *An Arthur A. Cohen Reader: Selected Fiction and Writings on Judaism, Theology, Literature, and Culture*. Detroit: Wayne State University Press, 1998.

Stewart, Carlyle Fielding, III. "The Method of Correlation in the Theology of James H. Cone." *Journal of Religious Thought* 40 (Fall–Winter 1983–1984): 27–28.

Sundquist, Eric J. *Strangers in the Land: Blacks, Jews, Post-Holocaust America*. Cambridge, MA: The Belknap Press of Harvard University Press, 2005. 1–4, 15, 17–30, 37–38, 66, 75, 96, 110, 152, 160.

Tamez, Elsa. "The Woman Who Complicated the History of Salvation." In *New Eyes for Reading: Biblical and Theological Reflections by Women from the Third World*, edited by John S. Pobee and Barbel von Wartenberg-Potter. Geneva: WCC, 1986.

Terrell, Joanne. *Power in the Blood?: The Cross in the African-American Experience*. Eugene, OR: Wipf and Stock, 2005.

Thomas, Laurence Mordekhai. *Vessels of Evil: American Slavery and the Holocaust*. Philadelphia: Temple University Press, 1993.

Tillich, Paul. *Systematic Theology*. Vol. 1. Chicago: University of Chicago Press, 1951. 64, 66.

Townes, Emilie M., ed., *Embracing the Spirit: Womanist Perspectives on Hope, Salvation and Transformation*. Maryknoll, NY: Orbis, 1997.

———. *Troubling in My Soul: Womanist Perspectives on Evil & Suffering*. Maryknoll, NY: Orbis, 1993.

Trunk, Isaiah. *Jewish Responses to Nazi Persecution*. New York: Stein and Day, 1979.

Walker, Alice. *The Color Purple: A Novel*. New York: Harcourt, Brace, and Jovanovich, 1982.

———. *In Search of Our Mothers' Gardens: Womanist Prose*. San Diego: Harcourt, Brace, and Jovanovich, 1983. xi–xii.

Warrior, Robert Allen. "Canaanites and Conquerors," *Christianity and Crisis* 49 no. 12 (Sept. 11, 1989).

Weddle, David L. "The Liberator as Exorcist: James Cone and the Classic Doctrine of Atonement," *Religion in Life* 49 (Winter 1980): 477–487.

West, Cornel. *Prophecy Deliverance! An Afro-American Revolutionary Christianity*. Philadelphia: Westminster, 1982.

Wiesel, Elie. *The Gates of the Forest*. New York: Schocken, 1995.

———. *Night*. New York: Bantam, 1986.

———. *Trial of God*. New York: Schocken, 1995.

Williams, A. Roger. "A Black Pastor Looks at Black Theology." *Harvard Theological Review* 64 (1971): 559–567.

Williams, Delores S. "Afflicted with Racism." *Sojourners* 19 (1990): 21–22.

———. "After Liberation, What?" *Christian Century* 107 (Oct. 31 1990): 993.

———. "Black Women's Literature and the Task of Feminist Theology." In *Immaculate and Powerful: The Female in Sacred Image and Social Reality*, edited by Clarissa W. Atkinson, Constance H. Buchanan, and Margaret R. Miles. Boston: Beacon Press, 1985.

———. "The Boundaries that Betray Us." *Other Side* 31 (May–June 1995): 26–27.

———. "Building Community amid Troubles." *Christian Century* 107 (Oct. 3 1990): 867.

———. "Christmas Families." *Christianity and Crisis* 49 (Dec. 11 1989): 371–372.

———. "The Color of Feminism." *Christianity and Crisis* 45 (Apr. 29 1985): 164–165.

———. "'The Color Purple': What Was Missed." *Christianity and Crisis* 46 (July 14 1986): 230–232.

———. "Could It Happen Here?" *Other Side* 31 (Jan.–Feb. 1995): 46–47, 55.

———. "A Crucifixion Double Cross? The Violence of Our Images May Do More Harm than Good." *Other Side* 29 (Sep.–Oct. 1993): 25–27.

———. "Excellence beyond Standards." *Christian Century* 107 (Oct. 17 1990): 931.

———. "Exposing False Distinctions." *Sojourners* 19 (Aug.–Sep. 1990): 19–21.

———. "From Harlem to Huairou: A Theological Reflection." *Church and Society* 86 (May–June 1996): 52–61.

———. "James Cone's Liberation: Twenty Years Later." In *A Black Theology of Liberation: Twentieth Anniversary Edition*, James H. Cone. Maryknoll, NY: Orbis, 1990.

———. "Kairos Time: Challenge of the Centrisms." *Christianity and Crisis* 52 (Feb. 3 1992): 16–18.

———. "'Keep on Climbing Up': Spiritual Mentors." *Christian Century* 110 (Oct. 6 1993): 927–928.

———. "Lethargy in Christendom." *Christianity and Crisis* 53 (Apr. 12 1993): 90.

———. "Liberation: Summing up the Negatives." *Christianity and Crisis* 49 (June 12 1989): 183–184.

———. "Piety and Preparation for New Life." *Christian Century* 107 (Nov. 7 1990): 1020.

———. "The Raging Undercurrent." *Other Side* 30 (Jan.–Feb. 1994): 15–27.

———. "ReImagining Truth." *Other Side* 30 (May–June 1994): 53–55.

———. "Representatives and Partners." *Christian Century* 107 (Dec. 12 1990): 1163.

———. "Rituals of Resistance in Womanist Worship." In *Women at Worship: Interpretations of North American Diversity*, edited by Marjorie Procter-Smith and Janet R. Walton. Louisville: Westminster/John Knox Press, 1993.

———. "Rub Poor Lil' Judas's Head." *Christian Century* 107 (Oct. 24 1990): 963.

———. "The Salvation of Growth." *Christian Century* 107 (Oct. 10 1990): 899.

———. "The 'Sense' of Advent." *Christian Century* 107 (Nov. 21–28 1990): 1092.

———. "The Sent and the Sender." *Christian Century* 107 (Dec. 5 1990): 1130.

———. *Sisters in the Wilderness: The Challenge of Womanist God-Talk*. Maryknoll, NY: Orbis, 1993. 60–62, 70–71, 81, 108, 144, 146–147, 161–162, 164–165, 167, 198.

———. "Straight Talk, Plain Talk: Womanist Words about Salvation in a Social Context." In *Embracing the Spirit: Womanist Perspectives on Hope, Salvation and Transformation*, edited by Emilie M. Townes. Maryknoll, NY: Orbis, 1997.

———. "A Time of Decision for the Black Community." *Sojourners* 20 (1991): 22–23.

———. "Violence against God." *Other Side* 32 (Sep.–Oct. 1996): 19–20.

———. "Way Out Yonder, Longing for Home." *Other Side* 32 (Mar.–Apr. 1996): 32–33.

———. "What Does the Bible Say?" *Christian Century* 107 (Nov. 14 1990): 1059.

———. "Womanist/Feminist Dialogue: Problems and Possibilities." *Journal of Feminist Studies in Religion* 9 (Spring–Fall 1993): 67–73.

———. "A Womanist Perspective on Sin." In *A Troubling in My Soul: Womanist Perspectives on Evil & Suffering*, edited by Emilie M. Townes. Maryknoll, NY: Orbis, 1993.

———. "Womanist Theology: Black Women's Voices." *Christianity and Crisis* 47 (Mar. 2, 1987).

———. "Womanist Theology." In *Women's Visions: Theological Reflection, Celebration, Action*, edited by Ofelia Ortega. Geneva: WCC Publications, 1995.

———. "Women as Makers of Literature." In *Women's Spirit Bonding*, edited by Janet Kalven and Mary I. Buckley. New York: Pilgrim Press, 1984.

———. "Women's Oppression and Lifeline Politics in Black Women's Religious Narratives." *Journal of Feminist Studies in Religion* 1 no. 2 (Fall 1985): 59–71.

Williams, Preston N. "American Black Theology and the Development of Indigenous Theologies in India." *The Indian Journal of Theology* 30 no. 2 (Apr.–June 1981): 55–68.

Wilmore, Gayraud S. *Black Religion and Black Radicalism: An Examination of the Black Experience in Religion*. Garden City, NY: Anchor Press, 1973.

Wilmore, Gayraud S., Jr. and James H. Cone, eds., *Black Theology: A Documentary History*. Vol. 1, 1966–1979. Maryknoll, NY: Orbis, 1979.

———. *Black Theology: A Documentary History*. Vol. 2, 1980–1992. Maryknoll, NY: Orbis, 1993.

Young, Henry James. "Black Theology and the Work of William R. Jones." *Religion in Life* 44 (Spring 1975): 14–28.

Index

Adam and Eve (biblical), 189–90
  see also creation; Garden of Eden
Adler, Rachel, 146
affirmative action, 165–6
African American-Jewish relations
  see relations, African-American-Jewish
agency
  see freedom, human
akedah, 101–2
anti-apartheid movement, 194
anti-Semitism, 5–6, 63, 89, 139–40, 162,
    165, 223n
anti-theodicy, 197n
  see also theodicy
Auschwitz, 10, 12, 87, 96, 101, 115
  see also voice of Auschwitz,
      commanding

"banality of evil", 97–8
Bar Kochba revolts, 194
Barth, Karl, 19, 21–2, 33, 43, 46,
    93, 177
Baumel, Judith Tydor, 149
Berrigan, Daniel, 226n
Biko, Steve, 207n
black experience, 15, 18–20, 22–5, 31–3,
    41, 49, 78–9, 88, 91–2, 103, 173,
    177, 201–2n, 204n
black-Jewish relations
  see relations, African American-Jewish
black nationalism, 52, 54, 164
black power movement, 19, 24–5, 29,
    31, 33, 40, 51, 56, 163–4
blackness, 15–17, 24, 28, 36–8, 43, 53,
    161, 202–3n, 206
Braiterman, Zachary, 197n
Braxton, Edward K., 206n
Buber, Martin, 89, 93, 108, 152, 157
Buddhism, 135

Burkle, Howard R., 3–4, 64, 181, 231n
Burrow, Rufus, Jr., 211n

Call to Renewal, 194
Cannon, Katie, 71
Carson, Clayborne, 166
Charry, Ellen T., 222n
chosenness, 8–10, 23, 27, 38, 47, 73,
    106–8, 131–3, 135, 161
  see also covenant
Christian-Jewish relations
  see relations, Jewish-Christian
civil rights movement, 19, 56, 162–3, 194
class, socio-economic, 3, 16–17, 20,
    55–8, 61, 71–2, 162–3, 165
Cleage, Albert B., Jr., 26–30, 62
Cohen, Arthur A., 228, 231
cold war, 160
commanding voice of Auschwitz
  see voice of Auschwitz, commanding
commandments, 108, 113, 127–8
  see also voice of Auschwitz,
      commanding
communism, 57, 160, 164
Cone, James H., 5–6, 8–13, 15–63, 65,
    70–3, 76–9, 83, 85, 88, 91–2, 103,
    111, 132, 136, 138, 151, 159,
    172–80, 182–4, 188–9, 194–6
  on Barth, Karl, 19, 22, 33, 43
  on the Bible, 18, 22–3, 25–35, 38,
      41, 49, 51, 66–7, 173, 175–7,
      202n, 204n
  on black experience, 15, 18–20,
      22–5, 31–3, 41, 49, 173, 177,
      201–2n, 204n
  on black power, 19, 24–5, 29, 31, 33,
      40, 51, 198n
  on blackness, 15, 23–4, 28–9, 36–8,
      43, 202–3n, 206n

Cone, James H.—*continued*
  biography of, 18–21
  on chosenness, 23, 27, 38, 47
  on class, socio-economic, 20, 58
  compared with Cleage, Albert B., Jr.,
      26–30
  on covenant, 27, 34, 39
  on creation, 34, 41
  on divine activity, 30, 33–4, 38–40, 42,
      44, 46, 66–7, 173, 175, 178, 188
  on divine blackness, 28, 32, 37–8
  on divine goodness, 31–2, 39–40, 42,
      48, 59, 66–7
  on divine power, 12, 31, 34, 37, 39,
      45, 47–8, 58–60, 66–7, 176–8
  on divine presence, 12, 28, 30, 38–9,
      41, 44, 176–8
  on divine suffering, 48
  on Ecumenical Association of Third
      World Theologians (EATWOT),
      20, 58
  on Exodus, 23, 25, 27, 34, 39, 41, 44,
      46, 173
  on freedom, human, 34–7, 41, 43–7,
      49, 51, 53, 59, 176–7, 188–9
  on gender, 20, 58
  on humanism, 50, 66–7
  on image of God (*imago dei*), 27, 34,
      44–6, 188
  on Jesus Christ, 21–3, 25–6, 28–32,
      34–8, 41, 44, 46–8, 59, 63, 66–7,
      173, 175–6, 195, 204n
  on Jews, ancient, 27–8, 31, 34, 36,
      39, 47
  on Jones, William R., 66–7, 78
  on King, Martin Luther, Jr., 19–20, 48,
      50, 52–59, 198n, 205n, 223n
  on liberal theology, 42–3
  on liberation, 11, 20, 23, 25–7, 30,
      32–5, 37–9, 42, 44–52, 58–9,
      62–3, 66–8, 72, 77–9
  on liberation theology, Latin
      American, 20
  on Luke (4:18–19), 29
  on Malcolm X, 20, 50, 52–9, 198n,
      223n
  on Marx, Karl, 51
  on methodology, theological, 18,
      21–33, 35, 43, 50–1, 67, 78, 174,
      197–8n

  on neo-orthodox theology, 42–4
  on nonviolence, 49, 53–4, 58
  on Pinn, Anthony B., 78, 213n
  on race, 28–9, 40
  on racism, 15, 19, 24, 32–3, 37, 42–3,
      46, 49, 177
  on resistance, 18, 23, 39–41, 48–60,
      208n
  on revelation, 25–6, 28–30, 32–4,
      36–8
  on sin, 27–8, 43–6, 59, 177, 188–9,
      206–7n
  on slavery, 29, 33, 37, 39, 51–2
  on spirituals, 50–2, 223n
  on suffering, 13, 22, 30, 42, 47–8,
      51–2, 59, 66, 71, 177–8, 195,
      207n
  on theological anthropology,
      27, 34, 41–8, 51, 58–60, 178,
      188–9
  on third world, 20, 199n
  on Tillich, Paul, 22, 33
  on violence, 49, 53–4, 58, 208n
covenant, 27, 34, 39, 91–2, 94,
      100, 103, 105–8, 110, 113, 131–3,
      136–7, 144, 146, 150, 152, 155,
      167–8, 174–6, 178, 218n
  see also chosenness
creation, 34, 41, 111, 126, 148,
      189–90
  see also Adam and Eve (biblical);
      Garden of Eden
crucifixion
  see Jesus, death of

Day, Dorothy, 226n
deicide, 168
deism, 106
dialogue, interreligious, 13, 85–6, 141,
      159, 167–72
  see also pluralism, religious; relations,
      Jewish-Christian
diversity, religious
  see dialogue, interreligious; pluralism,
      religious
divine commanding presence
  see God, presence of
divine saving presence
  see God, presence of
Dorrien, Gary, ix

Eck, Diana, 169–71
Eckhart, Meister, 135
Ecumenical Association of Third World
    Theologians (EATWOT), 20, 58
Eden
    see Garden of Eden
Eisfeldt, Otto, 89
election
    see chosenness
Ellis, Marc H., 10–11, 88, 129, 131–2,
    138–44, 146
    on Fackenheim, Emil L., 10–11,
        138–40, 142
    on Israel, 10–11
    on Jewish theology of liberation,
        139–40, 142, 226–7n
Enlightenment, 104
"epoch-making events"
    see Fackenheim, Emil L., on
        "epoch-making events"
evil, 1–14, 16, 18, 42, 47–8, 53–5, 57,
    59, 66–7, 69–70, 75, 77, 83, 85–8,
    97–8, 101, 114, 120, 125, 136, 147,
    153, 157, 172, 180–1, 183, 186–91,
    193, 195–6
"excremental assault", 113–14, 148, 150
exile, 96, 100–1, 161, 173
Exodus, 23, 25, 27, 34, 39, 41, 44, 63,
    66, 72, 79–80, 94–5, 103, 107–8,
    140–1, 161, 164, 173, 175, 182, 185
Exodus (3:14), 80

Fackenheim, Emil L., 5–6, 8, 11–13, 18,
    50, 83, 85–129, 131–2, 136–40,
    142–54, 156–7, 160, 172–80,
    184–6, 188–9, 194–6
    on Auschwitz, 87, 96, 101, 115
    on "banality of evil", 97–8
    on Barth, Karl, 93
    on the Bible, 216n
    biography of, 88–91
    on Buber, Martin, 89, 93, 108
    on chosenness, 106–8
    on Christianity, 98, 101, 105–6, 178
    on commandments, 108, 113, 127–8
    on covenant, 91–2, 94, 100, 103,
        105–8, 110, 113, 175–6, 178, 218n
    on creation, 111, 126
    on divine activity, 88, 102–5, 107,
        109, 113, 126–7, 186, 188
    on divine goodness, 107, 112–13, 115,
        120, 184
    on divine hiding of the face, 99–100
    on divine mystery, 94
    on divine power, 12, 101, 103, 107,
        109–11, 113, 120, 126–7, 176,
        178–9, 184–5, 219n
    on divine presence, 12, 85, 87–8, 91,
        95, 99–101, 103–11, 114–15,
        119–20, 124–7, 136–8, 144,
        146–7, 149, 175–9, 184–6, 188,
        220–1n
    on divine suffering, 99–101
    on Eisfeldt, Otto, 89
    on Enlightenment, 104
    on "epoch-making events", 92, 94–6,
        102
    on evil, 114, 120, 125
    on "excremental assault",
        113–14
    on Exodus, 94–5, 103, 107–8, 175
    on freedom, human, 88, 98–9, 103,
        109–13, 120, 126, 176, 188–9,
        219n
    on Hegel, Georg Wilhelm Friedrich,
        90, 105
    on Heschel, Abraham Joshua, 112
    on Hiroshima, 96–7
    on Hitler, Adolf, 87, 94, 96, 102, 111,
        115–16, 176
    on Holocaust, uniqueness of, 87–8,
        96–9, 142, 216–7n, 226n
    on humanism, 110
    on image of God, 98–9
    on Israel, 91–4, 96, 103, 105, 108,
        111, 113, 119–20, 123–5, 129,
        143, 175, 178, 223n
    on *kabbalah*, 126–8, 185, 223–4n
    on Kant, Immanuel, 90, 116, 219n
    on Kierkegaard, Soren, 89
    on Lewinska, Pelagia, 115
    on liberal theology, 93
    on Maccabean revolt, 96
    on *mad midrash*, 119, 121, 129
    on martyrdom, 13, 101–2
    on Menzer, Paul, 89
    on messianic age, 93, 112
    on messianism, 105
    on methodology, theological, 88,
        91–103, 173–4, 216n

Fackenheim, Emil L.—*continued*
  on *midrash*, 96, 105, 107, 109,
      119–23, 129, 219n, 223n
  on *Muselmanner*, 98–9, 127
  on Nazism, 85, 87, 89–90, 94, 96–9,
      113–17, 124, 129
  on neo-orthodox theology, 89, 116
  on Noah (biblical), covenant with,
      106, 113
  on nonviolence, 117
  on Passover Haggadah, 95
  on philosophy, 217–18n
  on process theology, 110–11, 178
  on Red Sea, 94–5, 104, 107–8
  on resistance, 11, 50, 85, 88, 91, 97,
      99, 102–3, 108, 112, 114–29,
      188, 220n, 222n
  on revelation, 88, 92–6, 102–3,
      114–15, 117, 120
  on "root experiences", 92, 94–6,
      102–4, 120–1, 175–6
  on Rosenzweig, Franz, 89–90, 93
  on Sachsenhausen, 89, 114
  on *Shekhinah*, 126
  on sin, 111–12, 188–9
  on Sinai, 93–4, 96, 103–5, 108–9,
      113, 175
  on Six Day War, 90, 124–5
  on Spinoza, Baruch, 90
  on Strauss, Leo, 89
  on suffering, 88, 99–102, 176, 195
  on Temple, Second, destruction of, 96,
      99–100
  on *teshuva*, 126
  on theodicy, 103
  on theological anthropology, 94, 97–9,
      103, 105–6, 109–19, 126, 128,
      179, 186, 188–9, 221n
  on *tikkun olam*, 119–20, 124–29, 176,
      220n, 223–4n
  on Tillich, Paul, 92–3
  on Treblinka revolt, 118
  on violence, 118
  on voice of Auschwitz, commanding,
      8, 10–11, 85, 87, 91, 103, 111,
      115–16, 119–20, 124–5, 136,
      138, 144, 176, 179, 184, 220–3n
  on Warsaw Ghetto Uprising, 117
  on Wiesel, Elie, 122, 219n, 223n

  on Zionism, 123
feminist theology, 11, 71, 132, 135,
    145, 191
Fine, Lawrence, 224
free will
  see freedom, human
freedom, human, 7–9, 12, 34–7, 41,
    43–7, 49, 51, 53, 57–9, 62, 64, 66,
    68–70, 73, 76–81, 83, 85, 98–9,
    103, 109–13, 120, 126, 145, 154,
    172, 175–7, 181–3, 185, 187–91,
    194, 219n, 228n, 231n
  see also theological anthropology

Gandhi, Mohandas K., 16, 171, 194,
    205n
Garden of Eden, 189
  see also Adam and Eve (biblical);
      creation
God
  absence of, 69–70, 77, 133, 136, 144
  activity of, 7–8, 11–14, 23, 27–8, 30,
      34, 38–40, 42, 44, 46, 63, 66,
      72–3, 76–7, 79–80, 88, 102–5,
      107, 109, 113, 126–7, 131–3,
      135–7, 140, 145, 172–3, 175,
      177–9, 183–4, 186–8, 190–1,
      194, 196
  blackness of, 28, 32, 37–8
  goodness of, 2, 7–8, 10, 27, 31–2,
      39–42, 48, 52, 59, 61–8, 71, 73,
      77–81, 86, 107, 112–13, 115,
      120, 131–2, 137, 175–6, 179–87,
      190–1, 194–5
  hiding of the face of, 99–100
  as Holy Nothingness, 10, 131, 135–8,
      144
  image of, 7, 12, 27, 34, 44–6, 56, 81,
      83, 98–9, 148–50, 187–90
  mystery of, 94
  power of, 2, 7–8, 10–12, 30–1, 34, 37,
      39, 45, 47–8, 52, 57–68, 78–80,
      86, 101, 103, 107, 109–11, 113,
      120, 126–7, 132–3, 144, 151,
      173, 176–87, 189–91, 194, 196,
      219n
  presence of, 11–12, 28, 30, 38–9, 41,
      44, 62, 70, 74, 76–81, 85–8, 91,
      95, 99–101, 103–11, 114–15,

119–20, 124–7, 131–8, 144–51,
      155, 172–3, 175–9, 183–8,
      190–1, 194, 196, 220–1n
   suffering of, 48, 70, 99–101
   see also voice of Auschwitz,
      commanding
Good Samaritan, 191
Grant, Jacquelyn, 71, 198–9n
Greenberg, Cheryl Lynn, 162, 166
Greenberg, Irving, 138, 167–8
Grinnell College (Iowa), 3
Gruber, Heinrich, 132–3
Gutierrez, Gustavo, 21–2, 226n

Hagar (biblical), 10, 35, 72–4, 76–7
Hegel, Georg Wilhelm Friedrich, 90, 105,
   135
Heschel, Abraham Joshua, 4, 112, 231n
Hiroshima, 96–7
Hitler, Adolf, 87, 89, 94, 96, 102, 111,
   115–16, 133, 136, 138, 142, 145,
   176, 192–3
   see also Nazism
Holocaust, Jewish, 5–6, 11, 13–14,
      85–157, 161–3, 168, 173, 175–6,
      179–80, 184, 186, 188, 191
   uniqueness of, 6, 87–8, 96–9, 136,
      142, 216–17n, 226n
Holy Nothingness
   see God, as Holy Nothingness
homophobia, 41, 71
Hopkins, Dwight N., ix, 6, 10–11, 16–18,
      61–2, 70, 78–83, 151–2, 160, 172–3,
      180, 182, 186–8, 214–15n
   compared with Cone, James H., 78–80
   on humor, 10, 78, 82–3, 232n
   on Pinn, Anthony B., 70–1
Horowitz, Irving Louis, 216–17n
human nature
   see theological anthropology
humanism, 9–10, 12, 50, 61–71, 78, 80,
      110, 136, 184
humanocentric theism, 6–9, 11–12, 61–9,
      159–60, 172–3, 180–4, 186–7, 195
humor, 10, 12, 78, 82–3, 191–3, 232n
Hurston, Zora Neale, 74–5, 77

imago dei
   see God, image of

   see also theological anthropology
immanence
   see God, presence of
incarnation
   see Jesus, incarnation of
Israel, 10–11, 27–8, 31, 34, 36, 39, 47,
      86, 91–4, 96, 103, 105, 108, 111,
      113, 119–20, 123–5, 129, 131–2,
      134–6, 138–40, 142–8, 150,
      155–61, 164–5, 173–6, 178, 223n
   see also Zionism
Israeli-Palestinian relations
   see relations, Jewish-Palestinian

Jeremiah (biblical), 99
Jesus, 5, 13, 17, 21–3, 167, 173, 175–6,
      182–3
   birth of, 30
   blackness of, 28–9, 35–6, 46
   death of, 10, 23, 30–2, 35–6, 41,
      47–8, 59, 63, 67, 71–2, 75–7,
      173, 175–6, 182, 195
   incarnation of, 25–6, 28, 30–2, 35–8,
      41, 44, 46, 59, 66–7, 75–7, 80–1,
      175–6, 182, 195
   resurrection of, 23, 25, 27, 30–2,
      35–6, 38, 41, 46, 48, 59, 63, 67,
      76, 81, 173, 175–6, 182, 195
Jewish-African American relations
   see relations, African American-Jewish
Jewish-black relations
   see relations, African American-Jewish
Jewish-Christian relations
   see relations, Jewish-Christian
Jewish-Palestinian relations
   see relations, Jewish-Palestinian
Job (biblical), 99
Jones, William R., 6, 9, 11, 18,
      39, 48, 50, 61–9, 71, 80, 136, 160,
      172–3, 179–84, 186, 195, 210n
   on Cone, James H., 9, 39, 61–3, 65,
      67, 179–81
   on humanism, 61–5
   on humanocentric theism, 9, 61–6,
      180–4, 186

kabbalah, 126–8, 135, 138, 144, 148,
      151, 185, 223–4n
   see also tikkun olam

Kant, Immanuel, 90, 116, 154, 219n
Kasimow, Harold, 3–4, 85
Kierkegaard, Soren, 89, 177
King, Martin Luther, Jr., 15–16, 19–20,
    48, 50, 52–8, 82, 163, 171, 195,
    205n, 208n, 223n
Knitter, Paul, 231
Ku Klux Klan, 179
Kung, Hans, 4

Langer, Lawrence, 227–8n
Levi, Primo, 90, 98–9, 150, 154, 219n
    see also Muselmanner
Lewinska, Pelagia, 115
liberal theology, 42–3, 93
liberation, 7, 9–11, 13, 18, 20, 23, 25–7,
    30, 32–5, 37–9, 42, 44–52, 58–9,
    62–73, 76–83, 131, 140, 173, 177,
    180–3, 186–8, 190–1, 193–5
liberation theology, 1–83, 128, 139–43,
    159, 166, 180, 186
    black, 1–83, 131, 138, 145, 159,
        180, 186
    Jewish, *see* Ellis, Marc H., on Jewish
        theology of liberation
    Latin American, 20–1, 61
Lubarsky, Sandra, 220–21n
Luke (4:18–19), 29
Luria, Isaac
    see kabbalah

Maccabean revolt, 96
"mad *midrash*", 119, 129
    see also midrash
Malcolm X, 15, 19–20, 50, 52–7, 82,
    198n, 207–8n, 223n
    see also Muhammad, Elijah; Nation of
        Islam
Marley, Bob, 194
martyrdom, 13, 101–2, 133
Marx, Karl, 51
Maybaum, Ignaz, 132
McRobert, Laurie, 222–3
Mendelssohn, Moses, 152
Mendes-Flohr, Paul, ix, 197n
Menzer, Paul, 89
Merton, Thomas, 170
    see also simulacrum

messiah, 167
messianic age, 93, 112
messianism, 105, 107, 155–7
methodology, theological, 8, 18, 21–33,
    35, 43, 50–1, 67,
    72–3, 78–9, 83, 88, 91–103, 173–4
midrash, 52, 96, 015, 107, 109, 119–23,
    129, 152, 219n, 223n
    see also "mad *midrash*"
Morgan, Michael L., 11, 88, 129, 151–7
    on Fackenheim, Emil L., 151–4
    on "interim Judaism", 152, 154–7
Muhammad, Elijah, 55
    see also Nation of Islam; X, Malcolm
Muselmanner, 98–9, 127, 150, 154
music, 10, 24–5, 50–2, 65, 69, 134, 163,
    194, 223n
    see also Marley, Bob; spirituals

Nasser, Gamal Abdel, 163
Nation of Islam, 25, 53, 55
    see also Muhammad, Elijah; X,
        Malcolm
Nazism, 43, 85, 87, 89–90, 94, 96–9,
    113–17, 124, 129, 133, 148, 150,
    152, 16–2, 179
    see also Hitler, Adolf
Nebuchadnezzar (biblical), 133
neo-orthodox theology, 42–4, 89, 116,
    154
Niebuhr, Reinhold, 41, 112, 206n
Noah (biblical), 106, 113
nonviolence, 12, 20, 49, 53–8, 117, 163
    see also violence
Nostra Aetate, 168–9
    see also Second Vatican Council

omnibenevolence
    see God, goodness of
omnipotence
    see God, power of

paganism, 134, 137
Palestinians
    see relations, Jewish-Palestinian
Passover Haggadah, 95
patriarchy, 11, 32, 144–5, 151, 180, 184
    see also sexism

Pinn, Anthony B., ix, 9, 18, 48, 50, 61,
65–71, 78, 80, 136, 195, 231n
on Cone, James H., 9, 68–9, 71
on humanism, 9, 68–70
on Jones, William R., 67–9
on suffering, 68–71
Pinnock, Sarah Katherine, 197n
Plaskow, Judith, 146
pluralism, religious, 46, 106, 167,
169–72, 175
see also dialogue, interreligious;
relations, Jewish-Christian
postmodernism, 155
power, divine
see God, power of
presence, divine
see God, presence of
process theology, 7, 110–11, 178, 197n

race, 16, 17, 40
racism, 3, 5, 15, 19, 24, 32–3, 37, 42–3,
46, 49, 53–9, 61–4, 66, 68, 71, 73–4,
88, 160–1, 165–6, 177, 179, 223n
Raphael, Melissa, 6, 11–12, 88, 111,
129, 132, 144–51, 160, 172–3, 180,
184, 186–8, 191, 227–8n
on Fackenheim, Emil L., 11, 132,
144–6, 151, 180, 184
on *Shekhinah*, 12, 144, 147–51, 184,
186–7
on *Zehnerschaft*, 149
Rauschenbusch, Walter, 206n
Red Sea, 94–5, 104, 107–8
relations, African American-Jewish, 14,
159–66
relations, Jewish-Christian, 13–14,
132–3, 140–2, 159, 166–72, 230n
relations, Jewish-Palestinian, 138, 140–2,
147, 204–5n, 226n
resistance, 7–13, 18, 23, 25, 39–41,
48–61, 67, 72, 74–9, 81–3, 85,
88–9, 91, 97, 99, 102–3, 108, 112,
114–29, 133, 137–8, 141, 143–5,
148–51, 153–4, 159–60, 172,
179–80, 183–96, 208n, 220–2n
of care, 148–51, 191
of humor, 82–3, 191–3, 232n
see also theological anthropology

resurrection
see Jesus, resurrection of
revelation, 11, 25–6, 28, 30, 32–4, 36–8,
88, 92–6, 102–3, 114–15, 117, 120,
151–2
Roberts, J. Deotis, 62
"root experiences"
see Fackenheim, Emil L., on "root
experiences"
Rosenzweig, Franz, 89–90, 93, 157
Rubenstein, Richard L., 10, 88, 129,
131–9, 144
on Fackenheim, Emil L., 10, 131–2,
136–7
on God as Holy Nothingness, 10, 131,
135–8, 144

Sachsenhausen, 89, 114
Scholem, Gershom, 223–4n
Second Vatican Council, 168
see also *Nostra Aetate*
sexism, 17, 20, 41, 58, 61, 71, 73–4,
198–9n
see also patriarchy
Shekhinah, 126, 137, 144, 147–8,
150–1, 180, 184, 186
Shoah
see Holocaust, Jewish
simulacrum, 170
see also Merton, Thomas
sin, 27–8, 41, 43–6, 59, 75, 111–12,
177, 188–90, 206–7n
see also theological anthropology
Sinai, 93–6, 103–5, 108–9, 113, 146,
175
Six Day War (1967), 90, 124–5, 139,
163–4
614th commandment
see voice of Auschwitz, commanding
slavery, 5–6, 12, 29, 33, 37, 39, 51–2,
65, 72–4, 78–9, 81–2, 161, 182
Smith, Archie, Jr., 200
Smith, Wilfred Cantwell, 4
socialism, 57
Spinoza, Baruch, 90, 152
spirituals, 51–2, 223n
see also music
Stall, Steven, 201n

Stendahl, Krister, 167
Stonewall Rebellion, 194
Strauss, Leo, 89
Student Nonviolent Coordinating
    Committee (SNCC), 163
suffering, 1–14, 16, 18–19, 22, 30, 42,
    47–8, 51–2, 59, 61–3, 65–71, 75–8,
    83, 85, 88, 99–102, 133, 135–8,
    140–3, 145, 149–50, 162–3, 172,
    176–80, 182–3, 186–7, 194–6, 207n
    of God, *see* God, suffering of
Suffering Servant, 47
Sundquist, Eric, 160–2, 164, 166
Supersessionism, 166–8

Tamez, Elsa, 73, 213n
Tel Aviv University, 86
Temple, Second, destruction of, 96,
    99–100, 173
teshuva, 126, 142
theodicy, 1–14, 18, 59–63, 67–69, 77,
    103, 132, 136, 178, 183, 187, 197n,
    207n, 210n
theological anthropology, 11–12, 27, 34,
    41–8, 51, 56–60, 64, 66, 68–70, 73,
    76–8, 80–1, 83, 94, 97–9, 103,
    105–6, 109–19, 126, 128, 148–50,
    152, 156–7, 172, 179–83, 186–96,
    221n
    see also freedom, human; God, image
        of; resistance; sin
third world, 20, 54–8, 140, 199n
Thoreau, Henry David, 205n
tikkun olam, 11, 119–20, 124–9, 138,
    144, 147–8, 151, 157, 176, 220n,
    223–4n
    see also kabbalah
Tillich, Paul, 22, 33, 92–3, 135
Tracy, David, ix, 197n
transcendence
    see God, presence of
Treblinka revolt, 118
Turner, Nat, 25, 50–1, 82, 194

University of Chicago, ix, 16–17
University of Halle, 89
University of Toronto, 90

Vatican II
    see Second Vatican Council
Vietnam War, 57
violence, 12–13, 49, 53–7, 75–7, 118,
    160–1, 168, 208n
    see also nonviolence
voice of Auschwitz, commanding,
    8, 10–11, 85, 87, 91, 103, 111,
    115–16, 119–20, 124–5, 131,
    136–7, 139, 144–7, 151, 153, 176,
    179, 184, 220–3n

Walker, Alice, 69, 71, 74–5, 77, 191,
    211–12n
Warsaw Ghetto Uprising, 117,
    141, 194
Weddle, David L., 205n
Wiesel, Elie, 86–7, 90, 122, 138, 179,
    184, 219n, 223n
whiteness, 6, 13, 17, 55, 163, 165
Williams, Delores S., 10, 18, 34–5, 61,
    67, 71–7, 145, 195
    on Cone, James H., 71–3
    on Hagar (biblical), 10, 34–5,
        72–4, 76
    on Jesus Christ, 75–7
    on liberation, 10, 34–5, 71–3,
        76–7
    on suffering, 10, 73–7
    on surrogacy, 73–7
    on survival, 10, 35, 72–3, 75–7
womanist theology, 9–10, 61,
    71–5, 191

X, Malcolm
    see Malcolm X

yetzer ha ra, 112, 188
    see also theological anthropology
yetzer ha tov, 112, 188
    see also theological anthropology
Young, Henry James, 210n

Zapatista movement, 194
Zehnerschaft, 149
Zionism, 123, 142, 161
    see also Israel